AAT
FOUNDATION

REVISION **COMPANION** Units 1– 4

Unit 1: Income and Receipts

Unit 2: Payments

Unit 3: Ledger Balances and an Initial Trial Balance

Unit 4: Information for Management Control

BPP LEARNING MEDIA

Ninth edition May 2009
First edition 2001

ISBN 9780 7517 6714 8 (previous ISBN 9780 7517 4632 7)

British Library Cataloguing-in-Publication Data
A catalogue record for this book is available from the British Library

Published by

BPP Learning Media Ltd
BPP House,
Aldine Place,
London W12 8AA

Printed in the United Kingdom

www.bpp.com/learningmedia

Your learning materials, published by BPP Learning Media Ltd, are printed on paper sourced from sustainable, managed forests.

All our rights reserved. No part of this publication may be reproduced, stored in a retrieval system or transmitted, in any form or by any means, electronic, mechanical, photocopying, recording or otherwise, without the prior written permission of BPP Learning Media Ltd.

We are grateful to the AAT for permission to reproduce the specimen simulations, assessments and answers, of which the AAT holds the copyright. All other activities and answers have been produced by BPP Learning Media Ltd.

©
BPP Learning Media Ltd
2009

CONTENTS

		Questions	Answers
Introduction		(v)	
Chapter activities			
1	Introduction to business	1	421
2	Business documents – sales	3	423
3	Double entry bookkeeping	15	429
4	Accounting for credit sales	21	437
5	Receiving money	35	445
6	Recording receipts	47	447
7	The banking system	51	451
8	Communication with customers	55	453
9	Business documents – purchases	59	457
10	Accounting for credit purchases	77	461
11	Making payments to credit suppliers	91	467
12	Recording payments	99	473
13	Petty cash procedures	107	479
14	Payroll accounting procedures	111	481
15	Bank reconciliation statement	113	483
16	Control account reconciliations	121	487
17	Preparing an initial trial balance	131	493
18	Errors and the trial balance	135	495
19	Business transactions and the law	141	499
20	Introduction to management information	143	501
21	Elements of cost	145	503
22	Coding	151	507
23	Comparison of costs and income	161	517
AAT sample simulations	Unit 1 – Tubney Technology Ltd	165	519
	Unit 2 – Amica Printing Co	221	541
	Unit 3 – Weasley Supplies Ltd	295	579
	Unit 4 – Avontree Ltd	323	589
Practice exam 1 – Unit 3 – Flower Chain		347	595
Practice exam 2 – Unit 3 – First Fashions		365	607
Practice exam 3 – Unit 3 – Parker Paints		383	619
Practice exam 4 – Unit 3 – The Studio		401	631

INTRODUCTION

This is BPP Learning Media's Revision Companion for AAT NVQ Foundation Units 1-4. It is part of an integrated package of AAT materials.

It has been written in conjunction with the BPP Course Companion, and has been carefully designed to enable students to practise all aspects of the requirements of the Standards of Competence and performance criteria. It is fully up to date as at December 2008.

This Revision Companion contains these key features:

- graded activities corresponding to each chapter of the Course Companion
- the AAT's sample simulations and answers for each Unit
- a selection of the AAT's exams for Unit 3 set up to and including December 2008

VAT

You will find examples and questions throughout this companion which need you to calculate or be aware of a rate of VAT. This is stated at $17\frac{1}{2}\%$ in these examples and questions. Please use this rate when you are tackling these questions and not the temporary rate of 15% that applies at present.

Multiple Choice Questions

From January 2009 Unit 3 will be examined by multiple choice or objective test questions. Therefore each chapter in the Revision Companion relating to Unit 3 includes a selection of MCQ/OT questions.

The emphasis in all activities and questions is on the practical application of the skills acquired. All activities, practice assessments and simulations have full answers prepared by BPP Learning Media Ltd.

Tutors adopting our Companions (minimum of ten Course Companions and ten Revision Companions per Unit, or ten Combined Companions as appropriate) are entitled to free access to the Lecturers' Area resources, including the Tutor Companion. To obtain your log-in, e-mail lecturersvc@bpp.com.

Home Study students are also entitled to access to additional resources. You will have received your log-in details on registration.

If you have any comments about this book, please e-mail helendarch@bpp.com or write to Helen Darch, AAT range manager, BPP Learning Media Ltd, BPP House, Aldine Place, London W12 8AA.

chapter 1:
INTRODUCTION TO BUSINESS

1 What are the main differences between a sole trader, a partnership and a limited company in terms of:

- ownership and management

- liability for debts

- methods of taking out profit?

2 For each of the following transactions state whether they are cash or credit transactions:

		Cash or credit?
i)	purchase of goods for £200 payable by cash in one week's time	…………………
ii)	writing a cheque for the purchase of a new computer	…………………
iii)	sale of goods to a customer where the invoice accompanies the goods	…………………
iv)	receipt of a cheque from a customer for goods purchased today	…………………
v)	purchase of goods where payment is due in three weeks' time	…………………

3 For each of the following transactions state whether they are capital or revenue transactions:

Capital or revenue?

i) purchase of a new computer paid for by cheque ....

ii) purchase of computer disks by cheque ....

iii) purchase of a new business car on credit ....

iv) payment of road tax on a new business car ....

v) payment of rent for the business premises ....

4 Explain briefly the difference between a profit and loss account and a balance sheet.

chapter 2:
BUSINESS DOCUMENTS – SALES

1 On your desk is a pile of sales invoices that have already had the list price of the goods entered onto them and been totalled. You now have to calculate and deduct the 15% trade discount that is allowed on each of these invoices.

	List price total	Trade discount	Net total
i)	£416.70		
ii)	£105.82		
iii)	£ 96.45		
iv)	£263.46		
v)	£350.90		

2 There is a further pile of invoices which have the net total entered for which you are required to calculate the VAT charge.

	Net total	VAT	Invoice total
i)	£258.94		
ii)	£316.78		
iii)	£82.60		
iv)	£152.99		
v)	£451.28		

business documents – sales

3   You now discover that for each of the invoices from the previous activity a 3% settlement discount has been offered. Recalculate the VAT charge to correctly reflect the settlement discount.

	Net total	VAT	Invoice total
i)	£258.94	....	....
ii)	£316.78	....	....
iii)	£82.60	....	....
iv)	£152.99	....	....
v)	£451.28	....	....

4   You work in the accounts department for Southfield Electrical and on your desk are three purchase orders received from customers today. The purchase orders have already been checked to the purchase quotations and the prices are correct on each purchase order.

You also have on your desk the customer details file which gives you the following information about the three customers:

Customer name	Sales ledger code	Trade discount	Settlement discount
Whitehill Superstores	SL 44	10%	4% – 10 days
Quinn Ltd	SL 04	15%	–
Harper & Sons	SL 26	10%	3% – 14 days

You are now required to complete the three blank sales invoices given for each of these purchase orders. The last sales invoice sent out was 57103. Today's date is 8 January 2006. If no settlement discount is offered or taken then payment is due within 30 days.

PURCHASE ORDER

WHITEHILL SUPERSTORES
28 Whitehill Park
Benham DR6 5LM
Tel 0303446 Fax 0303447

To: Southfield Electrical
Industrial Estate
Benham DR6 2FF

Number: 32431

Date: 4 Jan 2006

Delivery address: Whitehill Superstores
28, Whitehill Park
Benham DR6 5LM

Product code	Quantity	Description	Unit list price £
6060	8	Hosch Tumble Dryer	300.00
4425	2	Zanpoint Dishwasher	200.00

Authorised by: *P. Williams* **Date:** 04/01/06

PURCHASE ORDER

QUINN LTD
High Rocks Estate
Drenchley
DR22 6PQ
Tel 0310442 Fax 0310443

To: Southfield Electrical
Industrial Estate
Benham DR6 2FF

Number: 24316

Date: 5 Jan 2006

Delivery address: As above

Product code	Quantity	Description	Unit list price £
3170	14	Temax Mixer	35.00
3174	6	Temax Mixer	46.00

Authorised by: *J. P. Walters* **Date:** 05/01/06

PURCHASE ORDER

HARPER & SONS
30/34 High Street
Benham DR6 4ST
Tel 0303419 Fax 0303464

To: Southfield Electrical
Industrial Estate
Benham DR6 2FF

Number: 04367

Date: 4 Jan 2006

Delivery address: 30/34 High Street
Benham DR6 4ST

Product code	Quantity	Description	Unit list price £
6150	3	Hosch Washing Machine	260.00

Authorised by: *S. Stevens*   Date: *05/01/06*

INVOICE

Southfield Electrical
Industrial Estate
Benham DR6 2FF
Tel 0303379 Fax 0303152
VAT Reg 0264 2274 49

To:

Invoice number:

Date/tax point:

Order number:

Account number:

Quantity	Description	Stock code	Unit amount £	Total £

Net total

VAT

Invoice total

Terms

INVOICE

Southfield Electrical
Industrial Estate
Benham DR6 2FF
Tel 0303379 Fax 0303152
VAT Reg 0264 2274 49

To:

Invoice number:

Date/tax point:

Order number:

Account number:

Quantity	Description	Stock code	Unit amount £	Total £

Net total	
VAT	
Invoice total	

Terms

INVOICE

Southfield Electrical
Industrial Estate
Benham DR6 2FF
Tel 0303379 Fax 0303152
VAT Reg 0264 2274 49

To:

Invoice number:

Date/tax point:

Order number:

Account number:

Quantity	Description	Stock code	Unit amount £	Total £
			Net total	
			VAT	
			Invoice total	

Terms

5 You have on your desk two further sales invoices that have been prepared by your assistant. You are required to check these invoices prior to them being sent out and note any errors that you find in the space given.

You are also given extracts from Southfield's price list and customer details listing.

PRICE LIST EXTRACT

CODE	DESCRIPTION	UNIT PRICE £
HOSCH		
6040	Tumble dryer	250.00
6050	Tumble dryer	280.00
6060	Tumble dryer	300.00
6140	Washing machine	220.00
6150	Washing machine	260.00
6160	Washing machine	300.00
6170	Washing machine	340.00
TEMAX		
3160	Food processor	100.00
3162	Food processor	120.00
3164	Food processor	140.00
3170	Mixer	35.00
3172	Mixer	40.00
3174	Mixer	46.00

CUSTOMER DETAILS EXTRACT

Customer name	Sales ledger code	Trade discount	Settlement discount
Weller Enterprises	SL 18	10%	4% - 14 days
QQ Stores	SL 37	12%	-

business documents – sales

Weller Enterprises –

QQ Stores –

INVOICE

Southfield Electrical
Industrial Estate
Benham DR6 2FF
Tel 0303379 Fax 0303152
VAT Reg 0264 2274 49

To: Q Q Stores

Invoice number: 57107

Date/tax point: 9 Jan 2006

Order number: 03611

Account number: SL 27

Quantity	Description	Stock code	Unit amount £	Total £
7	Temax Processor	3162	140.00	890.00
10	Temax Mixer	3170	35.00	350.00
				1,240.00
	Trade Discount			186.00

Net total	1,054.00
VAT	184.45
Invoice total	1,238.45

Terms
Net 30 days
E & OE

INVOICE

Southfield Electrical
Industrial Estate
Benham DR6 2FF
Tel 0303379 Fax 0303152
VAT Reg 0264 2274 49

To: Weller Enterprises

Invoice number:

Date/tax point:

Order number:

Account number:

Quantity	Description	Stock code	Unit amount £	Total £
3	Hosch Tumble Dryer	6060	300.00	900.00
7	Hosch Washing Machine	6160	300.00	2,100.00
				3,000.00
	Trade discount			300.00

Net total	2,700.00
VAT	472.50
Invoice total	3,172.50

Terms
Net 30 days
E & OE

chapter 3:
DOUBLE ENTRY BOOKKEEPING

1 James has just started up in business and in his first month had the following transactions:

i) James paid £20,000 into a business bank account in order to start the business;

ii) He paid an initial rental of £2,500 by cheque for the shop from which he is to trade;

iii) He purchased a van by cheque for £7,400;

iv) He purchased £6,000 of goods for resale on credit;

v) He sold goods for £1,000 - the customer paid by cheque;

vi) He sold goods on credit for £4,800;

vii) He paid shop assistant's wages by cheque totalling £2,100;

viii) He made further sales on credit for £3,900;

ix) He purchased a further £1,400 of goods for resale by cheque;

x) £3,700 was received from credit customers;

xi) He paid £3,300 to credit suppliers;

xii) He withdrew £800 from the business for living expenses.

State the two effects of each of these transactions in the space given below.

i) James paid £20,000 into a business bank account in order to start the business;

Effect 1   Effect 2

ii) He paid an initial rental of £2,500 by cheque for the shop from which he is to trade;

Effect 1   Effect 2

iii) He purchased a van by cheque for £7,400;

Effect 1   Effect 2

iv) He purchased £6,000 of goods for resale on credit;

Effect 1   Effect 2

v) He sold goods for £1,000 – the customer paid by cheque;

Effect 1   Effect 2

vi) He sold goods on credit for £4,800;

Effect 1   Effect 2

vii) He paid shop assistant's wages by cheque totalling £2,100;

Effect 1   Effect 2

viii) He made further sales on credit for £3,900;

Effect 1   Effect 2

ix) He purchased a further £1,400 of goods for resale by cheque;

   Effect 1   **Effect 2**

x) £3,700 was received from credit customers;

   Effect 1   **Effect 2**

xi) He paid £3,300 to credit suppliers;

   Effect 1   **Effect 2**

xii) He withdrew £800 from the business for living expenses.

   Effect 1   **Effect 2**

2 Using the information above about James's early transactions enter them into the given ledger accounts.

Bank account

£	£

Capital account

£	£

double entry bookkeeping

Rent account

| £ | £ |

Van account

| £ | £ |

Purchases account

| £ | £ |

Creditors account

| £ | £ |

Sales account

| £ | £ |

Debtors account

| £ | £ |

Wages account	
£	£

Drawings account	
£	£

3 Balance each of the ledger accounts from above that have more than one entry. Then prepare a trial balance.

4 During this first month of trading James decides that he must keep more detailed records of his sales and purchases on credit. Explain to James how he could do this by keeping a subsidiary ledger for sales and purchases as well as the main ledger accounts.

5 James decides to put your recommendations into practice and informs you of the details of his sales on credit and receipts from debtors during the first month.

	£
Sales:	
To H Simms	1,800
To P Good	3,000
To K Mitchell	910
To C Brown	2,990
Receipts:	
From H Simms	900
From P Good	1,400
From K Mitchell	910
From C Brown	490

You are now required to record these transactions in the main ledger accounts and in the subsidiary ledger, the sales ledger.

Main ledger

                                                Sales ledger control account

£	£

                                                  Sales account

£	£

Subsidiary ledger

                                                  H Simms account

£	£

                                                  P Good account

£	£

                                                  K Mitchell account

£	£

                                                  C Brown account

£	£

chapter 4:
ACCOUNTING FOR CREDIT SALES

1 Natural Productions is a small business that manufactures a variety of soaps and bath products which it sells directly to shops. During January 2006 the following credit sales took place:

2 Jan	Invoice No. 6237 to Hoppers Ltd £547 plus VAT
5 Jan	Invoice No. 6238 to Body Perfect £620 plus VAT
6 Jan	Invoice No. 6239 to Esporta Leisure £346 plus VAT
9 Jan	Invoice No. 6240 to Langans Beauty £228 plus VAT
12 Jan	Invoice No. 6241 to Body Perfect £548 plus VAT
16 Jan	Invoice No. 6242 to Superior Products £221 plus VAT
18 Jan	Invoice No. 6243 to Esporta Leisure £416 plus VAT
23 Jan	Invoice No. 6244 to Hoppers Ltd £238 plus VAT
26 Jan	Invoice No. 6245 to Langans Beauty £274 plus VAT

You are required to:

a) enter these transactions into the sales day book given below

b) cast the columns of the sales day book and check that they cross-cast

c) post the totals of the sales day book to the main ledger accounts given

d) post the individual entries to the subsidiary ledger, the sales ledger

Sales day book

Date	Customer	Invoice number	Gross £	VAT £	Net £

accounting for credit sales

Main ledger

Sales ledger control account

| £ | £ |

VAT account

| £ | £ |

Sales account

| £ | £ |

Subsidiary ledger

Hoppers Ltd account

| £ | £ |

Body Perfect account

| £ | £ |

accounting for credit sales

	Esporta Leisure account	
£		£

	Langans Beauty account	
£		£

	Superior Products account	
£		£

2 Given below are four sales invoices sent out by Short Furniture, a business that manufactures wooden garden furniture for sale to retail outlets. These are the only invoices that have been issued this week.

You are required to:

a) enter the invoices into the sales day book given

b) total and check the sales day book

c) post the sales day book to the main ledger and the subsidiary ledger, the sales ledger, given

INVOICE

Short Furniture
Eridge Estate
Benham DR6 4QQ
Tel 0303312 Fax 0303300
VAT Reg 0361 3282 60

To: Rocks Garden Suppliers
14 Windmill Lane
Benham

Invoice number: 08663

Date/tax point: 5 Jan 2006

Order number: 4513

Account number: SL 22

Quantity	Description	Stock code	Unit amount £	Total £
2	6 Seat Dining Table	DT613	344.00	688.00
	Trade Discount			103.20
			Net total	584.80
			VAT	102.34
			Invoice total	687.14

Terms
Net 30 days
E & OE

accounting for credit sales

INVOICE

Short Furniture
Eridge Estate
Benham DR6 4QQ
Tel 0303312 Fax 0303300
VAT Reg 0361 3282 60

To: Eridge Nurseries
Eridge Estate
Benham

Invoice number: 08664

Date/tax point: 7 Jan 2006

Order number: 61735F

Account number: SL 07

Quantity	Description	Stock code	Unit amount £	Total £
15	Plant Stands	PL006	23.85	357.75
			Net total	357.75
			VAT	62.60
			Invoice total	420.35

Terms
Net 30 days
E & OE

accounting for credit sales

INVOICE

Short Furniture
Eridge Estate
Benham DR6 4QQ
Tel 0303312 Fax 0303300
VAT Reg 0361 3282 60

To: Abergaven Garden Centre
Drenchley

Invoice number: 08665

Date/tax point: 7 Jan 2006

Order number: S129

Account number: SL 16

Quantity	Description	Stock code	Unit amount £	Total £
3	Lounger Chairs	LC400	285.00	855.00
	Trade discount			85.50
			Net total	769.50
			VAT	134.66
			Invoice total	**904.16**

Terms
Net 30 days
E & OE

INVOICE

Short Furniture
Eridge Estate
Benham DR6 4QQ
Tel 0303312 Fax 0303300
VAT Reg 0361 3282 60

To: Rother Nurseries
Rother Road
Benham

Invoice number: 08666

Date/tax point: 9 Jan 2006

Order number: 06112

Account number: SL 13

Quantity	Description	Stock code	Unit amount £	Total £
2	Coffee Table	CT002	96.00	192.00
6	Dining Chairs	DC416	73.00	438.00
			Net total	630.00
			VAT	110.25
			Invoice total	740.25

Terms
Net 30 days
E & OE

accounting for credit sales

a) and b)

Sales day book

Date	Customer	Invoice number	SL Ref	Gross £	VAT £	Net £

c)

Main ledger

Sales ledger control account
£ | £

VAT account
£ | £

Sales account
£ | £

Subsidiary ledger

	Eridge Nurseries	SL 07
£		£

	Rother Nurseries	SL 13
£		£

	Abergaven Garden Centre	SL 16
£		£

	Rocks Garden Supplies	SL 22
£		£

3 Returning to Natural Productions, during January the following credit notes were issued:

17 Jan   Credit note No. 1476 to Hoppers Ltd £68.70 plus VAT
23 Jan   Credit note No. 1477 to Esporta Leisure £89.23 plus VAT
30 Jan   Credit note No. 1478 to Superior Products £11.75 plus VAT

You are required to:

a) enter these transactions into the sales returns day book given below

b) cast the columns of the sales returns day book and check that they cross-cast

c) post the totals of the sales returns day book to the main ledger accounts given

d) post the individual entries to the subsidiary ledger accounts used in the earlier activity

accounting for credit sales

Sales returns day book

Date	Customer	Invoice number	SL Ref	Gross £	VAT £	Net £

Main ledger

Sales ledger control account

	£		£
31 Jan SDB	4,039.64		

VAT account

	£		£
		31 Jan SDB	601.64

Sales returns account

	£		£

30

4 Short Furniture also sent out a credit note on 9 January 2006 which is given below. Credit notes are not recorded in a separate returns day book but instead are recorded in the sales day book.

You are required to:

a) record the credit note in the partially completed sales day book given below

b) total and check the casting of the sales day book

c) post the totals to the main ledger accounts given below

d) post the individual entries to the subsidiary ledger accounts given below

---

CREDIT NOTE

SHORT FURNITURE
Eridge Estate
Benham DR6 4QQ
Tel 0303312 Fax 0303300
VAT Reg 0361 3282 60

Credit note to:

Rocks Garden Supplies
14 Windmill Lane
Benham

Credit note number: 1468
Date/tax point: 9 Jan 2006
Order number 4513
Account number: SL 22

Quantity	Description	Stock code	Unit amount	Total
			£	£
1	6 Seat Dining Table	DT613	344.00	344.00
	Trade Discount			51.60
			Net total	292.40
			VAT	51.17
			Gross total	343.57

Reason for credit note:

Damaged - two legs scratched

Sales day book

Date	Customer	Invoice number	SL Ref	Gross £	VAT £	Net £
5 Jan	Rocks Garden Supp	08663	22	687.14	102.34	584.80
7 Jan	Eridge Nurseries	08664	07	420.35	62.60	357.75
7 Jan	Abergaven G C	08665	16	904.16	134.66	769.50
9 Jan	Rother Nurseries	08666	13	740.25	110.25	630.00

Main ledger

Sales ledger control account

£	£

VAT account

£	£

Sales account

£	£

Subsidiary ledger

	Eridge Nurseries	SL 07
£		£

	Rother Nurseries	SL 13
£		£

	Abergaven Garden Centre	SL 16
£		£

	Rocks Garden Supplies	SL 22
£		£

chapter 5:
RECEIVING MONEY

1 Given below is a completed cheque.

Who is the drawee? –

Who is the payee? –

Who is the drawer? –

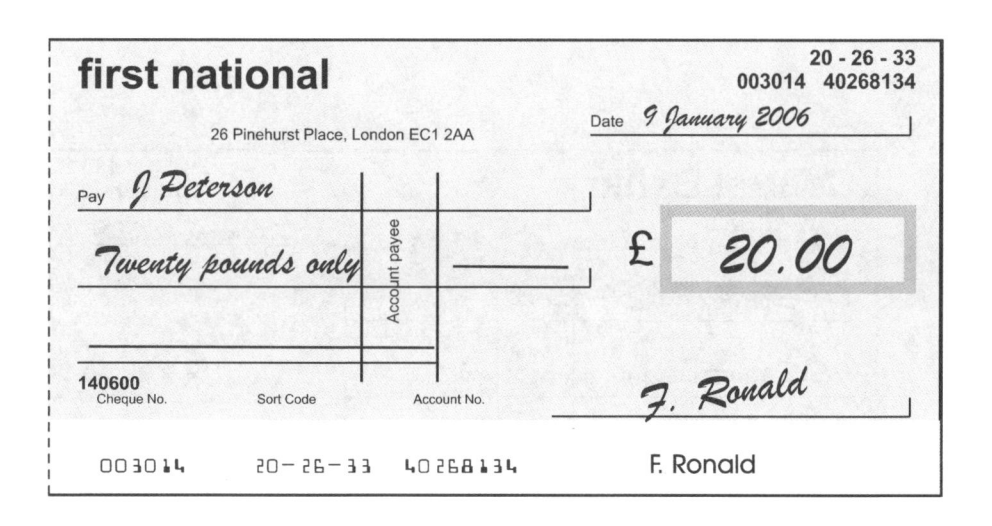

```
first national                                    20 - 26 - 33
                                                  003014  40268134
        26 Pinehurst Place, London EC1 2AA
                                            Date  9 January 2006

Pay  J Peterson

     Twenty pounds only                           £   20.00

140600
Cheque No.     Sort Code      Account No.         F. Ronald

003014      20-26-33      40268134       F. Ronald
```

receiving money

2 Given below are four cheques received by Southfield Electrical today 9 January 2006. Check each one thoroughly and make a note in the table provided of any errors or problems that you encounter.

	Comments
Cheque from B B Berry Ltd	
Cheque from Q Q Stores	
Cheque from Dagwell Enterprises	
Cheque from Weller Enterprises	

Central Bank
18 - 26 - 44
010629 32791641

44, Main Road, Walkingham

Date *5 January 2006*

Pay *Southfield Electrical*

Six hundred and seventy nine pounds and 83 pence

£ **697.83**

140600
Cheque No.   Sort Code   Account No.

010629   18-26-44   32791641

J. L. Smith

B. B. Berry Ltd

Northern Bank

High Street, Drenchley

22 - 44 - 16
10128 12976844

Date 7 January 2006

Pay Southfield Electrical

Two hundred and twenty eight pounds and 60 pence

£ 228.60

140600
Cheque No.   Sort Code   Account No.

10128   22-44-16   12976844

Q Q Stores

First Western

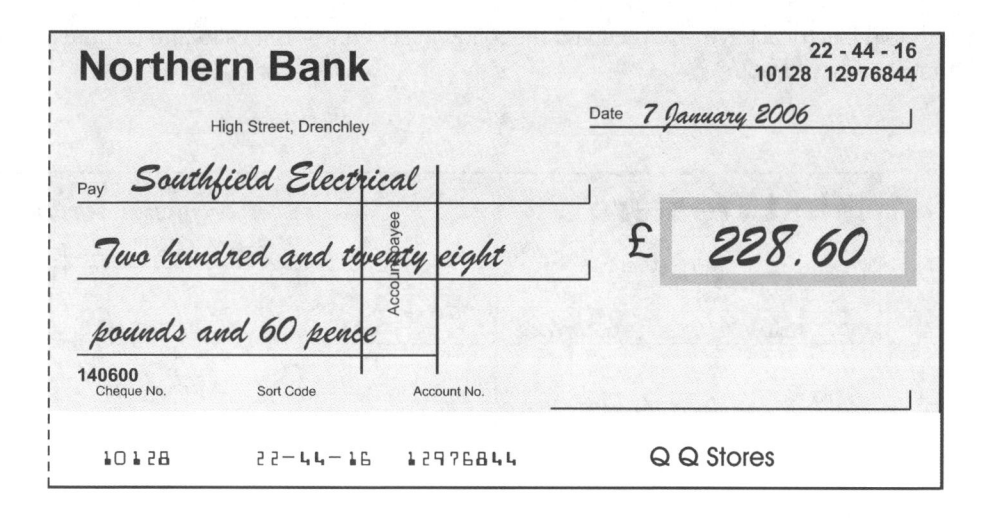

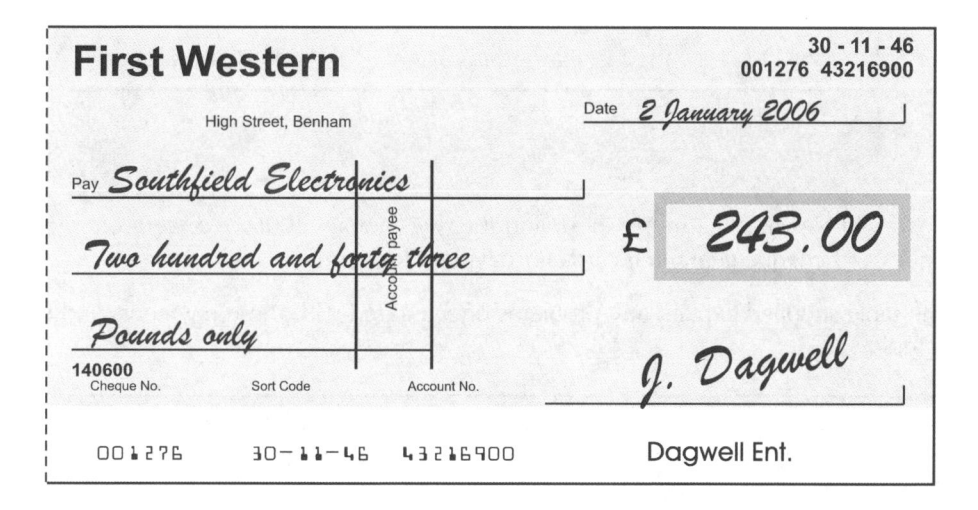

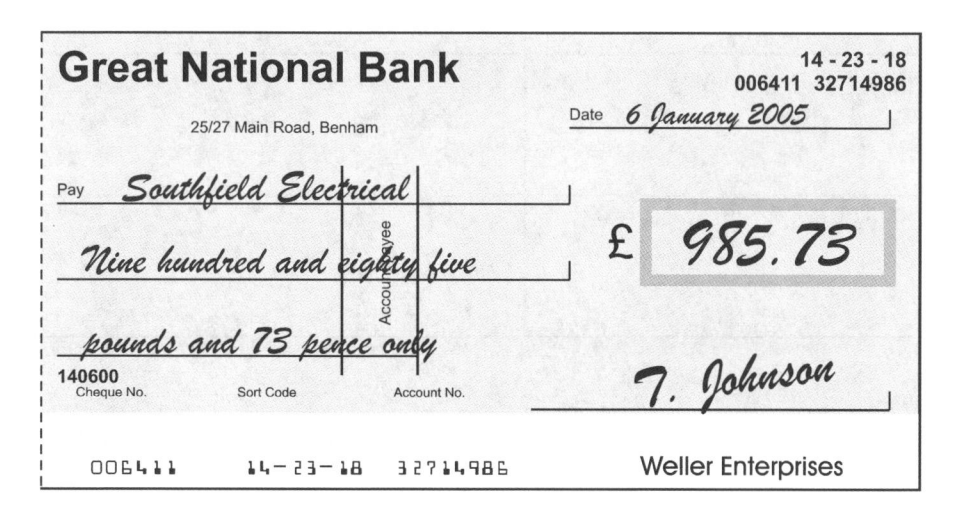

High Street, Benham

30 - 11 - 46
001276 43216900

Date 2 January 2006

Pay Southfield Electronics

Two hundred and forty three Pounds only

£ 243.00

J. Dagwell

140600
Cheque No.   Sort Code   Account No.

001276   30-11-46   43216900

Dagwell Ent.

Great National Bank

25/27 Main Road, Benham

14 - 23 - 18
006411 32714986

Date 6 January 2005

Pay Southfield Electrical

Nine hundred and eighty five pounds and 73 pence only

£ 985.73

T. Johnson

140600
Cheque No.   Sort Code   Account No.

006411   14-23-18   32714986

Weller Enterprises

receiving money

3 Southfield Electrical have also received the following cheque – is it valid and is there anything about it that you should note?

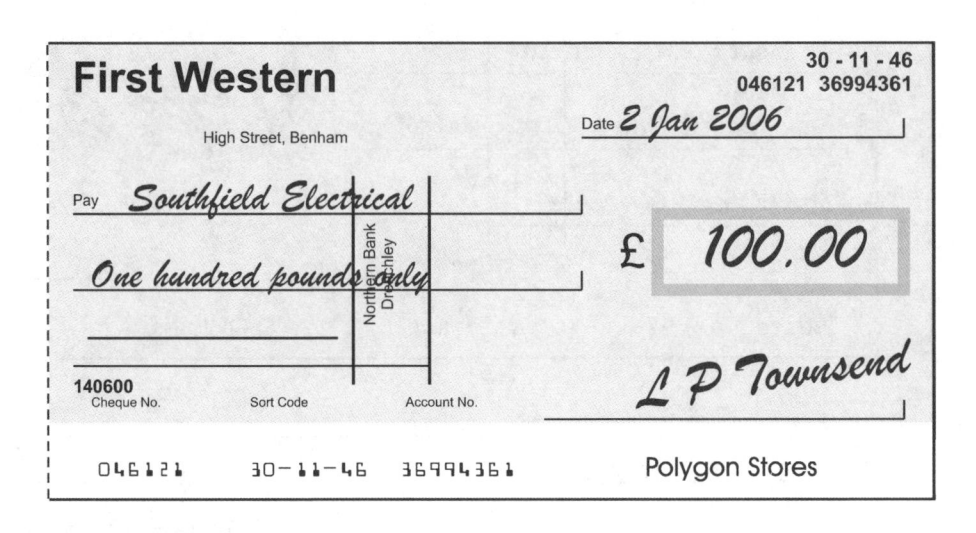

```
First Western                           30 - 11 - 46
                                        046121  36994361
         High Street, Benham
                                   Date 2 Jan 2006
Pay  Southfield Electrical
                                   £   100.00
     One hundred pounds only

                                        L P Townsend
140600
Cheque No.    Sort Code    Account No.

046121     30-11-46    36994361      Polygon Stores
```

4 You work in Newmans, a music shop, and today, 7 January 2006, you were offered the following cheques and cheque guarantee cards for payment for goods.

In the table supplied explain any problems encountered with these payments and the action that you took.

	Comment and action
Cheque from T M Spence	
Cheque from B Withers	
Cheques from C J Long	

receiving money

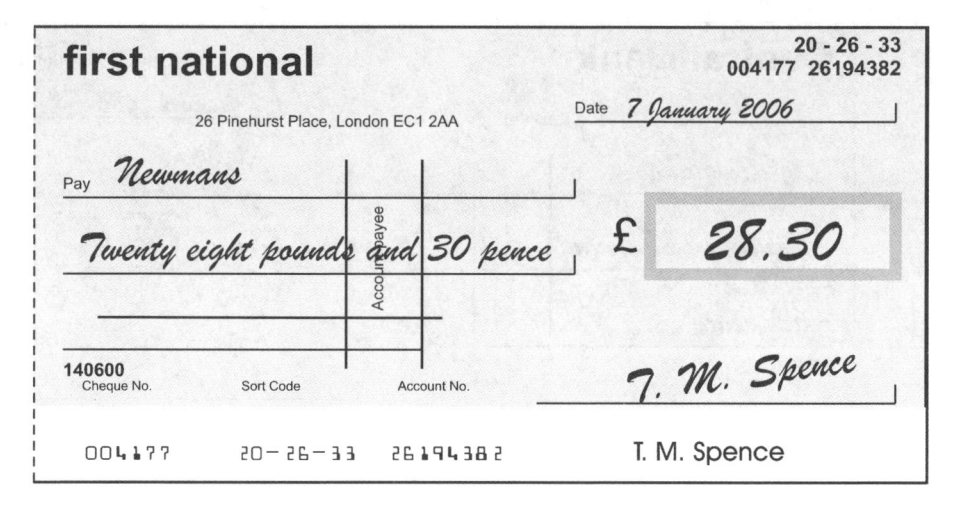

first national
20 - 26 - 33
004177 26194382
26 Pinehurst Place, London EC1 2AA
Date 7 January 2006
Pay Newmans
Twenty eight pounds and 30 pence
£ 28.30
140600 Cheque No.   Sort Code   Account No.
T. M. Spence
004177   20-26-33   26194382
T. M. Spence

This is given to you together with a cheque guarantee card – limit £200, sort code 20-26-33, account number 26194382, expiry date December 2005.

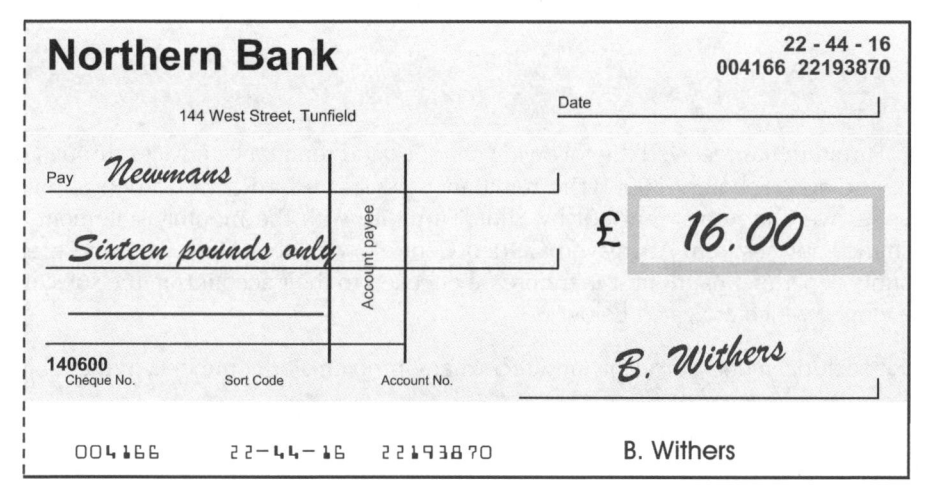

Northern Bank
22 - 44 - 16
004166 22193870
144 West Street, Tunfield
Date
Pay Newmans
Sixteen pounds only
£ 16.00
140600 Cheque No.   Sort Code   Account No.
B. Withers
004166   22-44-16   22193870
B. Withers

This is given to you together with a cheque guarantee card – limit £100, sort code 22-44-30, account number 22193621, expiry date May 2006.

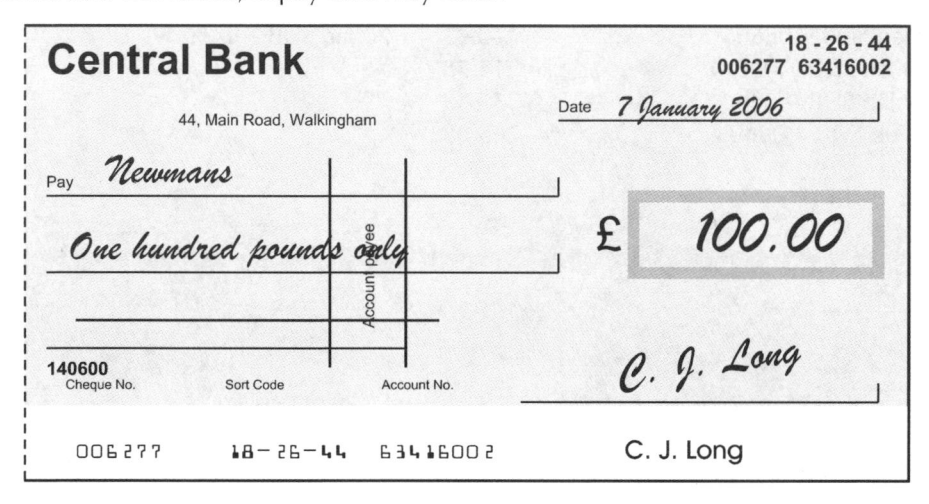

Central Bank
18 - 26 - 44
006277 63416002
44, Main Road, Walkingham
Date 7 January 2006
Pay Newmans
One hundred pounds only
£ 100.00
140600 Cheque No.   Sort Code   Account No.
C. J. Long
006277   18-26-44   63416002
C. J. Long

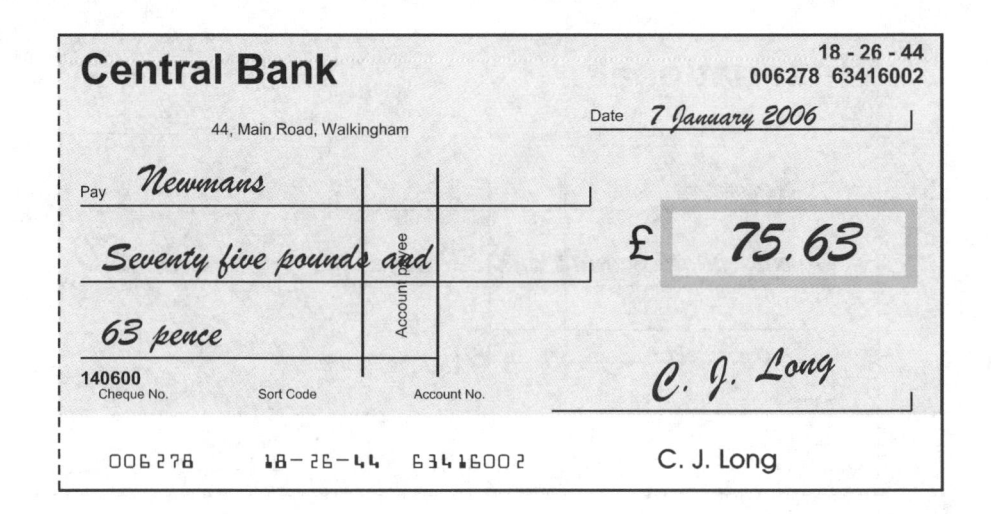

receiving money

Central Bank
18 - 26 - 44
006278 63416002

44, Main Road, Walkingham

Date 7 January 2006

Pay Newmans

Seventy five pounds and 63 pence

£ 75.63

140600
Cheque No.   Sort Code   Account No.

C. J. Long

006278   18-26-44   63416002   C. J. Long

These two cheques were given to you together with a cheque guarantee card – limit £100, sort code 18-26-44, account number 63416002, expiry date June 2006.

5 Short Furniture has received the following cheques and remittance advices through the post in the week ending 7 February 2006. The remittance advices from Rocks Garden Supplies and Eridge Nurseries were the ones sent out by Short Furniture with the monthly statement. However, the remittance advices from Abergaven Garden Centre and Rother Nurseries were prepared by their accounts department and must therefore be checked to their accounts in the subsidiary ledger, the sales ledger, which are given below.

Check each payment thoroughly and record any problems or comments in the table provided.

Subsidiary ledger

	Rother Nurseries		SL 16
	£		£
9 Jan SDB – 08666	740.25	20 Jan SDB – 1470	96.50
16 Jan SDB – 08674	214.78		
24 Jan SDB – 08681	337.89		
5 Feb SDB – 08695	265.98		

receiving money

	Abergaven Garden Centre		SL 17
	£		£
7 Jan SDB – 08665	904.16		
13 Jan SDB – 08672	623.56		
26 Jan SDB – 08685	316.58		
3 Feb SDB – 08692	415.76		

	Comments
Payment from Rocks Garden Supplies	
Payment from Eridge Nurseries	
Payment from Abergaven Garden Centre	
Payment from Rother Nurseries	

receiving money

First Western
30 - 11 - 46
001234 36142910

High Street, Benham

Date 4 February 2006

Pay *Short Furniture*

Seven hundred and seventy three pounds and 75 pence

£ 773.75

Account payee

140600
Cheque No.   Sort Code   Account No.

001234   30-11-46   36142910

P. S. Hammond

Rocks Garden Supplies

REMITTANCE ADVICE

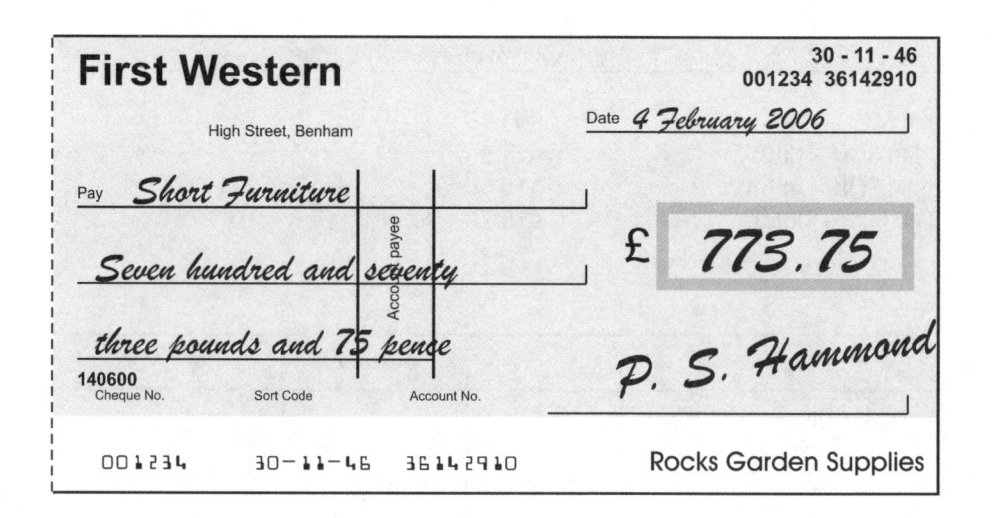

To: Short Furniture
Eridge Estate
Benham DR6 4QQ
Tel 0303312 Fax 0303300

From: Rocks Garden Supplies

Date: 4 February 2006

Reference	Amount £	Paid (✓)
08663	687.14	✓
1468	(343.57)	✓
08675	521.18	✓
08686	732.40	

CHEQUE ENCLOSED £773.75

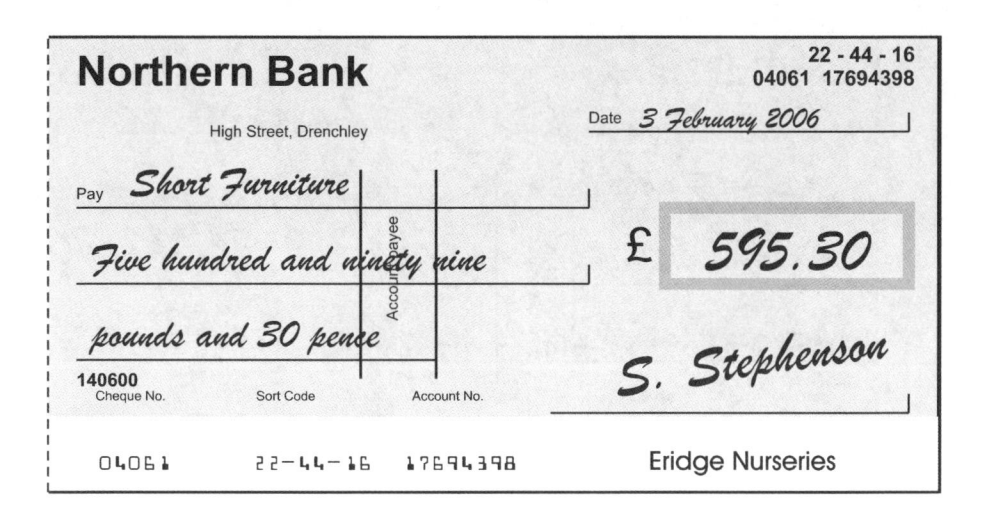

Northern Bank

22 - 44 - 16
04061 17694398

High Street, Drenchley

Date *3 February 2006*

Pay *Short Furniture*

Five hundred and ninety nine pounds and 30 pence

£ *595.30*

S. Stephenson

140600
Cheque No.   Sort Code   Account No.

04061   22-44-16   17694398   Eridge Nurseries

REMITTANCE ADVICE

To: Short Furniture
Eridge Estate
Benham DR6 4QQ
Tel 0303312 Fax 0303300

From: Eridge Nurseries

Date: 3 February 2006

Reference	Amount £	Paid (✓)
08664	420.35	✓
08676	381.18	✓
1471	(206.23)	✓
08687	640.20	
08690	381.62	

CHEQUE ENCLOSED	£595.30

receiving money

Central Bank

18 - 26 - 44
004621 31640390

44, Main Road, Walkingham

Date *4 February 2006*

Pay *Short Furniture*

One thousand eight hundred and forty four pounds and 30 pence

£ **1,844.30**

P. Oliver

140600
Cheque No.   Sort Code   Account No.

004621   18-26-44   31640390

Abergaven Garden Centre

REMITTANCE ADVICE

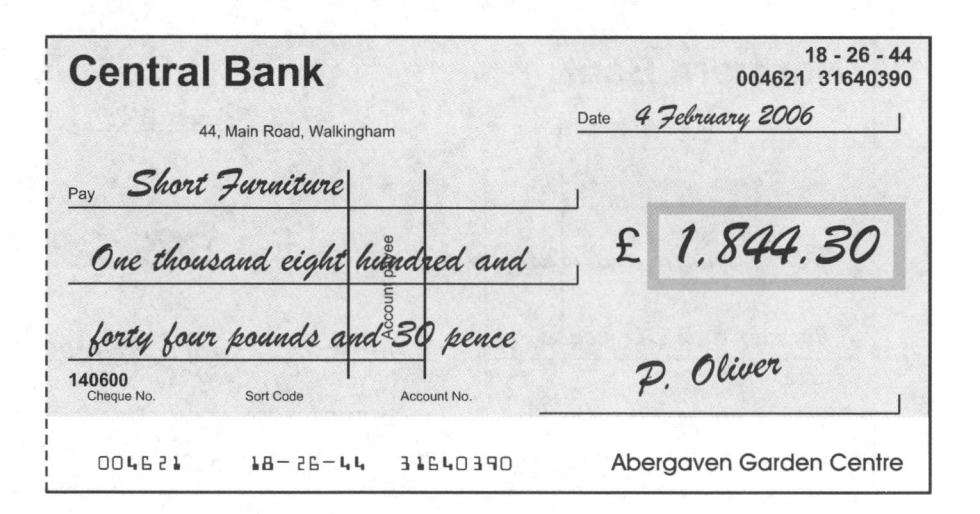

To: Short Furniture
Eridge Estate
Benham DR6 4QQ
Tel 0303312 Fax 0303300

From: Abergaven Garden Centre

Date: 4 February 2006

Reference	Amount £	Paid (✓)
08665	904.16	✓
08672	623.56	✓
08685	316.58	✓

CHEQUE ENCLOSED £1,844.30

Great National Bank

25/27 Main Road, Benham

14 - 23 - 18
001642 32660987

Date 3 February 2006

Pay *Rother Nurseries*

One thousand and ninety six pounds and 42 pence only

£ **1,096.42**

T. Johnson

140600
Cheque No.   Sort Code   Account No.

001642 14-23-18 32660987   Rother Nurseries

REMITTANCE ADVICE

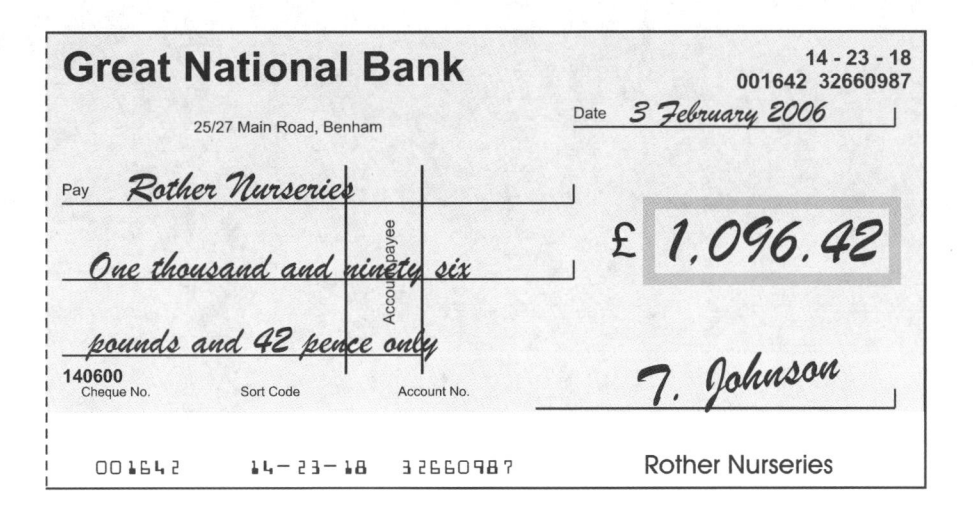

To: Short Furniture
Eridge Estate
Benham DR6 4QQ
Tel 0303312 Fax 0303300

From: Rother Nurseries

Date: 5 February 2006

Reference	Amount £	Paid (✓)
08666	740.25	✓
08674	114.78	✓
1470	(96.50)	✓
08681	337.89	✓

CHEQUE ENCLOSED £1,096.42

chapter 6:
RECORDING RECEIPTS

1 The following sales have been made inclusive of VAT. Calculate the amount of VAT on each sale and the net amount of the sale:

		VAT	Net amount
i)	£145.28	…………………………	…………………………
ii)	£68.90	…………………………	…………………………
iii)	£258.73	…………………………	…………………………
iv)	£35.82	…………………………	…………………………
v)	£125.60	…………………………	…………………………

2 You work for Natural Productions. One of your duties is to write up the cash receipts book. Natural Productions makes sales on credit to a number of credit customers and also has some cash sales from a small retail outlet attached to the factory.

The remittance list for the last week in January 2006 is given below.

REMITTANCE LIST	
23 Jan	£545.14 from Hoppers Ltd – cash discount £16.86
23 Jan	£116.70 from Superior Products
24 Jan	£128.46 from cash sales including VAT
24 Jan	£367.20 from Esporta Leisure – cash discount £11.36
25 Jan	£86.75 from cash sales including VAT
27 Jan	£706.64 from Body Perfect – cash discount £21.86
27 Jan	£58.90 from cash sales including VAT
27 Jan	£267.90 from Langans Beauty

recording receipts

You are required to:

i) record these receipts in the analysed cash receipts book given below

ii) total the cash receipts book and check that it cross-casts

Cash receipts book

Date	Details	Total	VAT	Cash sales	Sales ledger	Sundry	Discounts allowed
		£	£	£	£	£	£

3 What is the double entry required for discounts allowed to customers?

recording receipts

4 Returning to Natural Productions you are required to:

i) post the totals of the cash receipts book to the main ledger accounts given below

ii) post each individual receipt from sales ledger customers to their account in the subsidiary ledger given below

Main ledger

Sales ledger control account

	£		£
20 Jan SDB	3,438.04	20 Jan SRDB	80.72

VAT account

	£		£
20 Jan SRDB	12.02	20 Jan SDB	512.04

Sales account

	£		£
		20 Jan SDB	2,926.00

Discount allowed account

	£		£

Subsidiary ledger

Hoppers Ltd account

	£		£
2 Jan SDB – 6237	642.72	17 Jan SRDB – 1476	80.72

Body Perfect account

	£		£
5 Jan SDB - 6238	728.50		
12 Jan SDB – 6241	643.90		

Esporta Leisure account

	£		£
6 Jan SDB - 6239	406.55		
18 Jan SDB – 6243	488.80		

Langans Beauty account

	£		£
9 Jan SDB - 6240	267.90		

Superior Products account

	£		£
16 Jan SDB - 6242	259.67		

chapter 7:
THE BANKING SYSTEM

1 On 23 January 2006 Natural Productions received a cheque from Hoppers Ltd who bank with Central Bank, Drenchley. Natural Productions pays this cheque into its bank, the Benham branch of the First National Bank.

What happens to this cheque before it appears as cleared funds in Natural Production's bank account?

2 Given below is a summary of the contents of the cash till for a shop at the end of the day.

Notes/coins	Number
£50	3
£20	17
£10	26
£5	35
£2	7
£1	18
50p	15
20p	36
10p	47
5p	23
2p	41
1p	63

What is the total amount of cash in the cash till?

the banking system

3 Given below is the remittance list for Natural Productions for the last week in January 2006.

REMITTANCE LIST	
23 Jan	£545.14 from Hoppers Ltd – cash discount £16.86
23 Jan	£116.70 from Superior Products
24 Jan	£128.46 from cash sales including VAT
24 Jan	£367.20 from Esporta Leisure – cash discount £11.36
25 Jan	£86.75 from cash sales including VAT
27 Jan	£706.64 from Body Perfect – cash discount £21.86
27 Jan	£58.90 from cash sales including VAT
27 Jan	£267.90 from Langans Beauty

All of the cheques are to be paid into the bank today, 27 January 2006.

The cash in the till from the cash sales is made up of the following notes and coins:

Notes/coins	Number
£20	5
£10	12
£5	13
£2	1
£1	17
50p	9
20p	4
10p	15
5p	12
2p	16
1p	19

This is all to be paid into the bank other than the cash float which is always made up as follows:

Notes/coins	Number
£10	2
£5	2
£1	5
50p	2
10p	10
5p	10
2p	10
1p	10

You are required to fill in the paying-in slip given below for payment of the cheques and cash into the bank.

52

the banking system

	Date		Bank Giro Credit			**first national**
Date	Cashier's stamp and initials					

First National High Street, Benham

Account

No. of cheques

Paid in by

	£	p
Cash		
Cheques		
Total		

DE LA RUE 0514

Sorting code number: **20-26-33**
Account number: **40268134**
Transcode: **66**

£ p
Cash
Cheques +
£

Please do not write or mark below this line or fold this voucher

Please detail cash and cheques overleaf

000123 20−26−33 40268134 66

Cash	£	p		Cheques	£	p
£50 notes						
£20 notes						
£10 notes						
£5 notes						
£2 coins						
£1 coins						
Other coins						
Total				Total		

53

chapter 8: COMMUNICATION WITH CUSTOMERS

1 Given below are two debtors accounts. You are required to find the closing balance on each account:

<table>
<tr><td colspan="4" align="center">Harold & partners</td></tr>
<tr><td></td><td>£</td><td></td><td>£</td></tr>
<tr><td>1 May Opening balance</td><td>1,367.83</td><td>7 May CRB</td><td>635.78</td></tr>
<tr><td>5 May SDB – 27465</td><td>998.20</td><td>7 May CRB – discount</td><td>33.46</td></tr>
<tr><td>12 May SDB – 27499</td><td>478.92</td><td>15 May SRDB – CN0364</td><td>106.34</td></tr>
<tr><td>20 May SDB – 27524</td><td>258.29</td><td>30 May CRB</td><td>663.66</td></tr>
<tr><td></td><td></td><td>30 May CRB – discount</td><td>34.93</td></tr>
</table>

<table>
<tr><td colspan="4" align="center">T N Designs</td></tr>
<tr><td></td><td>£</td><td></td><td>£</td></tr>
<tr><td>1 May Opening balance</td><td>2,643.56</td><td>8 May CRB</td><td>1,473.28</td></tr>
<tr><td>11 May SDB – 27491</td><td>828.40</td><td>24 May SRDB CN0381</td><td>253.89</td></tr>
<tr><td>18 May SDB – 27513</td><td>1,083.65</td><td></td><td></td></tr>
</table>

communication with customers

2 You work in the accounts department for Short Furniture. On your desk this morning, 5 February 2006, is the debtor listing as at 31 January 2006, showing amounts outstanding and how long they have been outstanding for. Short Furniture's credit terms are that payment should be made within 30 days of the invoice date. Given below is an extract from that debtor listing:

AGED DEBTOR ANALYSIS

Date: 31 January 2006

Account number	Account name	Credit limit £	Balance £	Current £	> 30 days £	> 60 days £	> 90 days £
SL08	Sunshine Sales	2,000.00	1,979.40	558.38	1,421.02	–	–
SL09	Groom Nurseries	1,000.00	368.90	368.90	–	–	–
SL10	Bridge DIY	1,500.00	1,760.47	1,760.47	–	–	–
SL11	Erfield Gardens	500.00	435.77	–	–	435.77	–
SL12	Lye Nursery	2,500.00	2,100.45	1,743.67	267.46	–	89.32

You are required to comment on the credit position of each of the debtors in the table given below:

Debtor	Comment
Sunshine Sales	
Groom Nurseries	
Bridge DIY	
Erfield Gardens	
Lye Nursery	

3 Using the data from the aged debtor analysis above for Short Furniture draft a suitable letter to Erfield Gardens regarding their credit position on behalf of the Sales Ledger manager, Jane Trump. Today's date is 5 February 2006 and your reference code for the letter is EG11/01/01. The letterhead for Short Furniture is given below to use.

SHORT FURNITURE
ERIDGE ESTATE
BENHAM DR6 4QQ
Tel 0303312 Fax 0303300
VAT Reg 0361 3282 60

chapter 9:
BUSINESS DOCUMENTS – PURCHASES

1 Your name is Charlie Rubble and you work in the warehouse at Whitehill Superstores. You have just taken delivery of some goods supplied by Southfield Electrical, delivery note number 34976. You have checked and counted the goods with the following results:

3	Zanpoint fridge freezers	Stock code	4075
2	Zanpoint tumble dryers	Stock code	4120 (one of these is scratched and is returned to Southfield on the van)
1	Hosch washing machine	Stock code	6140

Your assistant Jim Davids has checked that this is correct. Today's date is 14 January 2006 and the last GRN number was 04883. The purchase order that this delivery relates to is 32581.

You are required to complete the goods received note given below.

GOODS RECEIVED NOTE

Whitehill Superstores

Supplier:

GRN number:

Date:

Order number:

Quantity	Description	Stock code

Received by: ....

Checked by: ....

Comments: ....

2 You work in the accounts department of Whitehill Superstores and one of your duties is to request credit notes from suppliers by sending debit notes. Regarding the delivery from Southfield Electrical above you are required to complete the debit note given below relating to this delivery. The purchase order that relates to this delivery is given below. Today's date is 15 January 2006 and the last debit note number used was 0612.

PURCHASE ORDER

WHITEHILL SUPERSTORES
28 Whitehill Park
Benham DR6 5LM
Tel 0303446 Fax 0303447

To: Southfield Electrical
Industrial Estate
Benham DR6 2FF

Number: 32581

Date: 10 Jan 2006

Delivery address: Whitehill Superstores
28, Whitehill Park
Benham DR6 5LM

Product code	Quantity	Description	Unit list price £
6140	1	Hosch Washing Machine	220.00
4075	3	Zanpoint Fridge Freezer	310.00
4120	2	Zanpoint Tumble Dryer	190.00

Authorised by: *T. Hampton*   **Date:** *10 Jan 2006*

DEBIT NOTE

WHITEHILL SUPERSTORES
28 Whitehill Park
Benham DR6 5LM
Tel 0303446 Fax 0303447

To:

Debit note number:

Date/tax point:

Order number

Delivery note number:

Quantity	Description	Stock code	Unit amount	Total
			£	£

Reason: ....

Authorised by: .... **Date:** ....

3 Your name is Anita Paul and you work in the accounts department of Short Furniture and one of your duties is to check invoices received from suppliers to purchase orders, delivery notes and GRNs.

Given below are three invoices from suppliers and the related supporting documentation. You are required to check each invoice carefully to the supporting documentation and note any discrepancies and the action required to be taken in the table given.

Supplier	Comment
A1 Wood Supplies	
Polish People	
Woodwards Woods	

INVOICE

A1 Wood Supplies
Heath Park
Drenchley DR22 6KL
VAT Reg 4621 3117 04

To: Short Furniture
Eridge Estate
Benham DR6 4QQ

Invoice number: 764910

Date/tax point: 5 Jan 2006

Order number: 04672

Account number: 504

Quantity	Description	Stock code	Unit amount £	Total £
20m	Stripped Pine	P4612	12.38	247.60
50m	Oak	02611	15.87	793.50
				1,041.10
	Trade Discount			156.17

Net total	884.93
VAT	150.21
Invoice total	1,035.14

Terms
3% settlement discount for payment within 14 days, otherwise 30 days net
E & OE

PURCHASE ORDER

SHORT FURNITURE
Eridge Estate
Benham DR6 4QQ
Tel 0303312 Fax 0303300

To: A1 Wood Supplies
    Heath Park
    Drenchley

Number: 04672

Date: 2 Jan 2006

Delivery address: As above

Product code	Quantity	Description	Unit list price £
04612	20m	Stripped Pine	12.38 per m + VAT
02611	50m	Oak	15.87 per m + VAT

Authorised by: *K. Palmer*   Date: *2 Jan 2006*

DELIVERY NOTE

A1 Wood Supplies
Heath Park
Drenchley DR22 6KL
VAT Reg 4621 3117 04

Delivery address:

Short Furniture
Eridge Estate
Benham DR6 4QQ

Number: DN41268
Date: 5 Jan 2006
Order number: 04672

Product code	Quantity	Description
P4612	20m	Stripped Pine
02611	45m	Oak

Received by: [Signature] *A. Hall* **Print name:** *A. HALL*

Date: *5 Jan 2006*

GOODS RECEIVED NOTE

Short Furniture

Supplier: A1 Wood Supplies

GRN number: 07904
Date: 5 Jan 2006
Order number: 04672

Quantity	Description	Stock code
45m	Oak	02611
20m	Stripped Pine	P4612

Received by: *A. Hall*
Checked by: *J. Finch*
Comments: —

business documents – purchases

INVOICE

Polish People
23/25 Main Street
Wakeham DR17 4ZF
VAT Reg 692 9417 63

To: Short Furniture
Eridge Estate
Benham DR6 4QQ

Invoice number: 06694

Date/tax point: 4 Jan 2006

Order number: 04668

Account number: SL 13

Quantity	Description	Stock code	Unit amount £	Total £
48 litres	Exterior Wood Polish – cherry	88631	3.16	151.68
24 litres	Exterior Wood Polish – teak	88413	2.83	67.92
			Net total	219.60
			VAT	38.43
			Invoice total	258.03

Terms
Net 30 days
E & OE

PURCHASE ORDER

SHORT FURNITURE
Eridge Estate
Benham DR6 4QQ
Tel 0303312 Fax 0303300

To: Polish People
23/25 Main Street
Wakeham DR17 4ZF

Number: 04668

Date: 23 Dec 2005

Delivery address: As above

Product code	Quantity	Description	Unit list price £
88413	24 litres	Exterior Wood Polish – teak	2.83 per litre + VAT
88631	48 litres	Exterior Wood Polish – cherry	2.99 per litre + VAT

Authorised by: *K. Palmer*　　　　　**Date:** *23 Dec 2005*

business documents – purchases

DELIVERY NOTE

Polish People
23/25 Main Street
Wakeham DR17 4ZF
VAT Reg 692 9417 63

Delivery address:

Short Furniture
Eridge Estate
Benham DR6 4QQ

Number: 17792
Date: 3 Jan 2006
Order number: 04668

Product code	Quantity	Description
88631	48 litres	Exterior Wood Polish – cherry
88413	24 litres	Exterior Wood Polish – teak

Received by: [Signature] *A. Hall*   **Print name:** *A. HALL*

Date: *3 Jan 2006*

GOODS RECEIVED NOTE

Short Furniture

Supplier: Polish People

GRN number: 07903
Date: 4 Jan 2006
Order number: 04668

Quantity	Description	Stock code
24 litres	Exterior Wood Polish – teak	88413
48 litres	Exterior Wood Polish – cherry	88631

Received by: A. Hall
Checked by: J. Finch
Comments: –

INVOICE

Woodwards Woods
Inchpark House
Westfield Road
Benham DR6 4PL
VAT Reg 6671 4289 83

To: Short Furniture
Eridge Estate
Benham DR6 4QQ

Invoice number: 46692

Date/tax point: 5 Jan 2006

Order number: 04671

Account number: SL 56

Quantity	Description	Stock code	Unit amount £	Total £
110m	Teak 10cm planks	T10P	7.23	795.90
	Trade Discount			159.06

Net total	636.24
VAT	108.55
Invoice total	744.79

Terms
2.5% settlement discount for payment within 20 days, otherwise 30 days net
E & OE

PURCHASE ORDER

SHORT FURNITURE
Eridge Estate
Benham DR6 4QQ
Tel 0303312 Fax 0303300

To: Woodwards Woods
Inchpark House
Westfield Road
Benham DR6 4PL

Number: 04671

Date: 2 Jan 2006

Delivery address: As above

Product code	Quantity	Description	Unit list price £
T10P	110m	Teak 10cm planks	7.23 per metre + VAT

Authorised by: *K. Palmer*   Date: *2 Jan 2006*

business documents – purchases

DELIVERY NOTE

Woodwards Woods
Inchpark House
Westfield Road
Benham DR6 4PL

Delivery address:

Short Furniture
Eridge Estate
Benham DR6 4QQ

Number: 646921
Date: 5 Jan 2006
Order number: 04671

Product code	Quantity	Description
T10P	~~110m~~ 95m	Teak 10cm plank

Received by: [Signature] *A. Hall*   **Print name:** *A. HALL*

Date: *5 Jan 2006*

GOODS RECEIVED NOTE

Short Furniture

Supplier: Woodwards Woods

GRN number: 07905
Date: 5 Jan 2006
Order number: 04671

Quantity	Description	Stock code
95m	Teak 10cm plank	T10P

Received by: A. Hall

Checked by: J. Finch

Comments: -

chapter 10:
ACCOUNTING FOR CREDIT PURCHASES

1   Natural Productions is a small business that manufactures a variety of soaps and bath products. It buys materials for the manufacturing process from a number of suppliers on credit. It also buys other items such as stationery and packaging on credit. During January 2006 Natural Productions received the following invoices from credit suppliers:

4 Jan	Invoice No. 03576 from P J Phillips £357 plus VAT for materials
6 Jan	Invoice No. 18435 from Trenter Ltd £428 plus VAT for materials
9 Jan	Invoice No. 43654 from W J Jones £210 plus VAT for stationery
12 Jan	Invoice No. 03598 from P J Phillips £413 plus VAT for materials
16 Jan	Invoice No. 28423 from Packing Supplies £268 plus VAT for packaging
19 Jan	Invoice No. 18478 from Trenter Ltd £521 plus VAT for materials
20 Jan	Invoice No. 84335 from O & P Ltd £624 plus VAT for materials
24 Jan	Invoice No. 28444 from Packing Supplies £164 plus VAT for packaging
28 Jan	Invoice No. 18491 from Trenter Ltd £368 plus VAT for materials
31 Jan	Invoice No. 43681 from W J Jones £104 plus VAT for stationery

You are required to:

a)   enter these transactions in the purchases day book given below

b)   cast the columns of the purchases day book and check that they cross-cast

c)   post the totals of the purchases day book to the main ledger accounts given

d)   post the individual entries to the subsidiary ledger, the purchases ledger, accounts given

Purchases day book

Date	Supplier	Invoice number	Gross £	VAT £	Purchases £	Stationery £	Packaging £

Main ledger

Purchases ledger control account

£	£

VAT account

£	£

accounting for credit purchases

Purchases account

£	£

Stationery account

£	£

Packaging account

£	£

Subsidiary ledger

P J Phillips account

£	£

Trenter Ltd account

£	£

W J Jones account

£	£

Packing Supplies account

£		£

O & P Ltd account

£		£

2 Given below are four purchase invoices received by Short Furniture, the only invoices received this week, the week ending 27 January 2006. You are also given an extract from the purchase ledger coding listing.

Purchase ledger coding listing

Calverley Bros	PL03
Cavendish Woods	PL14
Culverden & Co	PL23
Ephraim Supplies	PL39

You are required to:

a) enter the invoices in the purchases day book given - note that purchases are analysed into wood, polish and varnish and other

b) total and check the purchases day book

c) post the purchases day book totals to the main ledger accounts given

d) post the individual entries in the purchases day book to the supplier's accounts in the subsidiary ledger, the purchases ledger, given below

Purchases day book

Date	Supplier	Invoice number	Ref	Gross £	VAT £	Wood purchases £	Polish/ varnish purchases £	Other purchases £	Sundry £

INVOICE

Ephraim Supplies
24 Mount Street
Benham DR6 8PN

To: Short Furniture
Eridge Estate
Benham DR6 4QQ

Invoice number: 09642

Date/tax point: 24 Jan 2006

Order number: 04697

Account number: SL 02

Quantity	Description	Stock code	Unit amount £	Total £
75m	10cm Teak Pole	461127	4.85	363.75
	Trade Discount			72.75
			Net total	291.00
			VAT	49.39
			Invoice total	340.39

Terms
3% settlement discount for payment within 20 days, otherwise 30 days net
E & OE

INVOICE

Cavendish Woods
Earley House
Wakeham DR17 6TQ
VAT Reg 6291 3714 06

To: Short Furniture
Eridge Estate
Benham DR6 4QQ

Invoice number: 06932

Date/tax point: 23 Jan 2006

Order number: 04696

Account number: SL 14

Quantity	Description	Stock code	Unit amount £	Total £
70m	Teak	46117	11.85	829.50
	Trade Discount			124.43

Net total	705.07
VAT	123.38
Invoice total	828.45

Terms
Net 30 days
E & OE

accounting for credit purchases

INVOICE

Calverley Bros
Charter House
Main Street
Drenchley DR22 4XJ
VAT Reg 3929 4960 07

To: Short Furniture
Eridge Estate
Benham DR6 4QQ

Invoice number: 67671

Date/tax point: 23 Jan 2006

Order number: 04689

Account number: S03

Quantity	Description	Stock code	Unit amount £	Total £
40 litres	Exterior Wood Varnish – Colour 007	WV407	3.64	145.60
			Net total	145.60
			VAT	25.48
			Invoice total	171.08

Terms
Net 30 days
E & OE

INVOICE

Culverden & Co
Channing Park Estate
Wakeham DR17 4LF
VAT Reg 1273 4522 16

To: Short Furniture
Eridge Estate
Benham DR6 4QQ

Invoice number: 36004

Date/tax point: 24 Jan 2006

Order number: 04691

Account number: SL 10

Quantity	Description	Stock code	Unit amount £	Total £
20 dozen	3/4" nails	664327	2.87	57.40
			Net total	57.40
			VAT	9.84
			Invoice total	67.24

Terms
2% settlement discount for payment within 20 days, otherwise net 30 days
E & OE

accounting for credit purchases

Main ledger

Purchases ledger control account

| £ | £ |

VAT account

| £ | £ |

Wood purchases account

| £ | £ |

Polish/varnish purchases account

| £ | £ |

Other purchases account

| £ | £ |

Subsidiary ledger

	Calverley Bros account		PL 03
	£		£

	Cavendish Woods account		PL 14
	£		£

	Culverden & Co account		PL 23
	£		£

	Ephraim Supplies account		PL 39
	£		£

accounting for credit purchases

3 Returning to Natural Productions, during January the following credit notes were received:

10 Jan Credit note No. 04216 from P J Phillips £98 plus VAT
16 Jan Credit note No. CN 0643 from W J Jones £56 plus VAT
30 Jan Credit note No. CN 1102 from O & P Ltd £124 plus VAT

You are required to:

a) enter these transactions in the purchases returns day book given below

b) cast the columns of the purchases returns day book and check that they cross-cast

c) post the totals of the purchases returns day book to the main ledger accounts given

d) post the individual entries to the subsidiary ledger accounts also given below

Purchases returns day book

Date	Supplier	Invoice number	Gross £	VAT £	Purchases £	Stationery £	Packaging £

Main ledger

Purchases ledger control account

£		£
	31 Jan PDB	4,061.96

VAT account

£		£
31 Jan PDB	604.96		

accounting for credit purchases

Purchases account

	£		£
31 Jan PDB	2,711.00		

Stationery account

	£		£
31 Jan PDB	314.00		

Packaging account

	£		£
31 Jan PDB	432.00		

Subsidiary ledger

P J Phillips account

	£		£
		4 Jan PDB 03576	419.47
		12 Jan PDB 03598	485.27

W J Jones account

	£		£
		9 Jan PDB 43654	246.75
		31 Jan PDB 43681	122.20

O & P Ltd account

	£		£
		20 Jan PDB 84335	733.20

chapter 11:
MAKING PAYMENTS TO CREDIT SUPPLIERS

1 Given below is a list of suppliers' invoices that require paying and their payment terms. When a cheque is written to a supplier it generally takes two days to reach the supplier. It is your organisation's policy to take advantage of any settlement discounts wherever possible but, if a discount cannot be taken, to pay the invoice after 30 days. Where settlement discounts are not offered it is your organisation's policy to take the longest period of credit allowed by the supplier. Today's date is 17 January 2006.

	Invoice date	Payment terms	Invoice amount £
i)	9 Jan	30 days	£372.48 plus VAT
ii)	9 Jan	2.5% settlement discount for receipt within 10 days	£275.68 plus VAT
iii)	10 Jan	5% settlement discount for receipt within 7 days	£624.59 plus VAT
iv)	10 Jan	30 days	£168.90 plus VAT
v)	11 Jan	3% settlement discount for receipt within 10 days	£527.00 plus VAT
vi)	11 Jan	3% settlement discount for receipt within 14 days	£473.80 plus VAT

You are required to complete the schedule given below showing the date that the cheque must be sent to the supplier according to your organisation's policies and the amount of the cheque to be sent. There is space after the schedule for any workings that may be required.

Invoice No	Payment date	Amount £
i)		
ii)		
iii)		
iv)		
v)		
vi)		

making payments to credit suppliers

2 You work for Newmans, the music shop, in the accounts department and one of your responsibilities is to organise the payments to suppliers. You have been off sick for the last week and a half and therefore it is urgent that you consider the invoices that are on your desk requiring payment.

Newman's policy is to pay any invoices that are due each Friday. If a settlement discount is offered by a supplier then this should be taken if it can validly be taken each Friday. Otherwise the policy is to take the maximum amount of credit available. When a cheque is written on a Friday it does not then reach the supplier until Monday, ie three days later.

Today's date is Friday 27 January 2006. Thereafter, the following payment dates are 3 February, 10 February and 17 February. Remember that, as payments take three days to reach the supplier, then any invoice dated earlier than 7 January with a 30-day credit limit must be paid today as if they are delayed until 3 February then the payment will not be received until 6 February, more than 30 days.

The invoices that are on your desk are scheduled below:

Invoice date	Supplier	Terms	Gross £	VAT £	Net £
5 Jan	Henson Press	30 days	329.00	49.00	280.00
8 Jan	GH Publications	30 days	133.95	19.95	114.00
12 Jan	Ely Instruments	20 days 2% discount otherwise 30 days	749.76	109.76	640.00
15 Jan	Hams Instruments	14 days 2.5% discount otherwise 30 days	362.89	52.89	310.00
19 Jan	CD Supplies	10 days 3% discount otherwise 30 days	135.22	19.62	115.60
22 Jan	Jester Press	10 days 3.5% discount otherwise 30 days	149.14	21.54	127.60
22 Jan	Henson Press	30 days	299.62	44.62	255.00
23 Jan	CD Supplies	10 days 3% discount otherwise 30 days	76.50	11.10	65.40
25 Jan	Jester Press	10 days 3.5% discount otherwise 30 days	46.17	6.67	39.50
25 Jan	Buser Ltd	7 days 5% discount otherwise 30 days	285.73	40.73	245.00

In the schedule given below show the date that each invoice should be paid and the amount for which the cheque should be written out.

making payments to credit suppliers

Invoice		Payment date	Amount of cheque
5 Jan	Henson Press		
8 Jan	GH Publications		
12 Jan	Ely Instruments		
15 Jan	Hams Instruments		
19 Jan	CD Supplies		
22 Jan	Jester Press		
22 Jan	Henson Press		
23 Jan	CD Supplies		
25 Jan	Jester Press		
25 Jan	Buser Ltd		

3   Given below are six blank cheques. Using the information for Newmans set out above, for each of the payments to be made today write out the cheque and cheque stub recording any discount taken on the cheque stub. You do not need to sign the cheque as this will be done by the authorised signatories.

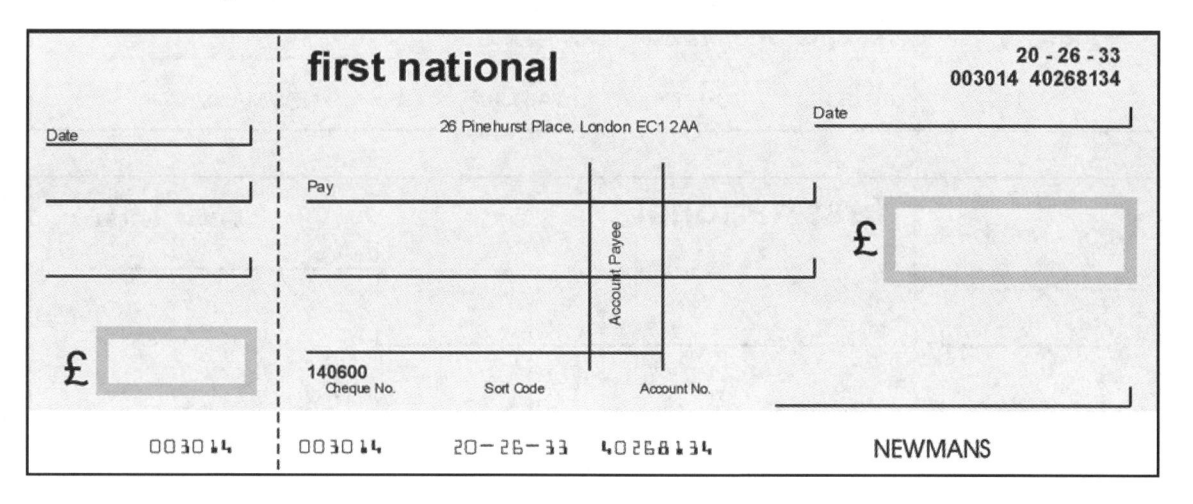

first national

26 Pinehurst Place, London EC1 2AA

Date

Pay

Account Payee

£

Date

£

140600
Cheque No.   Sort Code   Account No.

003014   003014   20-26-33   40268134   NEWMANS

20 - 26 - 33
003014 40268134

93

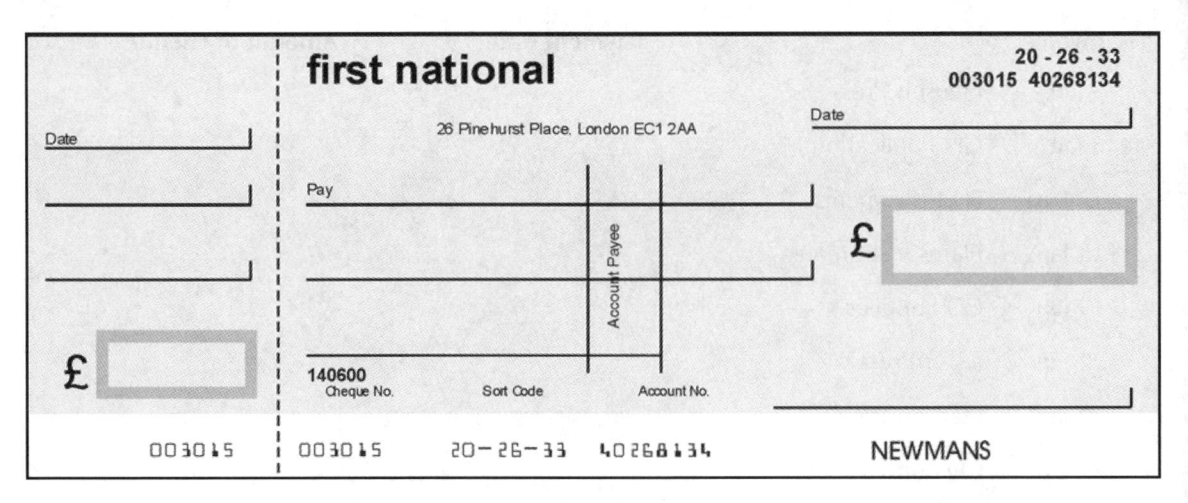

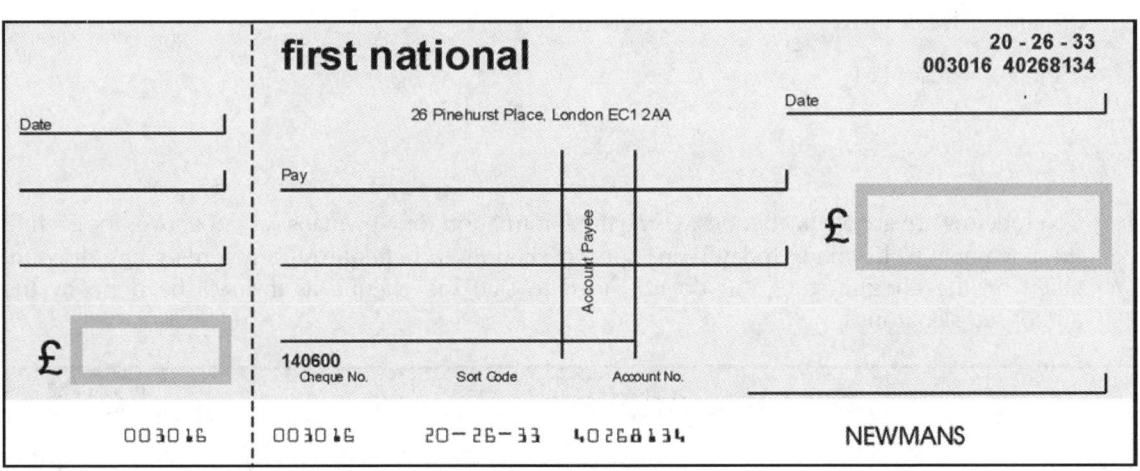

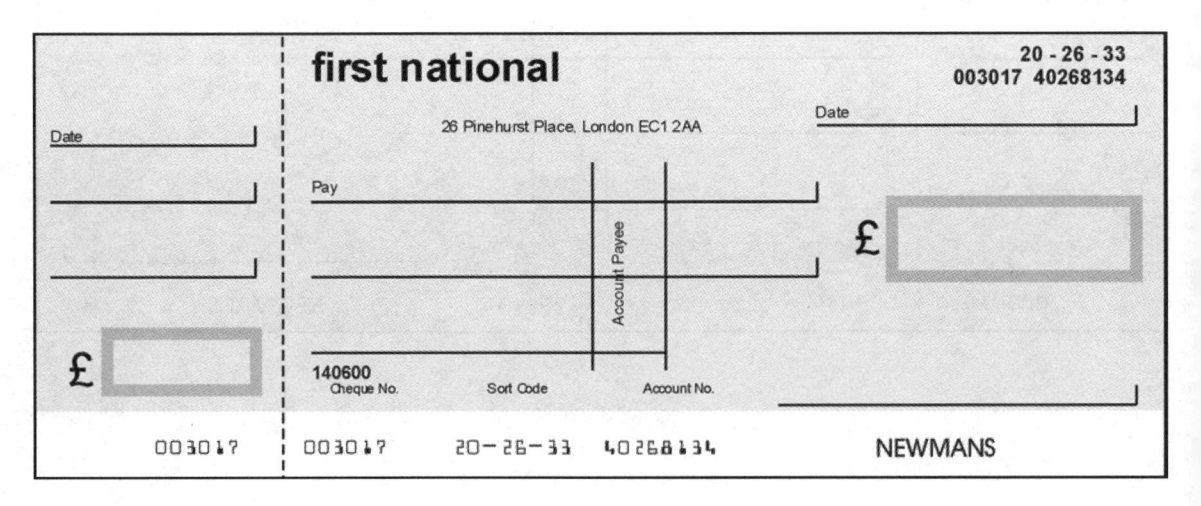

making payments to credit suppliers

94

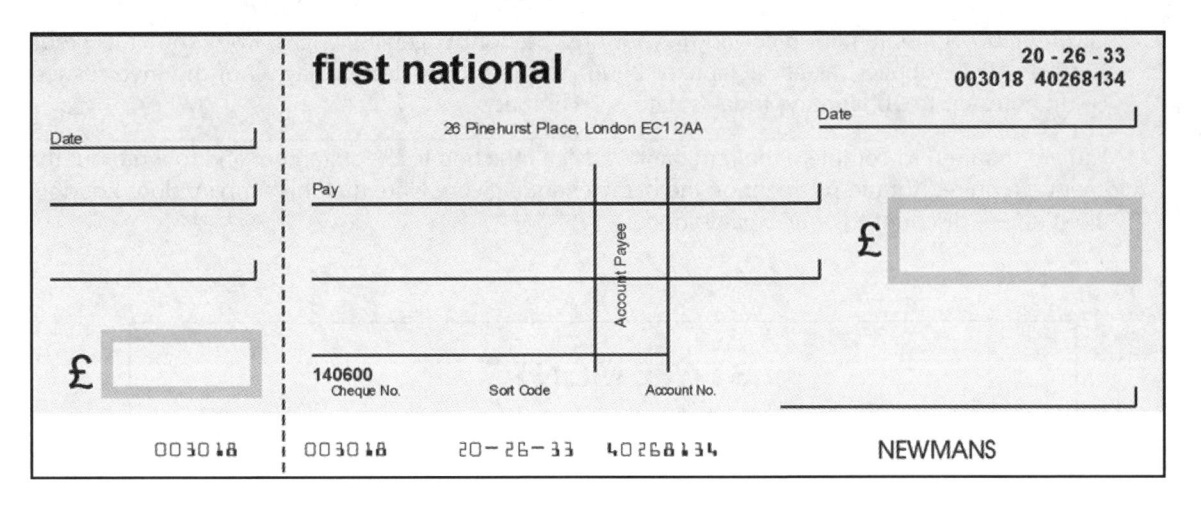

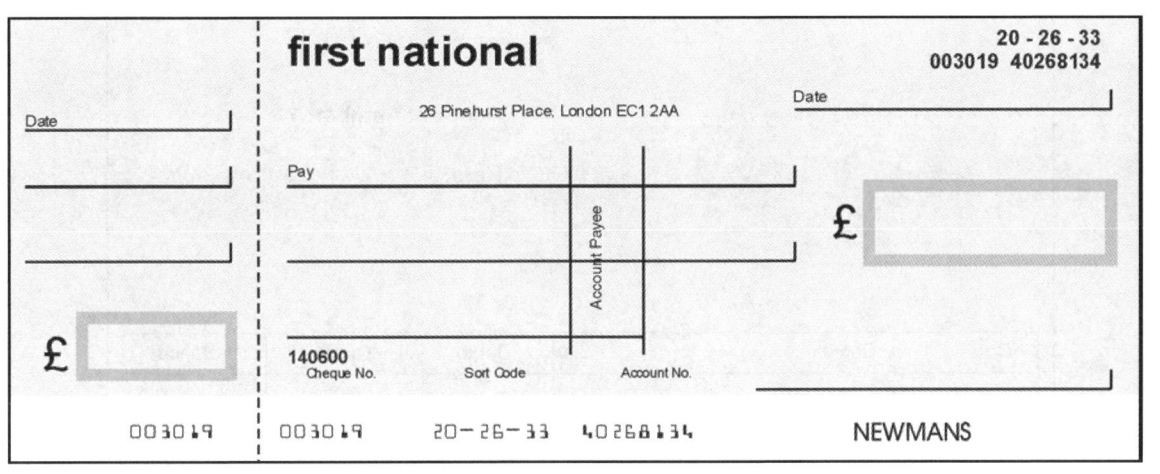

making payments to credit suppliers

first national

26 Pinehurst Place, London EC1 2AA

20 - 26 - 33
003018 40268134

Date

Date

Pay

£

Account Payee

£

140600
Cheque No.   Sort Code   Account No.

003018   003018   20-26-33   40268134   NEWMANS

---

first national

26 Pinehurst Place, London EC1 2AA

20 - 26 - 33
003019 40268134

Date

Date

Pay

£

Account Payee

£

140600
Cheque No.   Sort Code   Account No.

003019   003019   20-26-33   40268134   NEWMANS

4 Given below is a statement received by your organisation, Edgehill Designs, from one of its credit suppliers, P T Supplies, as at 31 January 2006. You are instructed to pay all of the invoices less credit notes up to 10 January. Today's date is 7 February.

You are required to complete the remittance advice attached to the statement and to write out the cheque required for the payment on the blank cheque given. Note that this supplier does not offer a settlement discount to your organisation.

STATEMENT

P. T. Supplies
28 Farm Court Road
Drenchley DR22 4XT

To: Edgehill Designs

Account number: SL 53

Date: 31 January 2006

Date	Details	Debit	Credit	Balance
2006				
1 Jan	Balance b/f	227.63		227.63
6 Jan	Inv 20671	107.22		334.85
8 Jan	Inv 20692	157.63		492.48
9 Jan	Payment - Thank you		227.63	264.85
10 Jan	CN 04722		28.41	236.44
17 Jan	Inv 20718	120.48		356.92
25 Jan	Inv 20734	106.18		463.10
30 Jan	CN 04786		16.15	446.95

Amount now due £446.95

REMITTANCE ADVICE

To: P.T. Supplies
28 Farm Court Road
Drenchley DR22 4XT

From: Edgehill Designs

Date: 7 February 2006

Reference	Amount £	Paid (✓)
20671	107.22	
20692	157.63	
CN 04722	(28.41)	
20718	120.48	
20734	106.18	
CN 04786	(16.15)	

CHEQUE ENCLOSED £

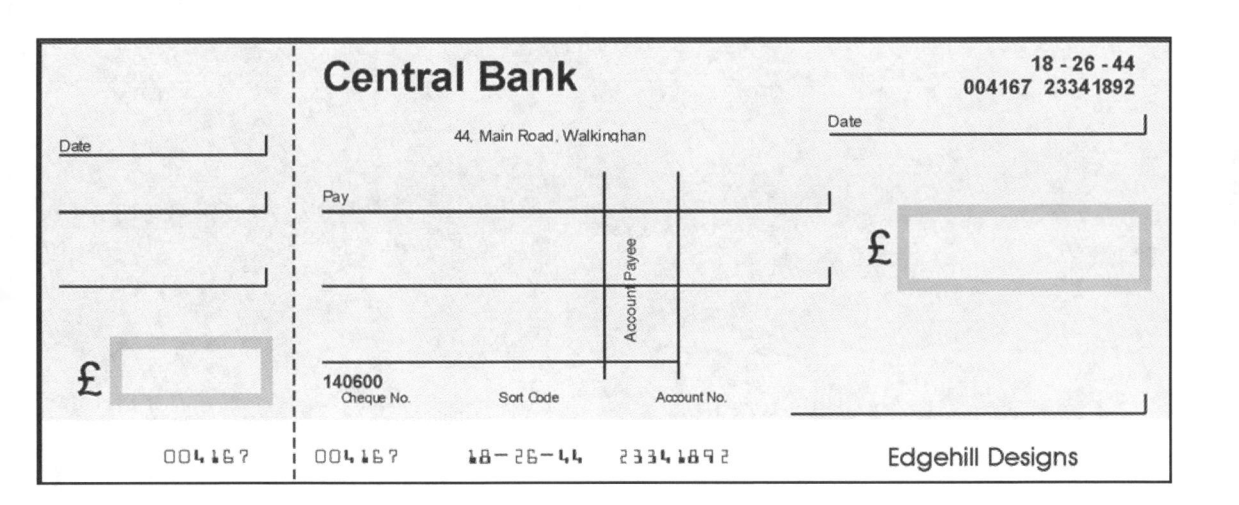

Central Bank

18 - 26 - 44
004167 23341892

44, Main Road, Walkinghan

Date

Pay

Account Payee

£

140600
Cheque No.   Sort Code   Account No.

004167   004167   18-26-44   23341892

Edgehill Designs

chapter 12:
RECORDING PAYMENTS

1 The following purchases have been made for cash inclusive of VAT. Calculate the amount of VAT on each purchase and the net amount of the purchase:

		VAT	Net amount
i)	£254.68	....	....
ii)	£159.28	....	....
iii)	£ 49.69	....	....
iv)	£104.28	....	....
v)	£ 62.48	....	....
vi)	£823.55	....	....

2 A payment is made to a supplier for £367.48 after a settlement discount of £12.50 has been taken. What is the double entry for this transaction?

recording payments

3 You work for Natural Productions and one of your duties is to write up the cash payments book. Most of the payments are to credit suppliers but there are some cash purchases of materials from small suppliers which include VAT.

The cheque payment listing for the week ending 27 January 2006 is given below:

Cheque Payment Listing

Date	Cheque number	Supplier	Amount £	Discount £
23 Jan	002144	Trenter Ltd	1,110.09	28.47
23 Jan	002145	Cash purchase	105.79	
24 Jan	002146	W J Jones	246.75	
24 Jan	002147	P J Phillips	789.60	
24 Jan	002148	Cash purchase	125.68	
25 Jan	002149	Packing Supplies	305.45	8.04
26 Jan	002150	O & P Ltd	703.87	18.72
27 Jan	002151	Cash purchase	95.00	

You are required to:

a) record these receipts in the analysed cash payments book given below

b) total the cash payments book and check that it cross-casts

c) post the totals of the cash payments book to the main ledger accounts given below

d) post each of the individual payments to the suppliers' accounts in the subsidiary ledger given below

Date	Details	Cheque No	Total £	VAT £	Cash purchases £	Purchases ledger £	Sundry £	Discounts received £

Main ledger

Purchases ledger control account

	£		£
31 Jan PRDB	326.65	31 Jan PDB	4,061.96

VAT account

	£		£
31 Jan PDB	604.96	31 Jan PRDB	48.65

Purchases account

	£		£
31 Jan PDB	2,711.00	31 Jan PRDB	222.00

Discounts received account

	£		£

Subsidiary ledger

P J Phillips account

	£		£
10 Jan PRDB 04216	115.15	4 Jan PDB 03576	419.47
		12 Jan PDB 03598	485.27

W J Jones account

	£		£
16 Jan PRDB CN0643	65.80	9 Jan PDB 43654	246.75
		31 Jan PDB 43681	122.20

recording payments

O & P Ltd account

	£		£
30 Jan PRDB CN1102	145.70	20 Jan PDB 84335	733.20

Trenter Ltd account

	£		£
		6 Jan PDB 18435	502.90
		28 Jan PDB 18491	432.40

Packing Supplies account

	£		£
		16 Jan PDB 28423	314.90
		24 Jan PDB 28444	192.70

4 Given below are the cheque stubs for the six payments made by Newmans on 27 January.

You have also looked at the standing order and direct debit instruction file and noted that there is a standing order due to be paid to the local council for business rates of £255.00 on the 27th of each month and a direct debit for rent of £500.00 also due on 27th of the month.

You are required to write up the cash payments book given below, total it and post it to the main ledger accounts given and the subsidiary ledger accounts given.

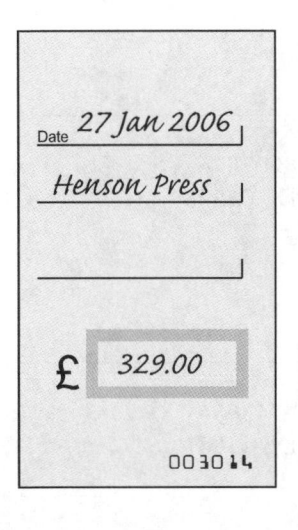

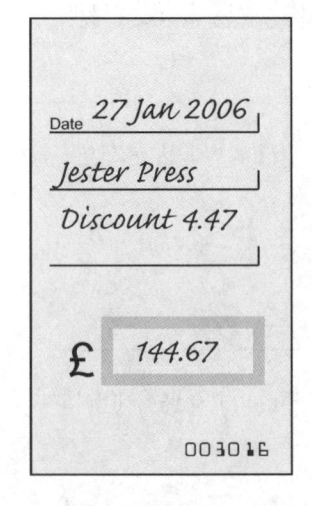

Date 27 Jan 2006
Henson Press
£ 329.00
003014

Date 27 Jan 2006
Ely Instruments
Discount 12.80
£ 736.96
003015

Date 27 Jan 2006
Jester Press
Discount 4.47
£ 144.67
003016

recording payments

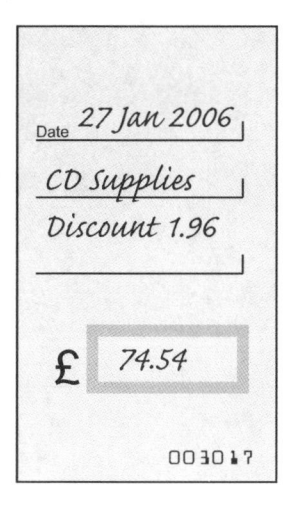

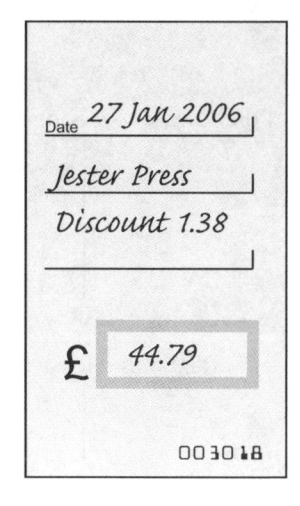

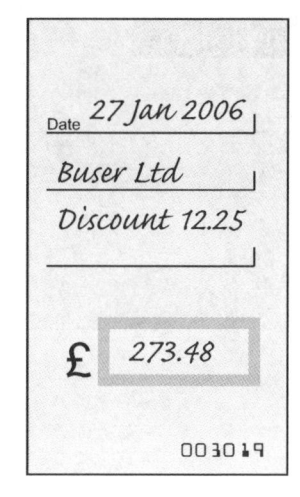

Date	CD Supplies	Jester Press	Buser Ltd
27 Jan 2006	Discount 1.96	Discount 1.38	Discount 12.25
£	74.54	44.79	273.48
	003017	003018	003019

Cash payments book

Date	Details	Cheque No	Total £	VAT £	Purchases ledger £	Rent & rates £	Sundry £	Discounts received £

recording payments

Main ledger

Purchases ledger control account

	£		£

Rent and rates account

	£		£

Discounts received

	£		£

Subsidiary ledger

Buser Ltd

	£		£

CD Supplies

	£		£

Ely Instruments

	£		£

Henson Press

	£		£

Jester Press

	£		£

recording payments

5 You have received an invoice from a regular supplier for £1,000 plus VAT. However, upon checking the supplier master file, you note that normally this supplier gives your company a 20% trade discount. Draft the wording of a letter to the supplier explaining the problem and requesting a credit note for a suitable amount.

chapter 13:
PETTY CASH PROCEDURES

1. Natural Productions has a petty cash system based on an imprest amount of £100 which is replenished weekly. On Friday 20 January 2006 the total of the vouchers in the petty cash box was £68.34. How much cash is required to replenish the petty cash box?

2. Newmans, the music shop, has an imprest petty cash system based upon an imprest amount of £120.00. During the week ending 27 January 2006 the petty cash vouchers given below were presented, authorised and paid.

PETTY CASH VOUCHER

Number: 0726   Date: 27 Jan 2006

Details		Amount
Computer disks		9 - 35
	Net	9 - 35
	VAT	1 - 63
	Gross	10 - 98

Claimed by: D. Player
Authorised by: J. Clarke

PETTY CASH VOUCHER

Number: 0721   Date: 23 Jan 2006

Details		Amount
Coffee		3 - 99
	Net	3 - 99
	VAT	-
	Gross	3 - 99

Claimed by: T. Richards
Authorised by: J. Clarke

PETTY CASH VOUCHER

Number: 0722
Date: 23 Jan 2006

Details		Amount
10 Books Postage Stamps		24 - 00
	Net	24 - 00
	VAT	-
	Gross	24 - 00

Claimed by: D. Player
Authorised by: J. Clarke

PETTY CASH VOUCHER

Number: 0723
Date: 24 Jan 2006

Details		Amount
Taxi fare		8 - 94
	Net	8 - 94
	VAT	1 - 56
	Gross	10 - 50

Claimed by: P. L. Newman
Authorised by: J. Clarke

PETTY CASH VOUCHER

Number: 0724
Date: 24 Jan 2006

Details		Amount
Printer paper		2 - 99
Envelopes		2 - 95
	Net	5 - 94
	VAT	1 - 03
	Gross	6 - 97

Claimed by: T. Richards
Authorised by: J. Clarke

PETTY CASH VOUCHER

Number: *0725*   Date: *26 Jan 2006*

Details		Amount
Train fare		*13 - 60*
	Net	*13 - 60*
	VAT	*-*
	Gross	*13 - 60*

Claimed by: *P. L. Newman*

Authorised by: *J. Clarke*

You are required to:

a) write up the petty cash vouchers in the petty cash book

b) total the petty cash payments side and check that it cross-casts

c) post the totals of the payments side to the main ledger accounts given

RECEIPTS			PAYMENTS							
Date	Details	Amount £	Date	Details	Voucher number	Total £	VAT £	Travel £	Post £	Stationery £	Office supplies £
16 Jan	Bal b/f	120.00									

109

petty cash procedures

Main ledger

VAT account

£ | £

Travel expenses account

£ | £

Postage account

£ | £

Stationery account

£ | £

Office supplies account

£ | £

chapter 14:
PAYROLL ACCOUNTING PROCEDURES

1 Peter Knight is one of the employees at Short Furniture and has a gross weekly wage of £440.00. For this week his income tax payable through the PAYE system is £77.76. The employee's National Insurance Contribution for the week is £43.18 and 5% of his gross wage is deducted each week as a pension contribution. The employer's National Insurance Contribution for the week is £49.35.

a) Calculate Peter's net wage for the week.

b) What payments and to whom will Short Furniture be making in regard to Peter's wages this week?

c) Show how all of the elements of this wage payment would be entered into the accounting records by writing up the ledger accounts given.

Wages expense account	
£	£

payroll accounting procedures

Gross wages control account

£	£

PAYE/NIC creditor account

£	£

Pension contribution account

£	£

2 Short Furniture has five employees who are paid on a monthly basis. For each one you are required to calculate their net monthly salary.

Each employee has a personal allowance of £4,300 and they pay income tax at a rate of 10% on the first £1,500 per annum and 22% on the remainder.

National Insurance contributions are calculated at 10% of the gross salary but the first £300 of monthly income is exempt from this.

In the table given below show the calculation of the net annual pay for each employee.

Employee	Gross annual salary £	Taxable annual salary £	Income tax @ 10% £	Income tax @ 22% £	NIC £	Net annual salary £
J Short	30,000					
P Nielson	24,000					
J Taylor	17,400					
M Harris	15,500					
J Philpott	14,600					

chapter 15:
BANK RECONCILIATION STATEMENT

1 Would each of the following transactions appear as a debit or a credit on the bank statement?

	Transaction	Debit or credit?
i)	£470.47 paid into the bank	....
ii)	standing order of £26.79	....
iii)	cheque payment of £157.48	....
iv)	interest earned on the bank balance	....
v)	BACS payment for wages	....

2 Given below is the cash payments book for Newmans for the week ending 27 January 2006.

Cash payments book

You are given information about the receipts during the same week:

Date	Cheque No	Details	Total £	VAT £	Purchases ledger £	Rent and rates £	Sundry £	Discounts received £
27 Jan	003014	Henson Press	329.00		329.00			
27 Jan	003015	Ely Instr	736.96		736.96			12.80
27 Jan	003016	Jester Press	144.67		144.67			4.47
27 Jan	003017	CD Supplies	74.54		74.54			1.96
27 Jan	003018	Jester Press	44.79		44.79			1.38
27 Jan	003019	Buser Ltd	273.48		273.48			12.25
27 Jan	SO	Rates	255.00			255.00		
27 Jan	DD	Rent	500.00			500.00		

bank reconciliation statement

From Tunfield District Council £594.69
From Tunshire County Orchestra £468.29 – discount taken of £14.48
Cash sales for music (no VAT) £478.90
From Tunfield Brass Band £1,059.72 – discount taken of £33.03
Cash sales from instruments (including VAT) £736.58
Cash sales from CDs (including VAT) £251.67

You are required to write up and total the cash receipts book given below:

Cash receipts book

Date	Details	Total £	VAT £	Sales ledger £	Music sales £	Instrument sales £	CD sales £	Discounts allowed £	Sundry £

3 Given below is the bank statement for Newmans for the week ending 27 January 2006. You are required to compare the cash payments book and cash receipts book from earlier in this chapter to the bank statement. Note any unmatched items in the space given below and state what action you would take.

Unmatched item	Action to be taken

bank reconciliation statement

STATEMENT

first national
26 Pinehurst Plance
London
EC1 2AA

NEWMANS

CHEQUE ACCOUNT

Account number: 20-26-33 40268134

Sheet 023

Date		Paid out	Paid in	Balance
2006				
20 Jan	Balance b/f			379.22 CR
24 Jan	BGC - Tunsfield		594.69	
	BGC - TunshireCo.		468.29	
24 Jan	SO - British Elec	212.00		1230.20 CR
25 Jan	BGC - Tunfield AOS		108.51	1338.71 CR
26 Jan	Cheque No 003014	329.00		
	Credit		478.90	1488.61 CR
27 Jan	Cheque No 003017	74.54		
	Cheque No 003015	736.96		
	Credit		1,059.72	
	Credit		736.58	
	SO - TDC	255.00		
	DD - Halpern Properties	500.00		
	Bank interest		3.68	1722.09 CR

4 Amend the cash receipts and payments books and find the balance on the cash books at 27 January. You can assume that the opening bank statement balance is the same as the opening cash book balance.

5 Prepare the bank reconciliation statement as at 27 January 2006.

bank reconciliation statement

Multiple choice questions

6 Which of the following items reconciling the cash book to the bank statement are referred to as timing differences?

i) Bank charges not recorded in the cash book

ii) Interest charged not recorded in the cash book

iii) Outstanding lodgements

iv) Unpresented cheques

A (i) and (ii)

B (iii) and (iv)

C (ii) and (iii)

D (i) and (v)

7 Your cash book at 31 December 20X3 shows a bank balance of £565 overdrawn. On comparing this with your bank statement at the same date, you discover the following:

A cheque for £57 drawn by you on 29 December 20X3 has not yet been presented for payment.

A cheque for £92 from a customer, which was paid into the bank on 24 December 20X3, has been dishonoured on 31 December 20X3.

The correct bank balance to be shown in the balance sheet at 31 December 20X3 is

A £714 overdrawn

B £657 overdrawn

C £473 overdrawn

D £53 overdrawn

8 The cash book shows a bank balance of £5,675 overdrawn at 31 August 20X5. It is subsequently discovered that a standing order for £125 has been entered twice, and that a dishonoured cheque for £450 has been debited in the cash book instead of credited.

The correct bank balance should be

A £5,100 overdrawn

B £6,000 overdrawn

C £6,250 overdrawn

D £6,450 overdrawn

bank reconciliation statement

9 Your firm's cash book at 30 April 20X8 shows a balance at the bank of £2,490. Comparison with the bank statement at the same date reveals the following differences:

	£
Unpresented cheques	840
Bank charges	50
Receipts not yet credited by the bank	470
Dishonoured cheque not in cash book	140

The correct balance on the cash book at 30 April 20X8 is

- A £1,460
- B £2,300
- C £2,580
- D £3,140

10 Your firm's bank statement at 31 October 20X8 shows a balance of £13,400. You subsequently discover that the bank has dishonoured a customer's cheque for £300 and has charged bank charges of £50, neither of which is recorded in your cash book. There are unpresented cheques totalling £2,400. Amounts paid in, but not yet credited by the bank, amount to £1,000. You further discover that an automatic receipt from a customer of £195 has been recorded as a credit in your cash book.

Your cash book balance, prior to correcting the errors and omissions, was:

- A £11,455
- B £11,960
- C £12,000
- D £12,155

11 Your firm's cashbook shows a credit bank balance of £1,240 at 30 April 20X9. Upon comparison with the bank statement, you determine that there are unpresented cheques totalling £450, and a receipt of £140 which has not been passed through the bank account. The bank statement shows bank charges of £74 which have not been entered in the cash book.

The balance on the bank statement is

- A £1,005 overdrawn
- B £930 overdrawn
- C £1,475
- D £1,550

12 Which of the following is NOT a valid reason for the cash book and bank statement failing to agree?
- A Timing difference
- B Bank charges
- C Error
- D Cash receipts posted to creditors

13 The bank statement at 31 December 20X1 shows a balance of £1,000. The cash book shows a balance of £750 in hand. Which of the following is the most likely reason for the difference?

  A Receipts of £250 recorded in cash book, but not yet recorded by bank

  B Bank charges of £250 shown on the bank statement, not in the cash book

  C Standing orders of £250 included on bank statement, not in the cash book

  D Cheques for £250 recorded in the cash book, but not yet gone through the bank account

14 The cash book balance at 30 November 20X2 shows an overdraft of £500. Cheques for £6,000 have been written and sent out, but do not yet appear on the bank statement. Receipts of £5,000 are in the cash book, but are not yet on the bank statement. What is the balance on the bank statement?

  A £1,500

  B £500 in hand

  C £1,500 in hand

  D £500 overdrawn

15 A bank reconciliation is needed to identify .... either in the cash book of the business or made by the ....

16 Your firm's cash book at 30 April 20X8 shows a balance at the bank of £2,490. Comparison with the bank statement at the same date reveals the following differences:

	£
Unpresented cheques	840
Bank charges not in cash book	50
Receipts not yet credited by the bank	470
Dishonoured cheque not in cash book	140

The correct bank balance at 30 April 20X8 is £ ....

chapter 16: CONTROL ACCOUNT RECONCILIATIONS

1 The balances on your organisation's sales ledger control account on 1 January 2006 were:

	£
Debit balances	12,589
Credit balances	900

The transactions that take place during January 2006 are summarised below:

	£
Credit sales	12,758
Sales returns	1,582
Cash received from debtors	11,563
Discounts allowed to debtors	738
Bad debt to be written off	389
Returned cheque	722

There were no credit balances on any debtor accounts at the end of January 2006.

You are required to write up the sales ledger control account for the month of January 2006 in the blank account given below.

Sales ledger control account

£	£

control account reconciliations

2 The opening balance on your organisation's purchases ledger control account at 1 January 2006 was £8,347. The transactions for the month of January have been summarised below:

	£
Credit purchases	9,203
Purchases returns	728
Payments to creditors	8,837
Discounts received	382

You are required to write up the purchases ledger control account for the month of January 2006 in the blank account given below.

Purchases ledger control account

	£		£

3 When considering the reconciliation of sales ledger and purchases ledger control accounts to the list of balances from the subsidiary ledger, would the following errors affect the relevant control account, the list of balances or both?

		Control account	List of balances	Both
i)	Invoice entered into the sales day book as £980 instead of £890	....	....	....
ii)	Purchase day book overcast by £1,000	....	....	....
iii)	Discounts allowed of £20 not entered into the cash receipts book	....	....	....
iv)	An invoice taken as £340 instead of £440 when being posted to the subsidiary ledger	....	....	....
v)	Incorrect balancing of a subsidiary ledger account	....	....	....
vi)	A purchase return not entered into the purchases returns day book	....	....	....

control account reconciliations

4 In an earlier chapter we came across James who had just completed his first month of trading. James makes sales on credit to four customers and the transactions during his second month of trading were as follows:

	£
Sales	
To H Simms	2,000
To P Good	2,700
To K Mitchell	1,100
To C Brown	3,800
Receipts	
From H Simms	2,400
From P Good	3,600
From K Mitchell	1,100
From C Brown	4,800

All the sales are inclusive of VAT.

You are required to:

a) show these transactions in total in the sales ledger control account given and in detail in the individual subsidiary ledger accounts given. Each of the accounts given shows the opening balance at the start of month two.

b) balance the sales ledger control account and the individual subsidiary ledger accounts

c) reconcile the list of subsidiary ledger balances to the balance on the control account in the pro-forma given

Main ledger

Sales ledger control account

	£		£
Opening balance	5,000		

Subsidiary ledger

H Simms account

	£		£
Opening balance	900		

control account reconciliations

P Good account

	£		£
Opening balance	1,600		

K Mitchell account

	£		£

C Brown account

	£		£
Opening balance	2,500		

Reconciliation of subsidiary ledger balances with control account balance

	£
H Simms	
P Good	
K Mitchell	
C Brown	
Sales ledger control account	

5 James also buys goods on credit from three suppliers. The transactions with these suppliers in month two are summarised below:

	£
Purchases:	
From J Peters	1,600
From T Sands	2,500
From L Farmer	3,200
Payments:	
To J Peters	1,700
To T Sands	3,200
To L Farmer	3,000

All the purchases are inclusive of VAT.

You are required to:

a) show these transactions in total in the purchases ledger control account given and in detail in the individual subsidiary ledger accounts given. Each of the accounts given shows the opening balance at the start of month two.

b) balance the purchases ledger control account and the individual subsidiary ledger accounts

c) reconcile the list of subsidiary ledger balances to the balance on the control account in the pro-forma given

Main ledger

Purchases ledger control account

£		£
	Opening balance	2,700

Subsidiary ledger

J Peters account

£		£
	Opening balance	300

T Sands account

£		£
	Opening balance	1,700

L Farmer account

£		£
	Opening balance	700

Reconciliation of subsidiary ledger balances with control account balance

                                                                                             £

J Peters
T Sands
L Farmer

Purchases ledger control account

---

6   The balance on a business's sales ledger control account at 30 June 2006 was £13,452. However the list of balances in the subsidiary ledger totalled to £12,614. The difference was investigated and the following errors were discovered:

i)   the sales returns day book was undercast by £100

ii)   a payment from one debtor had been correctly entered into the cash receipts book as £350 but had been entered into the subsidiary ledger as £530

iii)   a bad debt of £200 had been written off in the subsidiary ledger but had not been entered into the main ledger accounts

iv)   a balance of £358 due from one debtor had been omitted from the list of subsidiary ledger balances.

You are required to write up the corrected sales ledger control account and to reconcile this to the corrected list of subsidiary ledger balances.

7   The balance on an organisation's purchases ledger control account at 30 June 2006 was £26,677 whereas the total of the list of subsidiary ledger balances for creditors was £27,469. The following errors were discovered:

i)   one total in the purchases day book had been undercast by £1,000

ii)   a discount received from a supplier of £64 had not been posted to his account in the subsidiary ledger

iii)   a debit balance of £120 had been included in the list of subsidiary ledger balances as a credit balance

iv)   discounts received of £256 were credited to both the discounts received account and to the creditors' control account.

You are required to correct the purchases ledger control account and to reconcile the corrected balance to the corrected list of subsidiary ledger balances.

control account reconciliations

8 Short Furniture has a petty cash imprest system based upon an imprest amount of £150.00 each month. During the month of January 2006 the following petty cash vouchers were authorised and paid:

Voucher No.	£
0473	12.60
0474	15.00
0475	19.75
0476	9.65
0477	10.00
0478	13.84
0479	4.26
0480	16.40

The cash in the petty cash box at 31 January 2006 was made up as follows:

£10 note	1
£5 note	4
£2 coin	3
£1 coin	7
50p coin	5
20p coin	8
10p coin	9
5p coin	4
2p coin	11
1p coin	8

a) Reconcile the petty cash in the petty cash box and the vouchers at the end of January 2006 in the space below.

b) The petty cash control account in the main ledger is given below:

Petty cash control			
	£		£
1 Jan Balance b/d	150.00	31 Jan Petty cash book	101.50

You are to balance the petty cash control account and reconcile the balance to the amount of cash in the petty cash box on 31 January 2006.

127

Multiple choice questions

9 A credit balance of £917 brought down on Y Ltd's account in the books of X Ltd means that

    A   X Ltd owes Y Ltd £917

    B   Y Ltd owes X Ltd £917

    C   X Ltd has paid Y Ltd £917

    D   X Ltd is owed £917 by Y Ltd

10 A supplier sends you a statement showing a balance outstanding of £14,350. Your own records show a balance outstanding of £14,500.

The reason for this difference could be that

    A   The supplier sent an invoice for £150 which you have not yet received

    B   The supplier has allowed you £150 cash discount which you had omitted to enter in your ledger

    C   You have paid the supplier £150 which he has not yet accounted for

    D   You have returned goods worth £159 which the supplier has not yet accounted for

11 The sales ledger control account at 1 May had balances of £32,750 debit and £1,275 credit. During May, sales of £125,000 were made on credit. Receipts from debtors amounted to £122,500 and cash discounts of £550 were allowed. Refunds of £1,300 were made to customers. The closing balances at 31 May could be

    A   £35,175 debit and £3,000 credit

    B   £35,675 debit and £2,500 credit

    C   £36,725 debit and £2,000 credit

    D   £36,725 debit and £1,000 credit

12 The sales ledger control account had a closing balance of £8,500. It contained a contra to the purchase ledger of £400, but that had been entered on the wrong side of the control account.

The correct balance on the control account should be

    A   £7,700 debit

    B   £8,100 debit

    C   £8,400 debit

    D   £8,900 debit

control account reconciliations

13 Your purchase ledger control account has a balance at 1 October 20X8 of £34,500 credit. During October, credit purchases were £78,400, cash purchases were £2,400 and payments made to suppliers, excluding cash purchases, and after deducting cash discounts of £1,200, were £68,900. Purchase returns were £4,700.

The closing balance was:

A £38,100

B £40,500

C £47,500

D £49,900

14 A control account is an account in the nominal ledger in which a record is kept of the ....

15 Control accounts are useful chiefly for .... and ....

16 An invoice for £69 has been recorded in the sales day book as £96. When the sales ledger reconciliation is prepared, adjustments will be required to:

☐ The control account

☐ The list of balances

17 Bruce prepared the following purchase ledger reconciliation statement.

Balance on nominal ledger control account	£46,865 credit
Payment entered twice in nominal ledger control account	£573 credit
	£47,438 credit
Purchase daybook overcast	£900 debit
Total list of balances	£46,538

What is the correct figure for the balance on the purchase ledger control account?

£

18 What is the main reason for preparing a sales ledger control account reconciliation?

....

control account reconciliations

19 The total of the balances on the individual suppliers accounts in Arnold's purchase ledger is £81,649. The balance on the trade creditors control account in his nominal ledger is £76,961. He has discovered that an invoice for £4,688 has been posted twice to the correct supplier's account and that payments totalling £1,606 which he made by standing order have been omitted from his records.

What amount should be reported in Arnold's balance sheet for trade creditors?

£

chapter 17: PREPARING AN INITIAL TRIAL BALANCE

1. Given below are the sales ledger and purchases ledger control accounts for your organisation. You are required to balance the accounts and show the closing balance carried down and brought down.

Sales ledger control account

	£		£
Opening balance	16,387	Cash receipts	15,388
Sales	17,385	Discounts allowed	734
		Sales returns	1,297
		Bad debt written off	479

Purchases ledger control account

	£		£
Cash payments	10,756	Opening balance	11,529
Discounts received	529	Purchases	10,487
Purchases returns	926		

2. You are given the following account balances from the main ledger of your organisation. Would each balance be a debit or a credit balance in the trial balance?

Ledger account	Balance	Debit or credit?
Sales	625,679	....
Telephone	1,295	....
Debtors	52,375	....
Wages	104,288	....
Purchases returns	8,229	....
Bank overdraft	17,339	....
Purchases	372,589	....
Drawings	38,438	....
Sales returns	32,800	....
Motor car	14,700	....
Creditors	31,570	....

preparing an initial trial balance

3 Given below is the list of ledger balances for your organisation at 31 January 2006. You are required to prepare a trial balance as at 31 January 2006.

	£
Motor vehicles	76,800
Office equipment	36,440
Sales	285,600
Purchases	196,800
Bank overdraft	2,016
Petty cash	36
Capital	90,000
Sales returns	5,640
Purchases returns	4,320
Sales ledger control	42,960
Purchases ledger control	36,120
VAT (credit balance)	15,540
Stock	12,040
Telephone	1,920
Electricity	3,360
Wages	74,520
Loan	36,000
Discounts allowed	7,680
Discounts received	4,680
Rent	14,400
Bad debts written off	1,680

Multiple choice questions

4 The double-entry system of bookkeeping normally results in which of the following balances on the ledger accounts?

	Debit balances	Credit balances
A	Assets and revenues	Liabilities, capital and expenses
B	Revenues, capital and liabilities	Assets and expenses
C	Assets and expenses	Liabilities, capital and revenues
D	Assets, expenses and capital	Liabilities and revenues

5 A credit balance on a ledger account indicates

- A An asset or an expense
- B A liability or an expense
- C An amount owing to the organisation
- D A liability or a revenue

6 Which of the following balances would be a credit balance on a trial balance?

- A Opening stock
- B Sales returns
- C Discounts allowed
- D Bank overdraft

7   A business has the following balances at the year end:

	$
Opening stock	7,200
Loan	8,000
Purchases	72,300
Debtors	27,200
Fixed assets	40,600
Overdraft	5,600
Capital	41,500
Drawings	14,300
Expenses	17,600
Creditors	15,400
Sales	108,700

What is the trial balance total at the end of the year?

A   £173,600
B   £179,200
C   £164,900
D   £186,400

8   Which of the following balances would be found on the same side of the trial balance?

A   Bad debts expense and sales
B   Discounts received and bad debts expense
C   Discounts allowed and a bank loan
D   Discounts received and purchases returns

9   The ………………………… lists all the balances in every account in the nominal ledger at the end of a period.

chapter 18:
ERRORS AND THE TRIAL BALANCE

1 Given below are two ledger accounts. Examine them carefully and then re-write them correcting any errors that have been made.

Sales ledger control account

	£		£
Sales	15,899	Balance b/d	1,683
Discounts allowed	900	Cash received	14,228
Sales returns	1,467	Bad debts written off	245
		Balance c/d	2,110
	18,266		18,266

VAT account

	£		£
VAT on sales	2,368	Balance b/d	2,576
VAT on purchases returns	115	VAT on purchases	1,985
Balance c/d	2,078		
	4,561		4,561

errors and the trial balance

2 Given below is a trial balance that does not balance. Examine it carefully and then re-draft it having corrected any errors that you can find – it should then balance.

	£	£
Motor vehicle	18,720	
Stock	2,520	
Bank (debit balance)	10,956	
Sales ledger control	5,280	
Purchases ledger control		3,840
Capital		48,000
Sales		78,000
Sales returns		6,000
Purchases	50,400	
Purchases returns		3,240
Bank charges	120	
Discounts allowed		1,080
Discounts received	720	
Wages and salaries	26,160	
Rent and rates		7,440
Telephone	1,224	
Electricity	3,060	
Bad debts written off	840	
	120,000	147,600

	£	£
Motor vehicle		
Stock		
Bank (debit balance)		
Sales ledger control		
Purchases ledger control		
Capital		
Sales		
Sales returns		
Purchases		
Purchases returns		
Bank charges		
Discounts allowed		
Discounts received		
Wages and salaries		
Rent and rates		
Telephone		
Electricity		
Bad debts written off		

3 The trial balance of Harry Parker & Co has been prepared by the bookkeeper and the total of the debit balances is £428,365 whilst the total of the credit balances is £431,737. The difference was dealt with by setting up a suspense account and then the ledger accounts were investigated to try to find the causes of the difference. The following errors and omissions were found:

i) the sales day book was undercast by £1,000

ii) the balance on the electricity account of £1,642 had been completely omitted from the trial balance

iii) discounts allowed of £865 had been entered on the wrong side of the discounts allowed account

iv) receipts from debtors of £480 had been entered into the accounts as £840

v) a discount received of £120 had been completely omitted from the cash payments book

You are required to:

a) draft journal entries to correct each of these errors or omissions

b) write up the suspense account showing clearly the opening balance and how the suspense account is cleared after correction of each of the errors

errors and the trial balance

Multiple choice questions

4 When posting an invoice received for building maintenance £980 was entered on the building maintenance expense account instead of the correct amount of £890.

What correction should be made to the building maintenance expenses account?

A	Debit	£90
B	Credit	£90
C	Debit	£1,780
D	Credit	£1,780

5 A business receives an invoice from a supplier for £2,800 which is mislaid before any entry has been made, resulting in the transaction being omitted from the books entirely.

This is an

A   error of transposition

B   error of omission

C   error of principle

D   error of commission

6 An error of commission is one where

A   a transaction has not been recorded

B   one side of a transaction has been recorded in the wrong account, and that account is of a different class to the correct account

C   one side of a transaction has been recorded in the wrong account, and that account is of the same class as the correct account

D   a transaction has been recorded using the wrong amount

7 A suspense account was opened when a trial balance failed to agree. The following errors were later discovered.

– A gas bill of £420 had been recorded in the gas account as £240

– A discount of £50 given to a customer had been credited to discounts received

– Interest received of £70 had been entered in the bank account only

The original balance on the suspense account was

A	Debit	£210
B	Credit	£210
C	Debit	£160
D	Credit	£160

8 Which ONE of the following is an error of principle?

A   A gas bill credited to the gas account and debited to the bank account

B   The purchase of a fixed asset credited to the asset at cost account and debited to the creditor's account

C   The purchase of a fixed asset debited to the purchases account and credited to the creditor's account

D   The payment of wages debited and credited to the correct accounts, but using the wrong amount

9 Where a transaction is entered into the correct ledger accounts, but the wrong amount is used, the error is known as an error of

A   Omission

B   Original entry

C   Commission

D   Principle

10 When a trial balance was prepared, two ledger accounts were omitted:

Discounts received   £6,150

Discounts allowed   £7,500

To make the trial balance balance, a suspense account was opened. What was the balance on the suspense account?

A   Debit   £1,350

B   Credit   £1,350

C   Debit   £13,650

D   Credit   £13,650

11 If a purchase return of £48 has been wrongly posted to the debit of the sales returns account, but has been correctly entered in the creditors account, the total of the trial balance would show

A   The credit side to be £48 more than the debit side

B   The debit side to be £48 more than the credit side

C   The credit side to be £96 more than the debit side

D   The debit side to be £96 more than the credit side

12 The debit side of a trial balance totals £50 more than the credit side. This could be due to

A   A purchase of goods for £50 being omitted from the creditor's account

B   A sale of goods for £50 being omitted from the debtor's account

C   An invoice of £25 for electricity being credited to the electricity account

D   A receipt for £50 from a debtor being omitted from the cash book

errors and the trial balance

13 A trial balance will not disclose the following types of errors:

– ....

– ....

– ....

– ....

14 Where a transaction is entered into the correct ledger accounts, but the wrong amount is used, the error is known as an error of [   ]

15 Preparing a trial balance will reveal the following errors. Tick the appropriate boxes to indicate your response.

	Yes	No
Omitting both entries for a transaction	☐	☐
Posting the debit entry for an invoice to an incorrect expense account	☐	☐
Omitting the debit entry for a transaction	☐	☐
Posting the debit entry for a transaction as a credit entry	☐	☐

16 Trevor's trial balance includes a suspense account with a debit balance of £900. He has discovered that:

– a supplier's invoice for £16,700 was posted to the correct side of the purchases account as £17,600 (the correct entry was posted to the creditors' control account); and

– a cheque for £900 has not been recorded in his ledger.

What is the balance on the suspense account after these errors are corrected?

£ .... debit/credit

17 Colin bought stationery on credit for £430 but recorded it as £340.

When he extracted his trial balance, the total of the debit balances was £157,728.

When the error is corrected, what is the revised total of the debit balances?

£

chapter 19:
BUSINESS TRANSACTIONS AND THE LAW

1. Short Furniture send out a purchase quotation to a customer, Rother Nurseries, for two dining tables at a cost of £340.00 plus VAT. Rother Nurseries respond by sending a purchase order for these tables.

    i) Who is the offeror and who is the offeree?

    ii) Is there a valid contract at this stage?

    iii) If Rother Nurseries state on the purchase order that the tables must be delivered the following day – is there a valid contract? Explain your answer.

2. Short Furniture place an advertisement in the local newspaper for their products. Unfortunately there is a typing error and a sun lounger has been shown at a price of £50 instead of £250. Three customers have telephoned to place orders for the sun lounger.

    Is Short Furniture obliged to sell the sun loungers at the advertised price of £50? Explain your answer.

business transactions and the law

3 Short Furniture have just employed a new salesman, Paul Finch. Paul has just taken a telephone call from a customer showing interest in a garden bench priced at £120 plus VAT. Paul has explained that this price is only available for the rest of this week and finished the conversation by saying to the customer "if I have not heard from you by Friday I will assume that you wish to go ahead with the purchase".

If the customer does not call back by Friday is there a contract of sale between the customer and Short Furniture? Explain your answer.

4 Paul Finch is also dealing with a further customer who is interested in the garden benches priced at £120 plus VAT. Paul has again explained that the price is only available this week and the customer agrees to send a purchase order for the benches.

The purchase order is not received until Tuesday of the following week although the post mark clearly shows that it was posted on the Friday of this week.

Does Short Furniture have to sell the garden benches to the customer at the price of £120 plus VAT? Explain your answer.

5 a) What type of information is covered by by the Data Protection Act 1998?

b) What are the eight principles of good information handling?

chapter 20:
INTRODUCTION TO MANAGEMENT INFORMATION

1   Given below are a number of different typical management tasks. For each one decide whether this is an example of management's role of decision-making, planning or control.

    Management task   **Management role**

    i)   Estimating advertising costs for the following year   ....

    ii)   Comparing this month' sales income to that for last month   ....

    iii) Considering the opening of an additional factory   ....

    iv)   Determining how many production employees are required
          for the following quarter's production   ....

    v)   Comparing the actual costs for the month to the budgeted costs   ....

    vi)   Considering taking out a loan to help fund expansion   ....

2   If the management of a business need to decide how many production employees are required for the next quarter what information might they need?

3 If the management of a business need to know the total cost of materials for the following quarter what budgets would be required?

chapter 21: ELEMENTS OF COST

1 Given below are a variety of costs that are incurred by Short Furniture, makers of wooden garden furniture. Classify each one as materials, labour or expense:

	Cost	Classification
i)	advertising costs in local paper	....
ii)	cost of imported wood	....
iii)	store keeper's wages	....
iv)	new blades for saws	....
v)	cost of wood polish	....
vi)	accountant's salary	....
vii)	repair cost of delivery van	....
viii)	insurance of the cutting machinery	....
ix)	telephone bill	....

2 Short Furniture has just received a delivery of wood which has been recorded on the following goods received note.

GOODS RECEIVED NOTE

Short Furniture

Supplier: A1 Wood Supplies

GRN number: 07904
Date: 5 Jan 2006
Order number: 04672

Quantity	Description	Stock code
45m	Oak	02611
20m	Stripped Pine	P4612

Received by: A. Hall
Checked by: J. Finch
Comments: –

You are required to write up the stock record cards given to reflect this delivery.

STOCK RECORD CARD

Stock code 02611

Date	In	Out	Balance
2006			
1 Jan			35 metres
2 Jan		25 metres	10 metres

STOCK RECORD CARD

Stock code P4612

Date	In	Out	Balance
2006			
1 Jan			15 metres
4 Jan		10 metres	5 metres

elements of cost

3 Short Furniture employs 15 weekly paid employees. There is one production supervisor, ten production workers and four administrative staff. There are three grades of production workers but the administrative staff are all paid at the same rate per hour.

The hourly rates of pay are:

Production supervisor		£10.20
Production workers –	Grade I	£8.50
	Grade II	£7.20
	Grade III	£6.50
Administrative staff		£7.10

All employees work a 35 hour week with any overtime being paid at time and a half.

The hours worked by each employee for the week ending 27 January are as follows:

Employee	Hours
Supervisor:	
P Knight	38
Production workers:	
P Anil (Grade II)	35
K Chappatte (Grade I)	39
H Dennis (Grade II)	37
K Fisher (Grade III)	38
J Hunt (Grade I)	40
D Jones (Grade III)	38
L Minns (Grade II)	41
S Percy (Grade II)	35
I Roberts (Grade I)	39
G Tracy (Grade III)	35
Administrative staff:	
F Albert	37
L Gill	35
J Norman	41
T Stevens	38

The employer's National Insurance Contribution is calculated at 12.8% of the weekly gross pay for each employee other than the first £97 each week which is exempt.

elements of cost

In the table below you are required to calculate the total gross pay and employer's NIC for each of the employees for the week ending 27 January.

Employee	Total hours	Basic hours	Overtime hours	Basic pay £	Overtime pay £	Total gross pay £	Employers' NIC £
P Knight P Anil K Chappatte H Dennis K Fisher J Hunt D Jones L Minns S Percy I Roberts G Tracy F Albert L Gill J Norman T Stevens							

4 Short Furniture has the following cost centres for management accounting purposes:

Production cost centres:

- cutting
- assembly
- finishing

Service cost centres:

- marketing
- administration

elements of cost

Summarised below are the total wage costs for the month to 27 January for the weekly paid employees together with the cost centre in which each employee works:

Employee	Cost centre	Gross wage £	Employer's NIC £
P Knight	(see note below)	1,612.70	159.59
P Anil	Assembly	1,008.00	84.00
K Chappatte	Cutting	1,327.55	123.94
H Dennis	Finishing	1,026.85	86.36
K Fisher	Assembly	1,026.40	86.30
J Hunt	Assembly	1,445.00	138.63
D Jones	Finishing	1,004.35	83.54
L Minns	Finishing	1,267.20	116.40
S Percy	Cutting	1,008.00	84.00
I Roberts	Assembly	1,284.60	118.58
G Tracy	Finishing	945.60	76.20
F Albert	Administration	1,079.20	92.90
L Gill	Marketing	994.00	82.25
J Norman	Marketing	1,234.70	112.34
T Stevens	Marketing	1,121.80	98.22
		17,385.95	1,543.25

P Knight is the production supervisor and as such works in all three production departments. His labour cost is to be split equally between all three production cost centres.

Short Furniture's policy is to allocate the employer's NIC as a labour cost to each cost centre as well as the total gross wage.

You are required to show the weekly labour cost for each cost centre in the table below:

	Cutting cost centre £	Assembly cost centre £	Finishing cost centre £	Marketing cost centre £	Admin cost centre £	Total £
Gross wages						
Employer's NIC						

150

chapter 22: CODING

1 Short Furniture makes sales to two types of organisation, garden centres/nurseries and high street stores. Each of these sales functions is a profit centre. It also has five cost centres, cutting, assembly, finishing, marketing and administration.

An extract from the coding manual is given below:

Profit centre codes:

110	Garden centres/nurseries
120	High street stores

The third digit of the sales code denotes the type of sale:

001	Dining furniture
002	Benches
003	Sun loungers
004	Coffee tables
005	Other

Cost centre codes:

210	Cutting
220	Assembly
230	Finishing
240	Marketing
250	Administration

coding

The third digit of the cost codes denotes the type of expense:

001	Wood
002	Screws/nails
003	Glue
004	Polish
005	Labour
006	Expenses

You are given below some sales invoices and purchase invoices from the end of the month of January 2006.

You are also given the coding listing which shows the total income or expense for each code to date.

INVOICE

Short Furniture
Eridge Estate
Benham DR6 4QQ
Tel 0303312 Fax 0303300
VAT Reg 0361 3282 60

To: Rother Nurseries
Rother Road
Benham

Invoice number: 08721
Date/tax point: 27 Jan 2006
Order number: 06148
Account number: SL 13

Quantity	Description	Stock code	Unit amount £	Total £
2	Coffee Table	CT002	96.00	192.00
6	Dining Chair	DC416	73.00	438.00
			Net total	630.00
			VAT	110.25
			Invoice total	740.25

Terms
Net 30 days
E & OE

coding

INVOICE

Short Furniture
Eridge Estate
Benham DR6 4QQ
Tel 0303312 Fax 0303300
VAT Reg 0361 3282 60

To: Fenband Stores
Victory Shopping Centre
Benham

Invoice number: 08722

Date/tax point: 27 Jan 2006

Order number: 43217

Account number: SL 61

Quantity	Description	Stock code	Unit amount £	Total £
7	Sunlounger	SL642	210.00	1,470.00
1	Bench	B443	110.00	110.00
				1,580.00
	Trade Discount			158.00
	Net total			1,422.00
	VAT			248.85
	Invoice total			1,670.85

Terms
Net 30 days
E & OE

coding

INVOICE

A1 Wood Supplies
Heath Park
Drenchley DR22 6KL
VAT Reg 4621 3117 04

To: Short Furniture
Eridge Estate
Benham DR6 4QQ

Invoice number: 764989

Date/tax point: 27 Jan 2006

Order number: 46794

Account number: S04

Quantity	Description	Stock code	Unit amount £	Total £
30m	Stripped Pine	P4612	12.38	371.40
40m	Oak	02611	15.87	638.80
				1,010.20
	Trade Discount			151.53

Net total	858.67
VAT	145.75
Invoice total	1,004.42

Terms
3% settlement discount for payment within 14 days, otherwise net 30 days
E & OE

INVOICE

Polish People
23/25 Main Street
Wakeham DR17 4ZF
Tel 0421666 Fax 0421667
VAT Reg 3692 9417 63

To: Short Furniture
Eridge Estate
Benham DR6 4QQ

Invoice number: 06715

Date/tax point: 27 Jan 2006

Order number: 04701

Account number: SL 13

Quantity	Description	Stock code	Unit amount £	Total £
40 litres	Exterior Wood Polish – cherry	88631	3.16	126.40
20 litres	Exterior Wood Polish – teak	88413	2.83	56.60
			Net total	183.00
			VAT	32.02
			Invoice total	215.02

Terms
Net 30 days
E & OE

coding

coding

INVOICE

J. T. Turner
Black Horse House
Budlett DR4 6TM
VAT Reg 3667 1294 61

To: Short Furniture
Eridge Estate
Benham DR6 4QQ

Invoice number: 06302

Date/tax point: 27 Jan 2006

Order number: 04699

Account number: SL 43

Quantity	Description	Stock code	Unit amount £	Total £
12 dozen	4" cross head 2/8 screws	S428	3.83	45.96
30 dozen	3" cross head 1/8 screws	S318	1.94	58.20
				104.16
	Trade Discount			15.62
			Net total	88.54
			VAT	14.87
			Invoice total	103.41

Terms
4% settlement discount for payment within 10 days, otherwise 30 days net
E & OE

Coding listing – Income and expenditure – January 2006

Code	Balance £	Amendment £	Updated balance £
111	16,387.50		
112	13,265.95		
113	9,326.20		
114	3,587.90		
115	1,037.00		
121	10,385.30		
122	7,256.30		
123	3,646.70		
124	3,027.60		
125	926.40		
211	35,287.74		
215	–		
216	–		
222	1,285.47		
223	1,036.80		
225	–		
226	–		
234	8,385.40		
235	–		
236	–		
245	–		
246	–		
255	–		
256	–		

You are required to code each of the invoices given and to enter the net amounts onto the coding listing for each code (ignore VAT as the management accounting records are only concerned with the net of VAT costs).

coding

2 Given below is the summary of the wages costs for the month to 27 January 2006 prepared earlier.

	Cutting cost centre £	Assembly cost centre £	Finishing cost centre £	Marketing cost centre £	Admin cost centre £	Total £
Gross wages	2,873.12	5,301.57	4,781.56	3,350.50	1,079.20	17,385.95
Employer's NIC	261.14	480.70	415.70	292.81	92.90	1,543.25
	3,134.26	5,782.27	5,197.26	3,643.31	1,172.10	18,929.20

You are required to code each total and to enter them into the coding listing for the relevant codes. The coding listing from the previous question is to be used.

3 Given below is the expense schedule for January 2006 produced earlier.

Expense	Total £	Cutting £	Assembly £	Finishing £	Marketing £	Admin £
Blades	340	340				
Electricity 60% x 1,560	1,560	936	156	156	156	156
Advertising	550				550	
Rent 2,100 x 1,000/7,000 2,100 x 3,000/7,000 2,100 x 2,000/7,000 2,100 x 500/7,000	2,100	300	900	600	150	150
Telephone 70% x 420 30% x 420	420				294	126
	4,970	1,576	1,056	756	1,150	432

You are required to code the totals and to enter them into the coding listing for the relevant codes. The coding listing from the earlier question is to be used.

coding

4 Finally you are required to complete the coding listing for January 2006 by calculating the updated balance for each code.

5 A business has the following balances on each of its cost codes at 1 June 2006.

Code	Balance £
10101	28,375
10102	13,773
10103	12,356
10201	17,365
10202	21,925
10203	11,482

During the month of June 2006 the following costs were incurred for each cost code.

Code	Cost £
10101	6,234
10102	3,154
10103	1,783
10201	4,254
10202	4,793
10203	2,015

Set up a computer spreadsheet to find the closing balance on each cost code at the end of June 2006.

	A	B	C	D	E
1					
2					
3					
4					
5					
6					
7					

chapter 23:
COMPARISON OF COSTS AND INCOME

1 During the month of December 2006 the production costs of Natural Productions were summarised as:

	£
Raw materials	2,968
Labour	1,635
Expenses	372

You are Jane Mitchell and you have been asked by the owner of the business, Phil McKenna, to compare these costs to those of the previous month. The costs for November 2006 are summarised as:

	£
Raw materials	5,216
Labour	2,667
Expenses	552

You mention to Phil that the November costs are much larger than those for December as production was greater due to Christmas demand. He therefore asks you to compare the December 2006 costs to those for December 2005. The relevant figures for December 2005 are:

	£
Raw materials	2,537
Labour	1,367
Expenses	350

You are required to prepare a memo to the owner showing separate comparisons of the December 2006 costs to those of the previous month and those of the corresponding month last year. Today's date is 5 January 2007.

comparison of costs and income

MEMO

To:

From:

Date:

Subject:

2 Phil McKenna has now asked you send him a note comparing the actual costs for December 2006 to the forecast costs for that month and showing any variances. You find the budgeted figures for December 2006 in the filing system and they are:

	£
Raw materials	2,700
Labour	1,650
Expenses	420

Prepare a note to Phil showing the comparison and the variances.

NOTE

To:

From:

Date:

comparison of costs and income

3   Newmans, the music shop, has an accounting year that runs from 1 July through to 30 June. The forecast sales for figures for the year from 1 July 2006 to 30 June 2007 are:

	July	Aug	Sept	Oct	Nov	Dec	Jan	Feb	Mar	Apr	May	June
£	8,700	8,100	9,800	8,600	8,500	9,900	7,400	7,800	8,400	8,500	8,700	8,800

The actual sales for the year to date are:

	July	Aug	Sept	Oct	Nov	Dec	Jan	Feb	Mar	Apr	May	June
£	8,500	8,500	9,900	9,000	8,500	9,600	7,100					

You have been asked to prepare a table that shows a comparison of the actual monthly sales and the cumulative sales to date to the forecast figures. Show the actual figures up to January 2007 but complete the forecast figures until June 2007 in order that the actual figures can be inserted when each month's sales are known.

4   The actual and budgeted costs for material, labour and expenses for a business for the last month are given:

	Actual £	Budget £
Materials	41,705	45,000
Labour	68,376	60,000
Expenses	25,357	22,500

All variances which exceed 5% of the budgeted figure are to be investigated.

Set up a computer spreadsheet to calculate each variance and the percentage that each variance is of the budgeted figure.

	A	B	C	D	E
1					
2					
3					
4					
5					
6					
7					

AAT

SAMPLE SIMULATION
UNIT 1

TUBNEY TECHNOLOGY LTD

This is the AAT's Sample Simulation for Unit 1. Its purpose is to give you an idea of what an AAT simulation looks like. It is not intended as a definitive guide to the tasks you may be required to perform.

This simulation is in two parts. It is suggested that you spend approximately 90 minutes on each part.

Total time: 3 hours

sample simulation – unit 1

Coverage of performance criteria and range statements

All performance criteria are covered in this simulation.

Element	PC Coverage
1.1	**Process documents relating to goods and services supplied.**
a)	Accurately prepare **invoices and credit notes** in accordance with organisational requirements and check against **source documents**.
b)	Ensure invoices and credit notes are correctly authorised and coded before being sent to customers.
c)	Ensure invoices and credit notes are correctly **coded**.
d)	Enter invoices and credit notes into **books of prime entry** according to organisational procedures.
e)	Enter invoices and credit notes in the appropriate **ledgers**.
f)	Produce **statements** of account for despatch to debtors.
g)	**Communicate** politely and effectively with customers regarding accounts, using the relevant information from the aged debtors analysis.
1.2	**Process receipts**
a)	Check **receipts** against relevant supporting information.
b)	Enter receipts in appropriate **accounting records**.
c)	Prepare paying-in documents and reconcile to relevant records.
d)	Identify **unusual features** and either resolve or refer to the appropriate person.

All range statements are covered in this simulation.

sample simulation – unit 1

DATA AND TASKS

INSTRUCTIONS

This simulation is designed to let you show your ability to record income and receipts.

You should read the whole simulation before you start work, so that you are fully aware of what you will have to do.

You are allowed **three hours** to complete your work.

Write your answers in the Answer Booklet provided on pages 199 to 222. If you need more paper for your answers, ask the person in charge.

You should write your answers in blue or black ink, **not** pencil.

You may use correcting fluid, but in moderation. You should cross out your errors neatly and clearly.

You may pull apart and rearrange your booklets if you wish to do so, but you must put them back in their original order before handing them in.

Your work must be accurate, so check your work carefully before handing it in.

You are not allowed to refer to any unauthorised material, such as books or notes, while you are working on the simulation. If you have any such material with you, you must hand it to the person in charge before you start work.

Any instances of misconduct will be reported to the AAT, and disciplinary action may be taken.

Coverage of performance criteria and range statements

It is not always possible to cover all performance criteria and range statements in a single simulation. Any performance criteria and range statements not covered must be assessed by other means by the assessor before a candidate can be considered competent.

Performance criteria and range statement coverage for this simulation is shown on page 166.

sample simulation – unit 1

THE SITUATION

Tubney Technology Limited is based at a business park in Oxford. It is a small company with a factory where it manufactures standard parts used in the production of computers and mobile phones. It also makes some special parts to the customer's specification.

You are Lynsey Jones, Accounts Assistant. You report directly to Samir Aleffi, who is the Accounts Manager of Tubney Technology Ltd.

All sales are made on credit to customers, which are computer and mobile phone manufacturers. Tubney Technology Ltd is registered for VAT and all its sales are standard rated at 17.5%.

A settlement discount of 3.5% for payment within 14 days is offered to all customers. Established customers also receive trade discount.

Accounting system

Tubney Technology Ltd operates a partially computerised sales and accounting system.

- Invoices and credit notes are prepared manually and details are input to a computer, which produces a Discount Analysis.

- The sales day book and sales returns day book are prepared manually. The relevant totals are entered by hand into the manual main ledger containing a sales ledger control account, and into the manual subsidiary (sales) ledger, which is not part of the double entry system.

- Receipts are entered first into the manual cash book, which is part of the main ledger, and this is posted manually to the other main ledger accounts and the subsidiary (sales) ledger. Details of receipts are also entered into the computer, which produces the Aged Debtors Analysis.

Today's date is Thursday 18 September 2006.

THE TASKS TO BE COMPLETED

PART 1 PROCESS DOCUMENTS RELATING TO GOODS AND SERVICES SUPPLIED (90 MINUTES)

Invoice preparation

All sales to customers are made against purchase orders received from the customer, or sales orders prepared by the Sales Manager, Mark Alberts. For sales of special parts there is also a quotation setting out the work to be done and the rates to be charged. Delivery notes accompany all deliveries to the customer. If the order and the delivery note do not agree in any respect, the sale is not invoiced but is referred back to Mark Alberts. The prices charged are calculated with reference to either the quotation or the price list on page 174 of this book. Trade discount details are taken from the Subsidiary (Sales) Ledger Account List, which is on page 174 of this book.

Task 1

Refer to the documents on pages 175-185 of this book.

- Check each order against the relevant delivery note. Make a note of any discrepancy on page 199 of the Answer Booklet.

- Prepare invoices for the sales that you have agreed. Use the invoice forms on pages 200-204 of the Answer Booklet. You do not need to fill in the customer's address. VAT, trade discount and settlement discount should be rounded down to the nearest penny.

Credit Note Preparation

Credit notes for parts returned are raised against return notes. The return notes are completed and signed by Ian Smith, the Factory Manager, to indicate that he has approved the return.

Task 2

Refer to the return notes on pages 186-187 of this book.

- Prepare credit notes using the credit note forms on pages 205-206 of the Answer Booklet. You do not need to fill in the customer's address.

sample simulation – unit 1

Task 3

Before invoices and credit notes are despatched to customers or recorded, they must be authorised.

- On page 207 of the Answer Booklet, make a note of who should authorise the invoices and credit notes for despatch: Mark Alberts (Sales Manager), Samir Aleffi (Accounts Manager) or Ian Smith (Factory Manager)?

Assume that you have obtained authorisation as required.

- Make appropriate entries in the sales day book and the sales return day book on pages 207-208 of the Answer Booklet.

- Calculate the total settlement discount that the computer's Discount Analysis will show is available to customers on the day's invoice. Make a note on page 207 of the Answer Booklet.

Task 4

- Total the entries in the sales day book and sales returns day book.

- Insert the appropriate main ledger and subsidiary (sales) ledger codes in the Day Books.

- Make the necessary entries in the main ledger and subsidiary (sales) ledger accounts on pages 209-213 of the Answer Booklet. (For some ledger accounts there will be no entries at this stage.)

Note: There are transactions already shown on some of the ledger accounts. You do NOT need to balance any accounts after you have made your entries.

sample simulation – unit 1

PART 2 PROCESS RECEIPTS (90 MINUTES)

Banking receipts

Cash and cheques received from customers are checked against supporting documentation and then entered into the cash book. Some customers make automated payments, which appear on the bank statement. These are entered into the cash book when they have been checked to the weekly bank statement, and the supporting documentation.

Where the receipt does not agree with supporting documentation, the payment is banked and entered into the cash book, but a communication is sent to the customer outlining the effect of the transaction on the debtor's account. Wrongly completed cheques are returned to the customer with a request for a correctly completed cheque to be issued.

Task 5

Refer to the documents on pages 188-192 of this book relating to amounts received, and the subsidiary (sales) ledger accounts on pages 211-213 of the Answer Booklet.

- Refer to the Discount Analysis printout on page 188 of this book and check the receipt and remittance advices on pages 188-192 of this book to ensure that any settlement discount taken by customers is allowable. You should bear in mind that only a 14-day period is offered and that the month of August has 31 days. Make notes on page 214 of the Answer Booklet of any queries, and the action that needs to be taken.

- On page 215 of the Answer Booklet, calculate a total for the cash received from Kendrick & Co, and agree this to the receipt that Samir gave to the customer.

- Check that the cheques have been correctly completed and agree with supporting documentation. If a cheque cannot be paid into the bank today, or does not agree with supporting documentation, make notes on page 214 of the Answer Booklet as to the reason, and the action that needs to be taken.

- Agree the automated receipt on the bank statement on page 193 of this book to the supporting documentation.

Task 6

- Write up the cash book (receipts side) on page 216 of the Answer Book for the cash and cheques that will be paid into the bank, and subtotal the amount to be paid in.

- Write up the cash book (receipts side) for the automated payment received.

Note: You do NOT need to calculate any totals in the cash book (receipts side) at this stage.

sample simulation – unit 1

Task 7

Prepare the paying-in slip on page 217 of the Answer Booklet for the cash and cheques that need to be paid into the bank today. Make sure that the total on the paying-in slip agrees with paying-in total in the cash book total (receipts side) that you calculated in Task 6.

Task 8

- Calculate the totals for the cash book (receipts side).
- Enter appropriate main ledger and subsidiary (sales) ledger codes into the cash book (receipts side) in preparation for posting.
- Post the cash book (receipts side) to the relevant main ledger and subsidiary (sales) ledger accounts.

Task 9

For the two customers for whom statements are provided on page 218 of the Answer Booklet:

- calculate a balance on the appropriate subsidiary (sales) ledger account;
- complete the statements as at today's date.

Chasing payments

The company policy for debtors who have debts which are more than 60 days old is to put the whole account on 'stop'. This means that that no more sales are made until settlement has been received as agreed.

Task 10

Refer to the extract from the Aged Debtor Analysis on page 194 of this book, and to the letter from Kendrick & Co to Mark Alberts on page 195 of this book. Samir has made some notes on both documents.

- Draft a letter to Slomax & Partners from Samir Aleffi, in accordance with Samir's notes on the Aged Debtor Analysis. Use the letterhead on page 219 of the Answer Booklet. Note that the contact name and address for the customer have been completed for you.
- Draft a memo to Mark Alberts concerning the letter from Kendrick & Co and Samir's notes on it. Use page 220 of the Answer Booklet.

Task 11

The Finance Director has asked Samir to find ways in which the computer can be used more fully by the accounts department without disrupting matters too much. Samir has asked you for some ideas.

- Using page 221 of the Answer Booklet, draft an email to Samir, with answers to the following points:

    - if we move to a fully computerised system, do we have to change the sequence of our invoice and credit note numbers and the ledger codes?

    - we already input details to the computer so that we have a Discount Analysis and an Aged Debtor Analysis. How will further computerisation help in completing the Day Books and the main and subsidiary ledgers, and in preparing statements?

MAIN LEDGER ACCOUNT CODES (EXTRACT)

Ledger code	Account name
1000	Cash
2000	Sales Ledger Control
3000	Discount Allowed
4000	Sales
5000	Returns
6000	VAT

SUBSIDIARY (SALES) LEDGER ACCOUNT CODES (EXTRACT)

Ledger code	Account name	Trade discount
100	Ardington plc	0
200	Dreadnought PC Ltd	5%
300	Kendrick & Co	0
400	Lineman plc	0
500	PrimeTime Mobiles	5%
600	Rondar plc	0
700	Slomax & Partners	0

TUBNEY TECHNOLOGY LTD: PRICE LIST

Part reference	£ per unit
AD897	0.35
DF014	3.60
GW208	12.80
MM936	0.50
PA220	5.55
RL188	9.75

QUOTATION

From: Tubney Technology Ltd, Oxford Business Park, Oxford OX2 8VN

To: Dreadnought PC Ltd
Saddleworth Laner
Halifax LS6 8WL

Date: 8 September 2006

Further to your enquiry, we have pleasure in providing this firm quotation to carry out the necessary work as per your specification.

Description

Manufacture and testing of 500 HighDensity 10 cm SIM cards as per your specification of 1 September 2006.

Including packing and delivery £1,950 plus VAT

Signed: M Alberts Date: 8 September 2006

PURCHASE ORDER

Ardington plc
90/94 Grove Road
Wantage OX16 9AS

To: Tubney Technology Ltd,
Oxford Business Park,
Oxford, OX2 8VN

Date: 15 September 2006

Please supply us with 2,000 AD897 and 1,000 MM936 parts as soon as possible.

Yours faithfully

C Timms

Ardington plc

DELIVERY NOTE

Tubney Technology
Oxford Business Park
Oxford
OX2 8VN

Delivery address:

Ardington plc
90/94 Grove Road
Wantage OX16 9AS

Date: 16 September 2006

Item	Quantity
MM936	1,000
AD897	2,000

Received by: [Signature] *C Timms*

Date: *16 September 2006*

PURCHASE ORDER

DREADNOUGHT PC Ltd
Saddleworth Lane
Halifax, LS6 8WL

To: Tubney Technology Ltd,
Oxford Business Park,
Oxford, OX2 8VN

Date: 10 September 2006

Please supply 500 special parts in accordance with your quotation of 8 September, which we accept.

Yours faithfully

S Parsons

Dreadnought PC Ltd

DELIVERY NOTE

Tubney Technology
Oxford Business Park
Oxford
OX2 8VN

Delivery address:

Dreadnought PC Ltd
Saddleworth Lane
Halifax LS6 8WL

Date: 16 September 2006

Item	Quantity
High Density 10 cm SIM cards as per quotation	500

Received by: [Signature] *S Parsons*

Date: *16 September 2006*

PURCHASE ORDER

Kendrick & Co
110-120 Banbury Road
Bicester OX6 9QW

To: Tubney Technology Ltd,
Oxford Business Park,
Oxford, OX2 8VN

Date: 15 September 2006

Please supply 100 PA220 parts as soon as possible.

Yours faithfully

O Kendrick

Kendrick & Co

DELIVERY NOTE

Tubney Technology
Oxford Business Park
Oxford
OX2 8VN

Delivery address:

Kendrick & Co
110-120 Banbury Road
Bicester OX6 9QW

Date: 17 September 2006

Item	Quantity
RL188	1,000

Received by: [Signature]   *O Kendrick*

Date: *17 September 2006*

SALES ORDER

Tubney Technology
Oxford Business Park
Oxford
OX2 8VN

Customer: Lineman plc

Delivery address:

Hamilton House
Oxford Science Park
Oxford OX3 3PR

Date: 15 September 2006

Item	Quantity
AD897	3,000
DF014	200
GW208	150

Received by: [Signature] *M Alberts*

Date: *15 September 2006*

DELIVERY NOTE

Tubney Technology
Oxford Business Park
Oxford
OX2 8VN

Delivery address:

Lineman plc
Hamilton House
Oxford Science Park
Oxford OX3 3PR

Date: 17 September 2006

Item	Quantity
GW208	150
DF014	200
AD897	3,000

Received by: [Signature] *P Patel*

Date: *17 September 2006*

SALES ORDER

Tubney Technology
Oxford Business Park
Oxford
OX2 8VN

Customer: PrimeTime Mobiles

Delivery address:

Penny Hinton Road
Morpath
Cambridge CB13 8DF

Date: 16 September 2006

Item	Quantity
PA220	250
MM936	3,000

Received by: [Signature]   *M Alberts*

Date: *16 September 2006*

DELIVERY NOTE

Tubney Technology
Oxford Business Park
Oxford
OX2 8VN

Delivery address:

```
PrimeTime Mobiles
Penny Hinton Road
Morpath
Cambridge CB13 8DF
```

Date: 17 September 2006

Item	Quantity
PA220　　　　　　　　　　　　　 MM936	250 3,000

Received by: [Signature]   *A Colley*

Date: *17 September 2006*

RETURN NOTE

Customer: Kendrick & Co

Tubney Technology
Oxford Business Park
Oxford
OX2 8VN

Date: 12 September 2006

Item	Quantity
GW208 see invoice 8900 8-Sept-05	20

Reason for return   Faulty parts

Received by: [Signature] *Ian Smith*

Date: *12 September 2006*

RETURN NOTE

Customer: Rondar plc

Tubney Technology
Oxford Business Park
Oxford
OX2 8VN

Date: 15 September 2006

Item	Quantity
PA220 see invoice 8905 10-Sept-05	15

Reason for return   Faulty parts

Received by: [Signature]   *Ian Smith*

Date: *15 September 2006*

sample simulation – unit 1

Discount analysis (extract)

Invoice number	Date 2006	Customer account	SDB folio	Invoice subtotal £	VAT £	Invoice total	Settlement discount £
8750	19 Sept	Dreadnought PC Ltd	200	8,550.00	1,443.88	9,993.88	299.25
8765	20 Aug	PrimeTime Mobiles	500	4,264.05	616.05	4,264.05	127.68
8790	22 Aug	Ardington plc	100	438.75	74.09	512.84	15.35
8890	5 Sept	Kendrick & Co	300	360.00	60.79	420.79	12.60
8910	8 Sept	Lineman plc	400	487.50	82.32	569.82	17.06

Receipt no: 51

18 September 2006

To: Barry Kendrick, Kendrick & Co

Receipt for cash received

Received with thanks £408.19 in full settlement of Invoice 8890 (discount taken: £12.60)

S Aleffi

Accounts Manager

Tubney Technology Ltd

REMITTANCE ADVICE

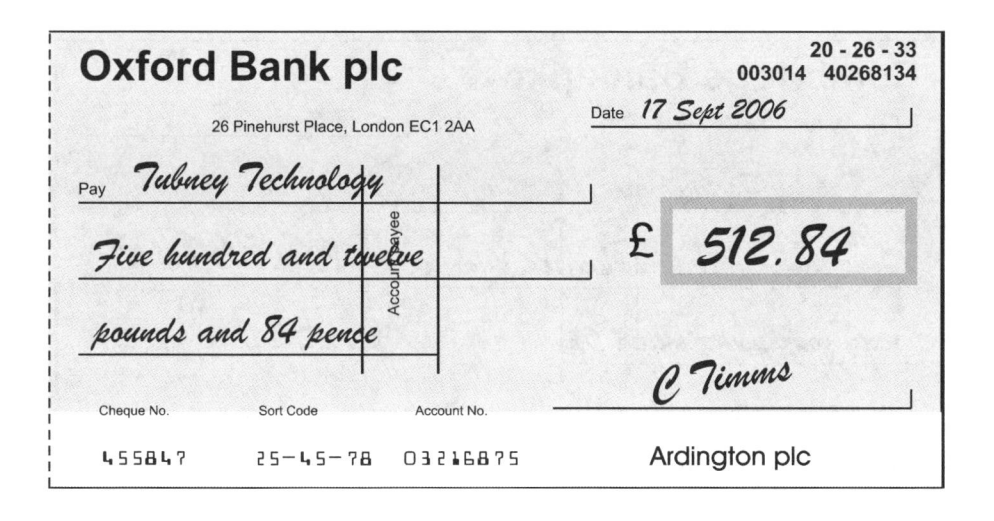

To: Tubney Technology Ltd,
Oxford Business Park,
Oxford, OX2 8VN

From: Ardington plc
90/94 Grove Road
Wantage, OX16 9AS

Date	Transaction reference	Amount (£)
28-Aug-06	Invoice 8790	512.84
17-Sept-06	Cheque attached	-512.84

Oxford Bank plc

26 Pinehurst Place, London EC1 2AA

20 - 26 - 33
003014 40268134

Date *17 Sept 2006*

Pay *Tubney Technology*

Five hundred and twelve pounds and 84 pence

£ *512.84*

C Timms

Cheque No.	Sort Code	Account No.
455847	25-45-78	03216875

Ardington plc

REMITTANCE ADVICE

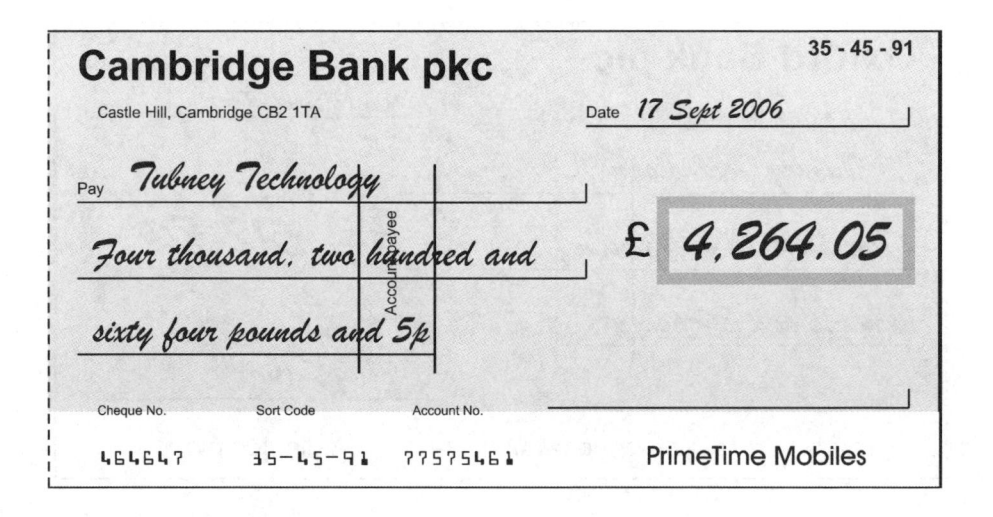

To: Tubney Technology Ltd,
Oxford Business Park,
Oxford, OX2 8VN

From: PrimeTime Mobiles,
Morpath, Cambridge,
CB13 8DF

Date	Transaction reference	Amount (£)
21-Aug-06	Invoice 8765	4,264.05
17-Sept-06	Cheque attached	-4,264.05

Cambridge Bank pkc

Castle Hill, Cambridge CB2 1TA

35 - 45 - 91

Date *17 Sept 2006*

Pay *Tubney Technology*

Four thousand, two hundred and sixty four pounds and 5p

£ *4,264.05*

Cheque No. 464647   Sort Code 35-45-91   Account No. 77575461

PrimeTime Mobiles

REMITTANCE ADVICE

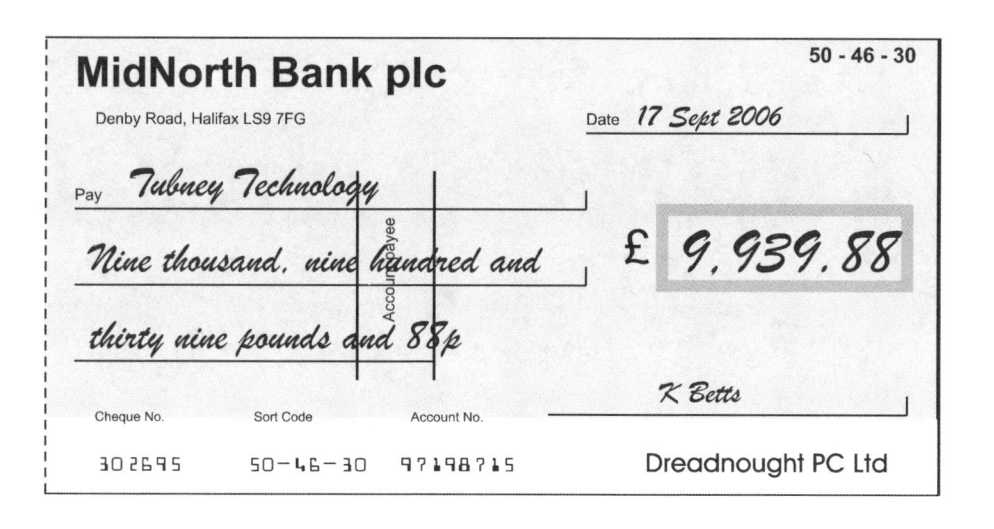

To: Tubney Technology Ltd,
Oxford Business Park,
Oxford, OX2 8VN

From: Dreadnought PC Ltd
Saddleworth Lane,
Halifax LS6 8WL

Date	Transaction reference	Amount (£)
19-Aug-06	Invoice 8750	9,939.88
17-Sept-06	Cheque attached	-9,939.88

MidNorth Bank plc   50 - 46 - 30
Denby Road, Halifax LS9 7FG

Date *17 Sept 2006*

Pay *Tubney Technology*

Nine thousand, nine hundred and thirty nine pounds and 88p

£ **9,939.88**

K Betts

Cheque No.	Sort Code	Account No.
302695	50-46-30	97198715

Dreadnought PC Ltd

REMITTANCE ADVICE

To: Tubney Technology Ltd,
Oxford Business Park,
Oxford, OX2 8VN

From: Lineman plc,
Hamilton House,
Oxford Science,
Oxford, OX3 3PR

Date	Transaction reference	Amount (£)
8-Sept 06	Invoice 8910	569.82
17-Sept-06	BACS	-552.76
17-Sept-06	Settlement discount taken	-17.06

STATEMENT

Oxford Bank plc
High Street,
Oxford,
OX2 7DF

Account name: Tubney Technology
Oxford Business Park
Oxford OX2 8VN

Account number: 98746510

Sort code: 25-45-78

Statement no: 109

Details	Date	Debit £	Credit £	Balance £
	2006			
Balance forward	11 Sept			25,946.46
CC	11 Sept		9,457.08	
Cheque 4900	11 Sept	15,789.43		
Cheque 4899	11 Sept	6,913.30		12,700.81
CC	12 Sept		12,879.63	
Cheques 4901	12 Sept	8,673.00		
CC	12 Sept		500.00	17,047.44
BACS payment - salaries	15 Sept	21,067.90		
CC	15 Sept		7,560.49	3,900.03
Cheque 4902	16 Sept	681.34		
BACS receipt	17 Sept		552.76	3,771.45

Key   CC: Cash and/or cheques   **BACS:** Banks automated clearing service

Aged Debtor Analysis

Customer	Subsidiary (sales) ledger code	Credit limit	Total	Not yet due 0-30 days £	30-60 days £	60+ days £	Action taken
Slomax & Partners	700	2,000.00	3,972.09	0.00	1,893.44	2,078.65	In error we allowed them to exceed their credit limit, then we received a cheque dated 16 September 2005 for £2,078.65, plus an order for goods worth £1,280.00. Draft a letter for my signature - point out why we could not bank this cheque (which we will return with the letter, asking for a corrected one), and confirm our company policy on the state of their account.

Kendrick & Co
111-120 Banbury Road
Bicester OX6 9QW
Phone: 01869 654641 Fax: 01869 567684

Mr M Alberts
Sales Manager
Tubney Technology Ltd
Oxford Business Park
Oxford OX2 8VN

16 September 2006

Dear Mark

As you know, I often pay your invoices in cash, so that we can take advantage of the settlement discount you offer. I have recently acquired a corporate credit card. If you are agreeable, I propose to pay our bills in future by this method. I shall pop in on Friday to settle our account as it stands in full with the card.

Yours sincerely

O Kendrick

Ollie Kendrick
Partner

Lynsey

Mark and his sales team are able to take credit card payments using vouchers, but our floor limit is only £100. And what is the state of Kendrick & Co's account currently? Will he be able to settle it in full on Friday? Please drop a memo to Mark about this, and let me have a copy.

Samir

ANSWER BOOKLET

ANSWERS (Task 1)

Errors or discrepancies

_____
_____
_____
_____
_____
_____

Action to be taken:

_____
_____
_____
_____
_____
_____

Invoice number

_____

ANSWERS (Task 1, continued)

INVOICE

Tubney Technology Ltd
Oxford Business Park
Oxford OX2 8VN
Phone: 01865 444555
Fax 01865 444666

To:

Invoice number: 8950

VAT Registration: 305 034 97 63

Date/tax point:

Subsidiary (sales) ledger code:

Item	Quantity	Price £	Total £

Goods total
Trade discount @   %
Sub-total
VAT @ 17.5%
Invoice total

Settlement discount: 3.5% for payment in 14 days
(to be deducted when computing VAT)

sample simulation – unit 1 – answer booklet

ANSWERS (Task 1, continued)

INVOICE

Tubney Technology Ltd
Oxford Business Park
Oxford OX2 8VN
Phone: 01865 444555
Fax 01865 444666

To:

Invoice number: 8951

VAT Registration: 305 034 97 63

Date/tax point:

Subsidiary (sales) ledger code:

Item	Quantity	Price £	Total £

Goods total
Trade discount @   %
Sub-total
VAT @ 17.5%
Invoice total

Settlement discount: 3.5% for payment in 14 days
(to be deducted when computing VAT)

sample simulation – unit 1 – answer booklet

ANSWERS (Task 1, continued)

INVOICE

Tubney Technology Ltd
Oxford Business Park
Oxford OX2 8VN
Phone: 01865 444555
Fax 01865 444666

To:

Invoice number: 8952

VAT Registration: 305 034 97 63

Date/tax point:

Subsidiary (sales) ledger code:

Item	Quantity	Price £	Total £
	Goods total		
	Trade discount @ %		
	Sub-total		
	VAT @ 17.5%		
	Invoice total		

Settlement discount: 3.5% for payment in 14 days
(to be deducted when computing VAT)

202

ANSWERS (Task 1, continued)

INVOICE

Tubney Technology Ltd
Oxford Business Park
Oxford OX2 8VN
Phone: 01865 444555
Fax 01865 444666

To:

Invoice number: 8953

VAT Registration: 305 034 97 63

Date/tax point:

Subsidiary (sales) ledger code:

Item	Quantity	Price £	Total £

Goods total	
Trade discount @ %	
Sub-total	
VAT @ 17.5%	
Invoice total	

Settlement discount: 3.5% for payment in 14 days
(to be deducted when computing VAT)

203

sample simulation – unit 1 – answer booklet

ANSWERS (Task 1, continued)

INVOICE

Tubney Technology Ltd
Oxford Business Park
Oxford OX2 8VN
Phone: 01865 444555
Fax 01865 444666

To:

Invoice number: 8954

VAT Registration: 305 034 97 63

Date/tax point:

Subsidiary (sales) ledger code:

Item	Quantity	Price £	Total £
		Goods total	
		Trade discount @ %	
		Sub-total	
		VAT @ 17.5%	
		Invoice total	

Settlement discount: 3.5% for payment in 14 days
(to be deducted when computing VAT)

ANSWERS (Task 2)

CREDIT NOTE

Tubney Technology Ltd
Oxford Business Park
Oxford OX2 8VN
Phone: 01865 444555
Fax 01865 444666

To:

Credit note number: 650

VAT Registration: 305 034 97 63

Date/tax point:

Subsidiary (sales) ledger code:

Item	Quantity	Price £	Total £

Goods total	
Trade discount @ %	
Sub-total	
VAT @ 17.5%	
Credit note total	

ANSWERS (Task 2, continued)

CREDIT NOTE

Tubney Technology Ltd
Oxford Business Park
Oxford OX2 8VN
Phone: 01865 444555
Fax 01865 444666

To:

Credit note number: 651

VAT Registration: 305 034 97 63

Date/tax point:

Subsidiary (sales) ledger code:

Item	Quantity	Price £	Total £

Goods total
Trade discount @   %
Sub-total
VAT @ 17.5%
Credit note total

ANSWERS (Tasks 3 and 4)

Invoices and credit notes should be authorised before despatch by: _____

Day's total settlement discount on invoices (to be agreed to discount analysis): _____

SALES DAY BOOK						Folio: SDB 38
Date 2006	Customer	Subsidiary (sales) ledger code: DR	Invoice number	Total £	VAT £	Net £
Totals						
Main ledger codes						

sample simulation – unit 1 – answer booklet

ANSWERS (Tasks 3 and 4, continued)

SALES RETURNS DAY BOOK   Folio: SRDB 9

Date 2006	Customer	Subsidiary (sales) ledger code: DR	Credit note number	Total £	VAT £	Net £
	Totals					
	Main ledger codes					

ANSWERS (Tasks 4 and 7)

MAIN LEDGER

2000 SALES LEDGER CONTROL ACCOUNT

Date 2006	Details	Folio	Amount £	Date 2006	Details	Folio	Amount £

3000 DISCOUNT ALLOWED

Date 2006	Details	Folio	Amount £	Date 2006	Details	Folio	Amount £

4000 SALES

Date 2006	Details	Folio	Amount £	Date 2006	Details	Folio	Amount £

sample simulation – unit 1 – answer booklet

ANSWERS (Tasks 4 and 7, continued)

MAIN LEDGER

5000 SALES RETURNS

Date 2006	Details	Folio	Amount £	Date 2006	Details	Folio	Amount £

6000 VAT

Date 2006	Details	Folio	Amount £	Date 2006	Details	Folio	Amount £

ANSWERS (Tasks 4 and 7, continued)

SUBSIDIARY (SALES) LEDGER

100 ARDINGTON PLC

Date 2006	Details	Folio	Amount £	Date 2006	Details	Folio	Amount £
22-Aug	Inv 8790	SDB 34	512.84				

200 DREADNOUGHT PC LTD

Date 2006	Details	Folio	Amount £	Date 2006	Details	Folio	Amount £
19-Aug	Inv 8750	SDB 34	9,993.38				

300 KENDRICK & CO

Date 2006	Details	Folio	Amount £	Date 2006	Details	Folio	Amount £
5-Sept	Inv 8890	SDB 36	420.79				
8-Sept	Inv 8900	SDB 37	1,496.16				

ANSWERS (Tasks 4 and 7, continued)

SUBSIDIARY (SALES) LEDGER

400 LINEMAN PLC

Date 2006	Details	Folio	Amount £	Date 2006	Details	Folio	Amount £
8-Sep	Inv 8910	SDB 37	569.82				

500 PRIMETIME MOBILES

Date 2006	Details	Folio	Amount £	Date 2006	Details	Folio	Amount £
20-Aug	Inv 8765	SDB 34	4,264.05				

600 RONDAR PLC

Date 2006	Details	Folio	Amount £	Date 2006	Details	Folio	Amount £
13-May	Inv 6535	SDB 7	169.86				
2-Jun	Inv 6590	SDB 10	210.87				

ANSWERS (Tasks 4 and 7, continued)

SUBSIDIARY (SALES) LEDGER

700 SLOMAX & PARTNERS

Date 2006	Details	Folio	Amount £	Date 2006	Details	Folio	Amount £
18-Sep	Balance		3,972.09				

ANSWERS (Task 5)

Notes

ANSWERS (Task 5, continued)

Contents of envelope handed in by Mark Albert with Kendrick & Co receipt

		£
£50	4	
£20	8	
£10	4	
£5	1	
£2	0	
£1	2	
50p	1	
20p	2	
10p	1	
5p	3	
2p	1	
1p	2	

sample simulation – unit 1 – answer booklet

ANSWERS (Tasks 6 and 8)

MAIN LEDGER

1000 CASH BOOK CB 38

RECEIPTS

Date 2006	Details	Ref	Receipt £	Discount allowed £	Customer account £	Subsidiary (sales) ledger code
	Main ledger codes					

sample simulation – unit 1 – answer booklet

ANSWERS (Task 7)

bank giro credit

Please detail cheques and cash overleaf

Date_____
Cashier's stamp

Oxford Bank plc
High Street, Oxford OX2 7DF

Account

Tubney Technology Ltd

Paid in by/Ref

£50 Notes	
£20 Notes	
£10 Notes	
£5 Notes	
£2	
£1	
50p	
20p	
10p, 5p	
2p, 1p	
Total cash	
Cheques, PO's	
£	

NO OF CHEQUES

25-45-78   98746510

Please do not write or mark below this line or fold this voucher

Details of cheques	Amount	
	£	P
Total cheques carried over		

sample simulation – unit 1 – answer booklet

ANSWERS (Task 9)

STATEMENT OF ACCOUNT
Tubney Technology Ltd, Oxford Business Park, Oxford OX2 8VN

Customer: Dreadnought PC Ltd
Date:
Subsidiary (sales) ledger code:

Date 2006	Transaction reference	Debit £	Credit £	Balance outstanding £
Balance outstanding				

Our terms are strictly 30 days, with 3.5% cash settlement discount available for payment within 14 days.

STATEMENT OF ACCOUNT
Tubney Technology Ltd, Oxford Business Park, Oxford OX2 8VN

Customer: Kendrick & Co
Date:
Subsidiary (sales) ledger code:

Date 2006	Transaction reference	Debit £	Credit £	Balance outstanding £
Balance outstanding				

Our terms are strictly 30 days, with 3.5% cash settlement discount available for payment within 14 days.

ANSWERS (Task 10)

Tubney Technology Ltd
Oxford Business Park, Oxford OX2 8VN
Phone: 01865 444555 Fax 01865 444666

Ms U Ogangwe
Slomax & Partners
Success House
200 Old Kent Road
London SE2 9CV

ANSWERS (Task 10, continued)

MEMO

To:
From:
CC:
Subject:
Date:

ANSWERS (Task 11)

EMAIL

From: lynsey.jones@tubneytech.co.uk
To: samir.aleffi@tubneytech.co.uk
CC:
Subject: Computerisation
Date: 18 September 2006

Message

If using this page, please state clearly which task you are answering.

AAT

SAMPLE SIMULATION
UNIT 2

AMICA PRINTING CO.

This is the AAT's Sample Simulation for Unit 2. Its purpose is to give you an idea of what an AAT simulation looks like. It is not intended as a definitive guide to the tasks you may be required to perform.

This simulation is in two parts. It is suggested that you spend approximately 90 minutes on each part.

Total time: 3 hours

Coverage of performance criteria and range statements

All performance criteria are covered in this simulation.

Element	PC Coverage
2.1	**Process documents relating to goods and services received**
a)	Check suppliers' invoices and credit notes against relevant **documents** for validity.
b)	Checked **calculations** on suppliers' invoices and credit notes for accuracy.
c)	Identify and deduct available **discounts**.
d)	Correctly **code** invoices and credit notes.
e)	Correctly enter invoices and credit notes into **books of prime entry** according to organisational procedures.
f)	Enter invoices and credit notes in the appropriate **ledgers**.
g)	Identify **discrepancies** and either resolve or refer to the appropriate person if outside own authority.
h)	**Communicate** appropriately with suppliers regarding accounts.
2.2	**Process payments**
a)	Calculate **payments** from relevant **documentation**.
b)	Schedule payments and obtain authorisation.
c)	Use the appropriate **payment method** and timescale, in accordance with organisational procedures.
d)	Enter payments into **accounting records**.
e)	Identify **queries** and resolve or refer to the appropriate person.
f)	Ensure security and confidentiality is maintained according to organisational requirements.

The following range statements are **not** covered in this simulation and should be assessed separately.

Element	Range Statement
2.1	**Code:** computerised systems
	Books of prime entry: relevant computerised records
	Ledgers: computerised ledgers
	Discrepancies: duplicated invoices
2.2	**Accounting records:** computerised records

DATA AND TASKS

INSTRUCTIONS

This simulation is designed to let you show your ability to make and record payments.

You should read the whole simulation before you start work, so that you are fully aware of what you will have to do.

You are allowed **three hours** to complete your work.

Write your answers in the Answer Booklet provided on pages 249-297. If you need more paper for your answers, ask the person in charge.

You should write your answers in blue or black ink, **not** pencil.

You may use correcting fluid, but in moderation. You should cross out your errors neatly and clearly.

You may pull apart and rearrange your booklets if you wish to do so, but you must put them back in their original order before handing them in.

Your work must be accurate, so check your work carefully before handing it in.

You are not allowed to refer to any unauthorised material, such as books or notes, while you are working on the simulation. If you have any such material with you, you must hand it to the person in charge before you start work.

Any instances of misconduct will be reported to the AAT, and disciplinary action may be taken.

Coverage of performance criteria and range statements

It is not always possible to cover all performance criteria and range statements in a single simulation. Any performance criteria and range statements not covered must be assessed by other means by the assessor before a candidate can be considered competent.

Performance criteria and range statement coverage for this simulation is shown on page 224.

sample simulation – unit 2

THE SITUATION

You are Hei Lam Cheng, Accounts Assistant at Amica Printing Company, a business situated in the town of Wantage. Your duties include accounting for purchases on credit, making payments and controlling petty cash. You report to Alex Cook, the Accountant. The business is owned by Sam Fisher.

Amica Printing Company prints brochures and leaflets for businesses and public sector organisations in the UK.

The company employs 20 people, most of whom work in the printing factory. The Factory Supervisor is Henry Lynch, who reports to Edward Hunt, the Factory Manager. Nearly all the factory staff are employed on a permanent basis, but there are three temporary factory staff to whom special payroll procedures apply. All staff are paid monthly by bankers automated clearing system (BACS), unless they do not have a bank account, in which case they are paid in cash.

Accounting system

Amica Printing Company operates a main ledger, which contains the cash book, the petty cash book and the purchase ledger control account. Each supplier has a separate account in the subsidiary (purchases) ledger, which is not part of the double entry system.

The company is registered for VAT.

Today's date is Tuesday 23 September 2006.

sample simulation – unit 2

THE TASKS TO BE COMPLETED

PART 1 PROCESSING DOCUMENTS RELATING TO GOODS AND SERVICES RECEIVED (90 MINUTES)

Handling Purchase Invoices

You are responsible for processing documents relating to goods and services received.

- Most of Amica Printing Company's purchases are made via the Internet. You match invoices received to the following supporting documentation: the supplier master file, printouts of Amica Printing Company purchase orders, delivery notes from the supplier, and Amica Printing Company goods received notes (for factory purchases only).

- If an invoice does not agree with the supporting documentation, the discrepancy is discussed initially with either Edward Hunt, the factory manager, or Alex Cook, the accountant. If appropriate, the invoice is recorded once it has been signed by one of them to show that the discrepancy has been resolved.

- For any other type of error, the invoice is not recorded but is returned to the supplier with a letter from you on headed notepaper, requesting a corrected invoice.

Task 1

Refer to the invoices on pages 249-260 of the Answer Booklet and the supporting documentation on pages 235-240 of this book. The last invoice recorded in the purchase day book was numbered 6069.

- Check each invoice against the supporting documentation, and check all the calculations, including settlement discount and VAT (which should always be rounded down to the nearest penny). Where appropriate, mark any errors or discrepancies beneath each invoice, and state the action to be taken.

- Allocate an invoice number to each invoice that can be recorded, and write the relevant number in the space beneath each document.

- If it is appropriate, prepare notes for conversations with either Edward Hunt or Alex Cook. Use page 261 of the Answer Booklet.

- If it is appropriate, prepare letters to suppliers. Use the letterheads on pages 262 and 263 of the Answer Booklet.

227

Handling Credit Notes

- Credit notes must be agreed to goods returned notes, which are prepared by Edward Hunt.

- A credit note which does not agree to the goods returned note is discussed with either Edward Hunt or Alex Cook, as appropriate. If the discrepancy is resolved by this method, the credit note is recorded once one of them has signed it.

- For any other type of error, the credit note is not recorded, but is returned to the supplier with a letter from you on headed notepaper, requesting a corrected credit note.

Task 2

Refer to the credit notes on pages 264-267 of the Answer Booklet and the supporting documentation on pages 237 and 240 of this book. The last credit note recorded in the purchase returns day book was numbered 286.

- Check each credit note against the supporting documentation, and check all the calculations, including discount and VAT (which should always be rounded down to the nearest penny). Where appropriate, mark any errors or discrepancies beneath each credit note, and state the action to be taken.

- Allocate a credit note number to each credit note to be recorded, and write the relevant number in the space provided beneath each document.

- If you have found any errors relating to the supporting documentation, prepare notes for conversations with either Edward Hunt or Alex Cook. Use page 261 of the Answer Booklet.

- If you have found any other errors, prepare a letter to the relevant supplier. Use the letterhead on page 268 of the Answer Booklet.

Task 3

For all invoices and credit notes in Tasks 1 and 2 that have not been queried with Edward Hunt or Alex Cook, and so can be recorded, enter and analyse the details of invoices in the purchase day book, and of credit notes in the purchase returns day book on pages 269-270 of the Answer Booklet.

Task 4

- Total the columns in the purchase day book and the purchase returns day book.

- Enter the relevant main ledger and subsidiary (purchase) ledger account codes in the day books in preparation for posting. Show which sides of the accounts will be posted by writing either 'DR' or 'CR' as appropriate.

- Make the required entries in the main ledger and subsidiary (purchase) ledger accounts on pages 271-276 of the Answer Booklet.

Note: There are transactions already shown on some of the ledger accounts. You do NOT need to balance any ledger accounts after you have made your entries.

sample simulation – unit 2

PART 2 PROCESS PAYMENTS (90 MINUTES)

Payments to suppliers and others

Twice a month you prepare cheque runs and BACS payments to be received by the payee on the second Friday and the last Friday of each month (the payment date). If settlement discount is available on any invoices at the payment date in question, you always take it. Otherwise, you take the maximum credit available according to the supplier's terms at the payment date. When assessing whether settlement discount is still available, you should treat the payment date for suppliers this week as 26 September 2006, as this is the date that cheques and BACS payments will be received by suppliers. The next payment date after the present one will be Friday 10 October 2006.

Task 5

Refer to the suppliers' statements on pages 277-281 of the Answer Booklet. Alex Cook has made a note on each statement of which invoices should be paid and how much settlement discount should be taken.

- Check the statements against the relevant ledger accounts on pages 275-276 of the Answer Booklet. On the ledger accounts, tick each item that is due for payment. Beneath each statement, write any settlement discount that is available. Also make a note of any discrepancies, and the action to be taken about them.

- Complete the remittance advices on pages 282-284 of the Answer Booklet for all payments to suppliers that will be made. You do not need to fill in the supplier's address.

- Refer to the cheque requisitions on page 241 of this book and check them against the supporting documentation on page 242 of this book. Make notes on page 285 of the Answer Booklet as to what further action is required, if any.

- Write up the cash book (payments side) on page 286 of the Answer Booklet with the amounts to be paid to suppliers and others today. In the Folio column, write the documentation that supports each payment.

Note: The BACS and cheque payments will be prepared later. You do not need to fill in relevant cheque numbers, and main and subsidiary (purchases) account numbers, nor total the cash book (payments side), at this stage.

Payroll payments

All staff are paid monthly in arrears on the last Friday of the month for the four (sometimes five) weeks ending the previous Friday. All factory staff are paid for a basic working week of 37.5 hours, plus overtime pay at time-and-a-half for hours over 37.5 hours per week. They can also receive occasional bonuses.

A payroll bureau, PrintPay Ltd, calculates gross pay and deductions and prepares payslips for all staff, and makes BACS payments by autopay to all permanent staff. You are sent a Factory Payroll with all amounts for permanent factory staff already inserted, plus payslips for temporary factory staff. Overtime and bonuses for temporary factory staff are listed on your Factory Pay List, which is signed by Edward

sample simulation – unit 2

Hunt and Alex Cook. You check this against the payslips, and then make the payments to any temporary factory staff from the payslips by cheque.

You raise queries about gross pay for temporary factory staff with Edward Hunt in person, and about the calculation and preparation of payslips with Robert Kane at PrintPay Ltd by phone.

You complete the Factory Payroll from the temporary factory staff payslips. Except where there is an error in the calculation of net pay you always include payslips for temporary staff in the Factory Payroll.

Task 6

- Check the payslips of the temporary factory staff shown on pages 287 and 288 of the Answer Booklet against the factory pay list and employee master file on page 243 of this book. Make notes beneath any payslip which contains an error or discrepancy, and state the action to be taken.

- Check the calculation of net pay on the payslips of each of the temporary staff.

Note: You do not need to check how the PAYE and NIC figures, and the year to date figures, are calculated, so you do not need tax tables to perform this task.

- Write up the factory payroll on page 289 of the Answer Booklet for the temporary factory staff payslips, indicating the amounts to be paid by cheque.

- Write up the cash book (payments side) on page 286 of the Answer Booklet with the amounts to be paid to individual temporary factory staff by cheque.

- Write up the cash book (payments side) for the total BACS payments by autopay that have been made by PrintPay Ltd to permanent factory staff.

Note: You need not fill in the references, nor total the cash book (payments side), at this stage.

Task 7

Refer to the email from Henry Lynch, the Factory Supervisor, on page 244 of this book.

- Draft an email to Henry in response to his memo, outlining the course of action you need to take. Use page 290 of the Answer Booklet.

Petty cash payments

Each day you are responsible for writing up petty cash vouchers from valid receipts for the expenditure paid out. Receipts are only valid if signed by the recipient and authorised by Alex Cook. Employees can only make petty cash claims up to £40. If they wish to claim for more than this amount, they are required to fill out an expenses claim form. You top up the petty cash to £300 each time the amount of cash in the petty cash box falls below £60.

sample simulation – unit 2

Task 8

Refer to the list of ledger accounts on page 233 and the authorised receipts on page 245 of this book.

- Complete vouchers on page 291 of the Answer Booklet, calculating VAT as appropriate (round VAT down to the nearest penny), for all receipts that you are able to pay from petty cash.

- Make notes on page 292 of the Answer Booklet on why you have not prepared a voucher for all the receipts.

- Refer to the list of notes and coin in the petty cash box on page 293 of the Answer Booklet. On this list, write in what notes and coin are being paid out in respect of the valid receipts. You should use the highest denominations of notes and coin that are available. Then calculate a revised total for notes and coin in the petty cash box.

Note: You can assume that the cash has now been paid to the recipients.

- Write up the petty cash book on page 294 of the Answer Booklet for the vouchers you have prepared and paid, analysing the expenditure.

- Total the petty cash book and calculate the balance. Ensure that the petty cash book balance agrees with the amount of cash in the petty cash box which you have just calculated.

- Calculate any necessary top-up for petty cash and include the payment for this in the cash book (payments side) on page 286 of the Answer Booklet. You do not need to fill in the cheque number at this stage.

- Enter the relevant main ledger codes in the petty cash book in preparation for posting to the main ledger.

- Write up the petty cash book for the top-up and calculate the balance at the end of the day.

Note: You may assume that all the payments you have listed out in the cash book (payments side) have been authorised by Alex Cook on behalf of Sam Fisher.

Task 9

- Complete the cheques on pages 295-297 of the Answer Booklet for all the items that you have written up in the cash book (payments side). These will be signed by Sam Fisher.

- Enter the cheque numbers in the cash book (payments side).

- Total the cash book (payments side) and insert the relevant main and subsidiary (purchase) ledger codes in preparation for posting to the ledgers.

Task 10

- From the cash book (payments side), the payroll and the petty cash book, make the appropriate entries in the ledger accounts on pages 271-276 of the Answer Booklet.

- Calculate the balance on the purchase ledger control account in the main ledger, and on all the subsidiary ledger accounts. Show also the balance brought down on 24 September for each of these accounts.

The following are extracts from the lists of ledger codes.

MAIN LEDGER

Ledger account	Ledger code
Administration	090
Cash book	100
Purchase ledger control account	110
Discount received	120
Factory wages control	130
Factory wages expense	140
PAYE/NIC creditor	150
Petty cash book	160
Postage	170
Production expense	180
Purchases	190
Purchases returns	200
Stationery	210
VAT	220

SUBSIDIARY (PURCHASES) LEDGER

Ledger account	Ledger code
Abingdon Paper Ltd	1101
Feltham Bindery Ltd	1102
Hamburg Print Plates Ltd	1103
Ilsley Inks Ltd	1104
Sidney Stationers	1105
Wantage Engineering	1106

sample simulation – unit 2

SUPPLIER MASTER FILE

Subsidiary (purchases) ledger account code	Name of supplier	Trade discount %	Settlement terms	Agreed payment methods	Bank account number	Sort code
1101	Abingdon Paper Ltd	5	30 days net	Cheque	N/a	N/a
1102	Feltham Bindery Ltd	0	30 days net	Cheque	N/a	N/a
1103	Hamburg Print Plates Ltd	0	3%/7 days, 30 days net	BACS	67461313	80-16-74
1104	Ilsley Inks Ltd	5	30 days net	Cheque	N/a	N/a
1105	Sidney Stationers	0	30 days net	Cheque	N/a	N/a
1106	Wantage Engineering Ltd	10	1%/21 days, 30 days net	Cheque	N/a	N/a

Hamburg Print Plates Ltd

Price list

Plate for:	£ (each)
Hamburg 250 print press	25.00
Hamburg 500 print press	30.00
Hamburg 1000 print press	35.00
Myobi 400 press	20.00
Myobi 600 press	37.50
Myobi 800 press	50.00

Amica Printing Company
McLaren Trading Estate, Wantage OX12 8SD Tel: 01235 687465

INTERNET PURCHASE ORDER

To: Abingdon Paper Ltd, Milton Park, Abingdon, Oxon OX13 9AS

Description of item(s) ordered	Quantity	Price from website (£)
100gsm Nordic White A1 (500 kg pack)	5	200.00
260 gsm Polar Ice A1 (500 kg pack)	4	350.00

Ordered: Edward Hunt   **Date:** 15 September 2006   **Expense classified as:** Purchases

---

Abingdon Paper Ltd
Milton Park, Abingdon, Oxon OX13 9AS   Tel: 01235 412 233

DELIVERY NOTE

To: Amica Printing Company, Mclaren Trading Estate, Wantage OX12 8SD

Description of item(s) ordered	Quantity
100gsm Nordic White A1 (500 kg pack)	5
260 gsm Polar Ice A1 (500 kg pack)	4

Signed for by: Edward Hunt   **Date:** 22 September 2006

Amica Printing Company
GOODS RECEIVED NOTE

From: Abingdon Paper Ltd

Description of item(s) ordered	Quantity	Received in good condition?
100gsm Nordic White A1 (500 kg pack)	5	Yes
260 gsm Polar Ice A1 (500 kg pack)	4	Yes

Signed: Edward Hunt   **Date:** 22 September 2006

Amica Printing Company
McLaren Trading Estate, Wantage OX12 8SD Tel: 01235 687465

PURCHASE ORDER

To: Feltham Bindery Ltd, Chertsey Road Trading Estate, Feltham, Mddx TW12 5AB

Description of item(s) ordered	Quantity	Fixed price agreed (£)
Consultancy report on installation of a fully automated binding line at the Wantage factory	1	3,250.00 plus VAT

Signed: Sam Fisher **Date:** 2 September 2006 **Expense classified as:** Production expenses

Lam,

I've received this report now so you can pay the bill when it comes in.

Sam 19 September 2006

Amica Printing Company
McLaren Trading Estate, Wantage OX12 8SD Tel: 01235 687465

INTERNET PURCHASE ORDER

To: Hamburg Print Plates Ltd, Highgrove Road, Newbury, Berks, NY9 4BW

Description of item(s) ordered	Quantity
Hamburg 250 print press plates	100
Hamburg 1000 print press plates	50
Myobi 600 press plates	70

Ordered: Edward Hunt   **Date:** 18 September 2006   **Expense classified as:** Purchases

---

Hamburg Print Plates
Highgrove Road, Newbury, Berks NY9 4BW

DELIVERY NOTE

To: Amica Printing Company, Mclaren Trading Estate, Wantage OX12 8SD

Description of item(s) ordered	Quantity
Myobi 600 press plates	70
Hamburg 1000 print press plates	50
Hamburg 250 print press plates	100

Signed for by: Edward Hunt   **Date:** 22 September 2006

Amica Printing Company
GOODS RECEIVED NOTE

From: Hamburg Print Plates Ltd

Description of item(s) ordered	Quantity	Received in good condition?
Myobi 600 press plates	70	Yes
Hamburg 1000 print press plates	50	Yes
Hamburg 250 print press plates	100	Yes

Signed: Edward Hunt   **Date:** 22 September 2006

sample simulation – unit 2

Amica Printing Company
McLaren Trading Estate, Wantage OX12 8SD Tel: 01235 687465

PURCHASE ORDER

To: Sidney Stationers, 40 Market Square, Wantage OX12 5KK

Description of item(s) ordered	Quantity	Rate agreed (£)
Red A4 lever arch files	200	1.49

Ordered: Alex Cook   **Date:** 16 September 2006   **Expense classified as:** Stationery

Sidney Stationers Ltd
40 Market Square, Wantage OX12 5KK

DELIVERY ORDER

To: Amica Printing Company, McLaren Trading Estate, Wantage OX12 8SD

Description of item(s) ordered	Quantity
Red A4 lever arch files	200

Ordered: Alex Cook   **Date:** 22 September 2006

Amica Printing Company
McLaren Trading Estate, Wantage OX12 8SD Tel: 01235 687465

INTERNET PURCHASE ORDER

To: Wantage Engineering Ltd, Grove Road, Wantage OX12 7SM

Description of item(s) ordered	Quantity	Price from website (£)
Machine Oil	10 litres	5.00/litre
Print press cleaning fluid	50 litres	6.50/litre
Press tester units	25	15.00 each

Ordered: Edward Hunt   **Date:** 15 September 2006   **Expense classified as:** Purchases

---

Wantage Engineering Ltd
Grove Road, Wantage OX12 7SM

DELIVERY NOTE

To: Amica Printing Company, Mclaren Trading Estate, Wantage OX12 8SD

Description of item(s) ordered	Quantity
Print press cleaning fluid	50 litres
Machine oil	10 litres
Press tester units	25

Agreed by: Edward Hunt   **Date:** 22 September 2006

Amica Printing Company
GOODS RECEIVED NOTE

From: Wantage Engineering Ltd

Description of item(s) ordered	Quantity	Received in good condition?
Print press cleaning fluid	50 litres	Yes
Machine oil	10 litres	Yes
Press tester units	25	Yes

Signed: Edward Hunt   **Date:** 22 September 2006

Amica Printing Company
GOODS RETURNED NOTE

To: Hamburg Print Plates

Description	Quantity	Rate agreed (£)
Hamburg 500 print press plates	5	On inspection, these plates are damaged and cannot be used in the printing machines

Signed: Edward Hunt   **Date:** 15 September 2006   **Return classified as:** Purchase returns

---

Amica Printing Company
GOODS RETURNED NOTE

To: Ilsley Inks Ltd

Description	Quantity	Rate agreed (£)
Special order pigment 291 - ordered at £25.00 per kilo	10 kilos	On examination, the ink is not of the correct pigment and cannot be used

Signed: Edward Hunt   **Date:** 15 September 2006   **Return classified as:** Purchase returns

Amica Printing Company

CHEQUE REQUISITION

Payee: *Yarnton Estates Ltd* Date: *22 September 2006*

Amount: *£150.00 + VAT*

Supporting documentation: *To follow*

Expense classified as: _____

Signed: *Henry Lynch, Factory Supervisor*

Amica Printing Company

CHEQUE REQUISITION

Payee: *Children in Need* Date: *22 September 2006*

Amount: *£300*

Supporting documentation: *This is the amount that our Pudsy Bear campaign raised. Please see the memo attached*

Expense classified as: *Administration*

Signed: *Henry Lynch, Factory Supervisor*

MEMO

To: All staff members
From: Sam Fisher
Subject: Children in Need – Pudsey Bear campaign
Date: 19 September 2006

As you know, we spent a very productive and enjoyable day this week doing silly things to help the Pudsey Bear campaign raise funds for Children in Need. I said to you that I would donate £300 to Children in Need if the day proved a success. I'm delighted that it exceeded even my expectations, so I'm happy to donate the £300.

I'd like to thank all those who took part.

Sam Fisher

> Alex
>
> Please issue a cheque for £300, and analyse it to Administration
>
> Sam   9-Sept-06

TO BE DISPLAYED ON ALL NOTICE BOARDS UNTIL 30 SEPTEMBER

Amica Printing Company

Factory Pay List - Temporary Factory Workers only

Date: 23 September 2006
Four weeks ending: 19 September 2006

Name	Basic hours	Overtime hours worked	Bonus
Pippa Allen	150.00	12	£15.00
Usha Gupta	37.50	4	£5.00

Signed Edward Hunt   **Authorised:** Alex Cook

Amica Printing Company

Employee Master File - Temporary Factory Workers

Name	Employee number	NI Number	Tax code	Basic hourly rate (£)	Pay by
Pippa Allen	FT683	KS 82 01 92 M	475L	5.50	Cheque
Ushta Gupta	FT685	WL 29 30 48 P	475L	5.50	Cheque

sample simulation – unit 2

EMAIL

To: heilamcheng@amica.co.uk
From: henrylynch@amica.co.uk
CC:
Subject: Larry Haynes
Date: 22 September 2006

Message

Hei Lam

Larry approached me yesterday to say that he has recently applied for a mortgage and the lender needs confirmation of his pay and benefits, plus copies of his last three payslips. He hasn't kept any of the documentation we have given him in the past on these matters, so I said I would get hold of copies and go through any queries he may have about him in person. Please leave these on my desk in the factory first thing tomorrow.

Henry

```
┌─────────────────────────────────────┐
│        POST OFFICE LTD              │
│        Mon 22 September 2006        │
│                                     │
│  Special Delivery                   │
│                                     │
│  2 @ £18.95                 37.90   │
│  2 @ £6.50                  13.00   │
│  Total due to Post Office   50.90   │
│  Cash from customer         50.90   │
│  Balance                     0.00   │
│                                     │
│  Dispatch of leaflets to customers  │
│  Martha Collins    23-Sep-06        │
│                                     │
│  Approved: Alex Cook                │
└─────────────────────────────────────┘
```

```
┌─────────────────────────────────────┐
│        Larkhill Stationers          │
│          VAT 0576761338             │
│                                     │
│  Stapler (inc VAT)           6.99   │
│  Total                       6.00   │
│  Cash tendered              10.00   │
│  Change amount               3.01   │
│                                     │
│  Date: 22 Sept 2006   Time 09.17    │
│                                     │
│  Office stapler to replace missing  │
│  stapler in factory.                │
│  Edward Hunt                        │
│                                     │
│  Approved: Alex Cook                │
└─────────────────────────────────────┘
```

```
┌─────────────────────────────────────┐
│         Sparkbrook Tools            │
│        Mon 22 September 2006        │
│                                     │
│                                     │
│  5" spanner                 15.99   │
│  Total due (inc VAT)        15.99   │
│  Cash from customer         20.00   │
│  Change                      4.01   │
│                                     │
│  Urgent purchase for factory        │
│  Larry Haynes                       │
│                                     │
│                                     │
│  Approved: Alex Cook                │
│                                     │
│  VAT 9870257119                     │
└─────────────────────────────────────┘
```

ANSWER BOOKLET

ANSWERS (Tasks 1 and 3)

INVOICE

Abingdon Paper Ltd
Milton Park
Abingdon
Oxon OX13 9AS
T: 01235 412233
F: 01235 412866

To: Amica Printing Company
McLaren Trading Estate
Wantage OX2 8SD

VAT Registration: 9175698745

Date/tax point: 22 September 2006

Quantity	Description	Unit amount £	Total £
5	100gsm Nordic White A1	200.00	1,000.00
4	260gsm Polar Ice A1	350.00	1,400.00
	Good total		2,400.00
	Trade discount @ 5%		120.00
	Sub-total		2,280.00
	VAT @ 17.5%		399.00
	Invoice total		2,679.00

Terms
30 days net
E & OE

sample simulation – unit 2 – answer booklet

Errors or discrepancies:
_____
_____
_____
_____
_____
_____

Action to be taken:
_____
_____
_____
_____
_____
_____

Invoice number:
_____

ANSWERS (Tasks 1 and 3, continued)

INVOICE
Feltham Bindery Ltd
Chertsey Road Trading Estate
Feltham
Middlesex TW12 5AB
T/F: 020 8371 5987

To: Amica Printing Company
McLaren Trading Estate
Wantage OX12 8SD

VAT Registration: 6873687344

Date/tax point: 22 September 2006

Description	Rate £	Total £
Consultancy report on installation of fully automated binding line, as per Sam Fisher's purchase order of 2 September 2006, and conversation with Alex Cook	4,250.00	4,250.00
Sub-total		4,250.00
VAT @ 17.5%		743.75
Invoice total		**4,993.75**

Terms: strictly 30 days net

Terms
30 days net
E & OE

sample simulation – unit 2 – answer booklet

Errors or discrepancies:
_____
_____
_____
_____
_____
_____

Action to be taken:
_____
_____
_____
_____
_____
_____

Invoice number:
_____

ANSWERS (Tasks 1 and 3, continued)

INVOICE

HAMBURG PRINT PLATES LTD
Highgrove Road
Newbury
Berks NY9 4BW
T: 01461 476431
F: 01461 547643

To: Amica Printing Company
McLaren Trading Estate
Wantage OX12 8SD

VAT Registration: 0547351034

Date/tax point: 22 September 2006

Description	Quantity	Rate £	Total £
Myobi 600 press plates	70	37.50	2,625.00
Hamburg 1000 print press plates	50	35.00	1,750.00
Hamburg 250 print press plates	100	25.00	2,500.00
		Goods total	6,875.00
		Trade discount @ 0%	0.00
		Sub-total	6,875.00
		VAT @ 17.5%	1,167.03
		Invoice total	**8,042.03**

Cash (settlement) discount: 3% for payment in 7 days
(to be deducted when computing VAT), otherwise 30 days net — £206.25

Errors or discrepancies:
_____
_____
_____
_____
_____
_____

Action to be taken:
_____
_____
_____
_____
_____
_____

Invoice number:
_____

ANSWERS (Tasks 1 and 3, continued)

INVOICE

Ilsley Inks Ltd
Ridgeway House
East Ilsley
Berks NY7 1LS
T: 01461 7576764
F: 01461 343463

To: Amica Printing Company
McLaren Trading Estate
Wantage OX12 8SD

VAT Registration: 0917757537

Date/tax point: 22 September 2006

Description	Quantity	Rate £	Total £
Cyan ink for Hamburg colour presses	15	20.00	300.00
Yellow ink for Myobi presses	20	12.50	250.00
Goods total			550.00
Trade discount @ 5%			27.50
Sub-total			522.50
VAT @ 17.5%			91.43
Invoice total			613.93

Terms: strictly 30 days net

sample simulation – unit 2 – answer booklet

Errors or discrepancies:
_____
_____
_____
_____
_____
_____
_____

Action to be taken:
_____
_____
_____
_____
_____
_____
_____

Invoice number:
_____

ANSWERS (Tasks 1 and 3, continued)

INVOICE

Sidney Stationers Ltd
40 Market Square
Wantage OX12 5KK
T: 01235 497611
F: 01235 576643

To: Amica Printing Company
McLaren Trading Estate
Wantage OX12 8SD

VAT Registration: 1473658734

Date/tax point: 22 September 2006

Description	Quantity	Price £	Total £
A4 lever arch files – red	200	1.49	298.00
		Goods total	298.00
	Trade discount	0%	0.00
		Sub-total	298.00
	VAT	17.5%	52.15
		Invoice total	350.13

Terms: strictly 30 days net

Errors or discrepancies:

_____
_____
_____
_____
_____
_____

Action to be taken:

_____
_____
_____
_____
_____
_____

Invoice number:

_____

ANSWERS (Tasks 1 and 3, continued)

INVOICE

Wantage Engineering Ltd
Grove Road
Wantage OX12 7SM
T: 01235 232155
F: 01235 235698

To: Amica Printing Company
McLaren Trading Estate
Wantage OX12 8SD

VAT Registration: 4654646446

Date/tax point: 22 September 2006

Description	Quantity	Price £	Total £
Print press cleaning fluid	50 litres	6.50	250.00
Machine oil	10 litres	5.00	60.00
Press tester units	25	15.00	475.00
		Goods total	785.00
	Trade discount	10%	78.00
		Sub-total	707.00
	VAT	17.5%	123.72
		Invoice total	**830.72**

Cash (settlement) discount: 1% for payment in 21 days
(to be deducted when computing VAT), otherwise 30 days net

£7.07

Errors or discrepancies:
_____
_____
_____
_____
_____
_____

Action to be taken:
_____
_____
_____
_____
_____
_____

Invoice number:
_____

ANSWERS (Tasks 1 and 2)

Notes for conversation with Alex Cook

Notes for conversation with Edward Hunt

sample simulation – unit 2 – answer booklet

ANSWERS (Task 1)

AMICA PRINTING COMPANY

McLaren Trading Estate, Wantage OX12 8SD

Tel: 01235 687465 Fax: 01235 687412

....

....

....

....

....

....

....

....

....

....

....

....

....

....

....

....

ANSWERS (Task 1, continued)

AMICA PRINTING COMPANY

McLaren Trading Estate, Wantage OX12 8SD

Tel: 01235 687465 Fax: 01235 687412

ANSWERS (Tasks 2 and 3)

CREDIT NOTE

HAMBURG PRINT PLATES LTD
Highgrove Road
Newbury
Berks NY9 4BW
T: 01461 476431
F: 01461 547643

To: Amica Printing Company
McLaren Trading Estate
Wantage OX12 8SD

VAT Registration: 0547351034

Date/tax point: 22 September 2006

Description	Quantity	Rate £	Total £
Hamburg 500 print press plates **Reason for credit** Damaged (part of batch delivered and invoiced 15 September 2006)	5	30.00	150.00
Goods total			150.00
Trade discount @ 0%			0.00
Sub-total			150.00
VAT @ 17.5%			25.46
Credit note total			175.46

Reduce cash (settlement) discount on original invoice by £4.50

Errors or discrepancies:

_____

_____

_____

_____

_____

_____

Action to be taken:

_____

_____

_____

_____

_____

_____

Invoice number:

_____

ANSWERS (Tasks 2 and 3, continued)

CREDIT NOTE

Ilsley Inks Ltd
Ridgeway House
East Ilsley
Berks NY7 1LS
T: 01461 7576764
F: 01461 343463

To: Amica Printing Company
McLaren Trading Estate
Wantage OX12 8SD

VAT Registration: 0917757537

Date/tax point: 22 September 2006

Description		Unit price £	Total £
Special order pigment 291 – 10 kilos		25.00	250.00
Reason for credit Incorrect pigment delivered and invoiced 15 September 2006			
	Goods total		250.00
	Trade discount @ 5%		12.50
	Sub-total		237.50
	VAT @ 17.5%		41.56
	Credit note total		279.06

Errors or discrepancies:
_____
_____
_____
_____
_____
_____

Action to be taken:
_____
_____
_____
_____
_____
_____

Invoice number:
_____

ANSWERS (Task 2)

AMICA PRINTING COMPANY

McLaren Trading Estate, Wantage OX12 8SD

Tel: 01235 687465 Fax: 01235 687412

ANSWERS (Tasks 3 and 4)

PURCHASE DAY BOOK   Folio: PDB 30

Invoice number	Supplier	Subsidiary (purchases) ledger code	Date 2006	Total £	VAT £	Purchases £	Stationery £
	Total						
Main ledger codes							

sample simulation – unit 2 – answer booklet

ANSWERS (Tasks 3 and 4, continued)

PURCHASE RETURNS DAY BOOK   Folio: PRDB 6

Credit note number	Supplier	Subsidiary (purchases) ledger code	Date 2006	Total £	VAT £	Purchases Returns £	Stationery £
	Total						
Main ledger codes							

ANSWERS (Tasks 4 and 10)

MAIN LEDGER

090 ADMINISTRATION

Date 2006	Details	Folio	Amount £	Date 2006	Details	Folio	Amount £

110 PURCHASE LEDGER CONTROL ACCOUNT

Date 2006	Details	Folio	Amount £	Date 2006	Details	Folio	Amount £
				22 Sept	Balance b/d		7,186.79

120 DISCOUNT RECEIVED

Date 2006	Details	Folio	Amount £	Date 2006	Details	Folio	Amount £

ANSWERS (Tasks 4 and 10, continued)

MAIN LEDGER

130 FACTORY WAGES CONTROL

Date 2006	Details	Folio	Amount £	Date 2006	Details	Folio	Amount £

140 FACTORY WAGES EXPENSE

Date 2006	Details	Folio	Amount £	Date 2006	Details	Folio	Amount £

150 PAYE/NIC CREDITOR

Date 2006	Details	Folio	Amount £	Date 2006	Details	Folio	Amount £

ANSWERS (Tasks 4 and 10, continued)

MAIN LEDGER

170 POSTAGE

Date 2006	Details	Folio	Amount £	Date 2006	Details	Folio	Amount £

180 PRODUCTION EXPENSES

Date 2006	Details	Folio	Amount £	Date 2006	Details	Folio	Amount £

190 PURCHASES

Date 2006	Details	Folio	Amount £	Date 2006	Details	Folio	Amount £

sample simulation – unit 2 – answer booklet

ANSWERS (Tasks 4 and 10, continued)

MAIN LEDGER

200 PURCHASES RETURNS

Date 2006	Details	Folio	Amount £	Date 2006	Details	Folio	Amount £

210 STATIONERY

Date 2006	Details	Folio	Amount £	Date 2006	Details	Folio	Amount £

220 VAT

Date 2006	Details	Folio	Amount £	Date 2006	Details	Folio	Amount £

ANSWERS (Tasks 4, 5 and 10)

SUBSIDIARY (PURCHASES) LEDGER

1101 ABINGDON PAPER LTD

Date 2006	Details	Folio	Amount £	Date 2006	Details	Folio	Amount £
				2 Sept	Invoice 5980	PDB27	2,511.56

1102 FELTHAM BINDERY LTD

Date 2006	Details	Folio	Amount £	Date 2006	Details	Folio	Amount £

1103 HAMBURG PRINT PLATES LTD

Date 2006	Details	Folio	Amount £	Date 2006	Details	Folio	Amount £
				5 Sept	Invoice 5982	PDB27	1,017.68
				15 Sept	Invoice 6040	PDB 29	1,754.62

ANSWERS (Tasks 4, 5 and 10, continued)

SUBSIDIARY (PURCHASES) LEDGER

1104 ILSLEY INKS LTD

Date 2006	Details	Folio	Amount £	Date 2006	Details	Folio	Amount £
				2 Sept	Invoice 5985	PDB27	726.46
				15 Sept	Invoice 6042	PDB29	1,088.34

1105 SIDNEY STATIONERS LTD

Date 2006	Details	Folio	Amount £	Date 2006	Details	Folio	Amount £
29 Aug	Credit note 250	PRDB5	17.62	28 Aug	Invoice 5965	PDB26	105.75

1106 WANTAGE ENGINEERING LTD

Date 2006	Details	Folio	Amount £	Date 2006	Details	Folio	Amount £

ANSWERS (Task 5)

STATEMENT

Lam,
Please pay ticked item.
Alex Cook

Abingdon Paper Ltd
Milton Park
Abingdon
Oxon OX13 9AS
T: 01235 412233
F: 01235 412866

To: Amica Printing Company
McLaren Trading Estate
Wantage OX12 8SD

VAT Registration: 9175698745

Date: 22 September 2006

Date	Transaction reference	Amount
1 Sept 2006	Invoice	2,511.56 ✓
22 Sept 2006	Invoice	2,679.00

Balance outstanding 5,190.56

Our terms are strictly net 30 days

Discount to be taken:

Discrepancies:

Action to be taken about discrepancies:

ANSWERS (Task 5, continued)

STATEMENT

HAMBURG PRINT PLATES LTD
Highgrove Road
Newbury
Berks NY9 4BW
T: 01461 476431
F: 01461 547643

Lam,
Please pay ticked items.
Cash discount of £201.75 to be taken on invoice and credit note dated 22 September 06.
Alex Cook

To: Amica Printing Company
McLaren Trading Estate
Wantage OX12 8SD

VAT Registration: 0547351034

Date: 22 September 2006

Date	Transaction reference	Amount
4 Sept 2005	Invoice	1,017.68 ✓
15 Sept 2006	Invoice	1,754.62
22 Sept 2006	Credit note	-175.46 ✓
22 Sept 2006	Invoice	8,042.03 ✓

Balance outstanding 10,638.87

3% settlement (cash) discount is available for payment within 7 days. Otherwise, our terms are strictly net 30 days.

Discount to be taken:

Discrepancies:

Action to be taken about discrepancies:

sample simulation – unit 2 – answer booklet

ANSWERS (Task 5, continued)

STATEMENT

Ilsley Inks Ltd
Ridgeway House
East Ilsley
Berks NY7 1LS
T: 01461 7576764 F: 01461 343463

Lam,
Please pay ticked item.
Alex Cook

To: Amica Printing Company
McLaren Trading Estate
Wantage OX12 8SD

VAT Registration: 0917757537

Date: 22 September 2006

Date	Transaction reference	Amount
1 Sept 2006	Invoice	726.46 ✓
22 Sept 2006	Invoice	1,088.34
22 Sept 2006	Credit note	-279.06

Balance outstanding 1,535.74

Our terms are strictly net 30 days

Discount to be taken:
....

Discrepancies:
....
....

Action to be taken about discrepancies:
....
....

ANSWERS (Task 5, continued)

STATEMENT

Sidney Stationers Ltd
40 Market Square
Wantage
OX12 5KK
T: 01235 497611
F: 01235 576643

Lam,
Please pay ticked items.
Alex Cook

To: Amica Printing Company
McLaren Trading Estate
Wantage OX12 8SD

VAT Registration: 1473658734

Date: 22 September 2006

Date	Transaction reference	Amount
27 Aug 2006	Invoice	105.75 ✓
28 Aug 2006	Credit note	-17.62 ✓
22 Sept 2006	Invoice	350.15

Balance outstanding 438.28

Our terms are strictly net 30 days

Discount to be taken:
___

Discrepancies:
___

Action to be taken about discrepancies:
___
___

ANSWERS (Task 5, continued)

REMITTANCE ADVICE

Amica Printing Company, McLaren Trading Estate, Wantage OX12 8SD
Tel: 01235 687465 Fax: 01235 687412

Supplier:

Subsidiary (purchase) ledger code:

Date	Transaction reference	Amount (£)

REMITTANCE ADVICE

Amica Printing Company, McLaren Trading Estate, Wantage OX12 8SD
Tel: 01235 687465 Fax: 01235 687412

Supplier:

Subsidiary (purchase) ledger code:

Date	Transaction reference	Amount (£)

ANSWERS (Task 5, continued)

REMITTANCE ADVICE

Amica Printing Company, McLaren Trading Estate, Wantage OX12 8SD
Tel: 01235 687465 Fax: 01235 687412

Supplier:

Subsidiary (purchase) ledger code:

Date	Transaction reference	Amount (£)

REMITTANCE ADVICE

Amica Printing Company, McLaren Trading Estate, Wantage OX12 8SD
Tel: 01235 687465 Fax: 01235 687412

Supplier:

Subsidiary (purchase) ledger code:

Date	Transaction reference	Amount (£)

ANSWERS (Task 5, continued)

REMITTANCE ADVICE

Amica Printing Company, McLaren Trading Estate, Wantage OX12 8SD
Tel: 01235 687465 Fax: 01235 687412

Supplier:

Subsidiary (purchase) ledger code:

Date	Transaction reference	Amount (£)

REMITTANCE ADVICE

Amica Printing Company, McLaren Trading Estate, Wantage OX12 8SD
Tel: 01235 687465 Fax: 01235 687412

Supplier:

Subsidiary (purchase) ledger code:

Date	Transaction reference	Amount (£)

ANSWERS (Task 5, continued)

sample simulation – unit 2 – answer booklet

ANSWERS (Tasks 5, 6, 9 and 10)

MAIN LEDGER

100 CASH BOOK (PAYMENTS) — CB 30

Date 2006	Details	Cheque number/ BACS ref	Folio	Payment £	Admin £	Factory wages £	Petty cash £	Suppliers £	Discount received £	Subsidiary (purchases) ledger codes

Main ledger codes	DR	
	CR	

ANSWERS (Task 6)

Amica Printing Company				
Employee: Pippa Allen	Employee no: FT683			
NI No: KS 82 01 92 M	Tax code: 475L		Date: 26 Sept 2006	Tax period: Mth 6
Pay for FOUR weeks ending: 19 September 2006	Hours	Rate (£)	AMOUNT (£)	YEAR TO DATE (£)
Basic hours	150.00	5.50	825.00	
Time and a half	12.00	8.25	99.00	
Bonus		15.00	15.00	
PAY FOR PERIOD			939.00	4,695.00
PAYE			149.93	899.57
Employees' NI (Employer's NI £61.28)			56.34	
TOTAL DEDUCTIONS			206.27	
NET PAY			732.73	

Errors or discrepancies:
_____
_____

Action to be taken:
_____

Amica Printing Company				
Employee: Usha Gupta	Employee no: FT685			
NI No: WL 29 30 48 P	Tax code: BR		Date: 26 Sept 2006	Tax period: Mth 6
Pay for FOUR weeks ending: 19 September 2006	Hours	Rate (£)	AMOUNT (£)	YEAR TO DATE (£)
Basic hours	37.50	5.50	206.25	
Time and a half	4.00	8.25	33.00	
Bonus		5.00	5.00	
PAY FOR PERIOD			244.25	244.25
PAYE			53.73	53.73
Employees' NI (Employer's NI £17.50)			14.65	
TOTAL DEDUCTIONS			68.38	
NET PAY			175.87	

Errors or discrepancies:
_____
_____

Action to be taken:
_____

ANSWERS (Tasks 6 and 10)

FACTORY PAYROLL MONTH 6						
Employee:	Employee number	Pay for period £	PAYE £	Employee's NIC £	Net pay £	Employer's NIC £
Temporary factory payroll total						
Permanent factory payroll total		5,014.96	1,002.99	351.04	3,660.93	347.77
Total factory payroll						
Main ledger codes DR		140	130	130		140
CR		130	150	150		150
Payment by BACS - permanent						
Payment by cheque						

sample simulation – unit 2 – answer booklet

ANSWERS (Task 7)

EMAIL

To: henrylynch@amica.co.uk

From: heilamcheng@amica.co.uk

CC:

Subject:

Date: 23 September 2006

Message:

ANSWERS (Task 8)

PETTY CASH VOUCHER	
Number: *099*	Date:
Expenditure	*Amount*
Total	
Supporting documentation:	
Paid to:	

PETTY CASH VOUCHER	
Number: *100*	Date:
Expenditure	*Amount*
Total	
Supporting documentation:	
Paid to:	

PETTY CASH VOUCHER	
Number: *101*	Date:
Expenditure	*Amount*
Total	
Supporting documentation:	
Paid to:	

ANSWERS (Task 8, continued)

ANSWERS (Task 8, continued)

PETTY CASH LISTING					
Notes and coin in box	In petty cash box as at 22-Sept-06 £	To be paid out 23-Sept-06			In petty cash box as at 23-Sept-06 £
		Voucher number: 099 £	Voucher number: 100 £	Voucher number: £	
£50	0.00				
£20	40.00				
£10	20.00				
£5	15.00				
£2	0.00				
£1	3.00				
50p	1.50				
20p	1.00				
10p	0.20				
5p	0.10				
2p	0.04				
1p	0.04				
Total					

sample simulation – unit 2 – answer booklet

ANSWERS (Tasks 8 and 10)

160 PETTY CASH BOOK   PCB 30

Date 2006	Details	Receipts £	Date 2006	Voucher number	Payments £	Postage £	Production expenses £	Stationery £	VAT £
22 Sept	Balance b/d	80.88							
					Totals				
					Balance c/d				
23 Sept	Balance b/d								
23 Sept	End of day balance								

Main ledger codes		
	DR	
	CR	

294

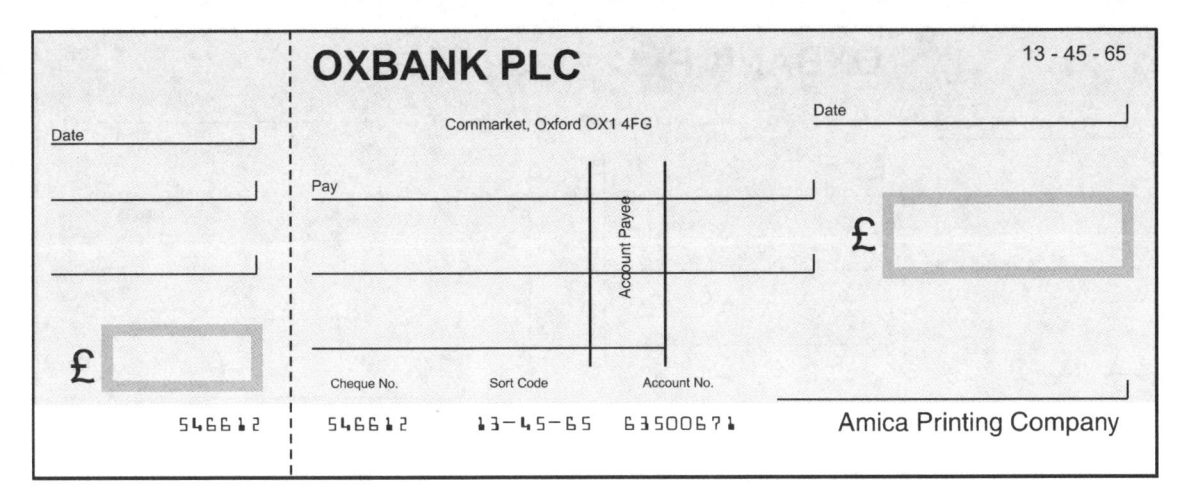

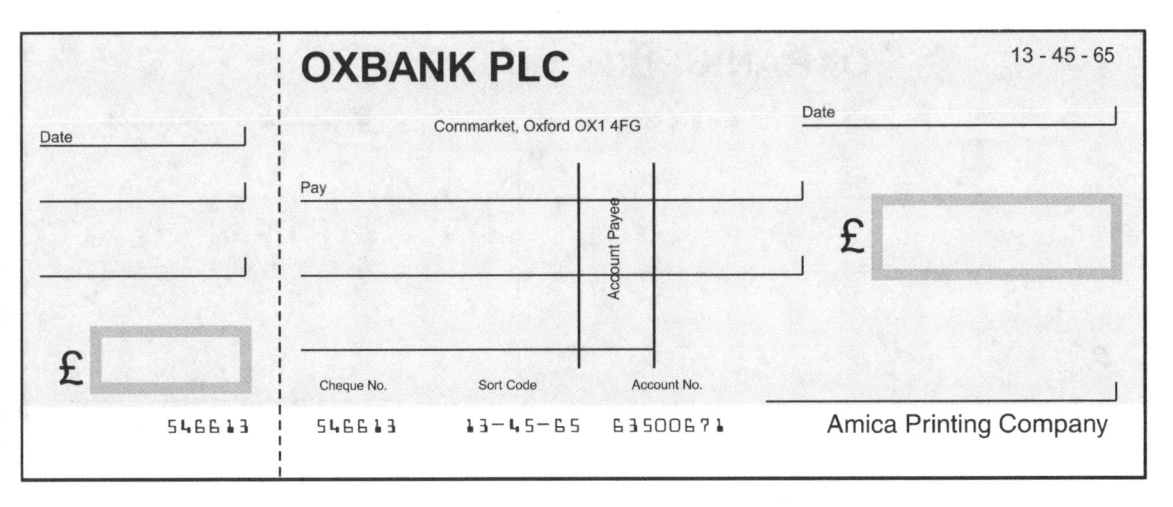

ANSWERS (Task 9)

	OXBANK PLC	13 - 45 - 65
Date	Cornmarket, Oxford OX1 4FG	Date
	Pay	£
£		
	Cheque No. Sort Code Account No.	
546612	546612 13-45-65 63500671	Amica Printing Company

	OXBANK PLC	13 - 45 - 65
Date	Cornmarket, Oxford OX1 4FG	Date
	Pay	£
£		
	Cheque No. Sort Code Account No.	
546613	546613 13-45-65 63500671	Amica Printing Company

sample simulation – unit 2 – answer booklet

ANSWERS (Task 9, continued)

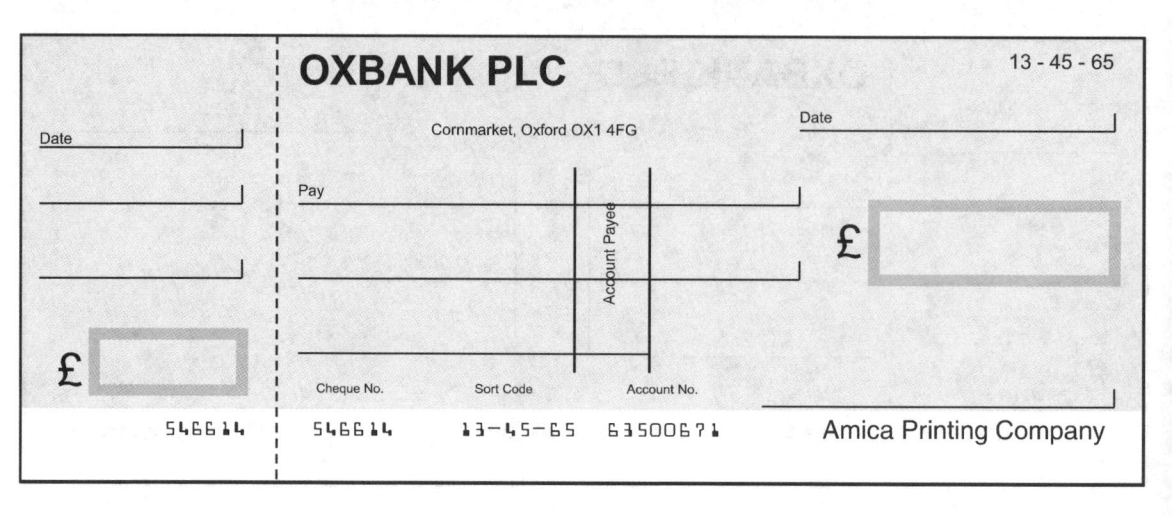

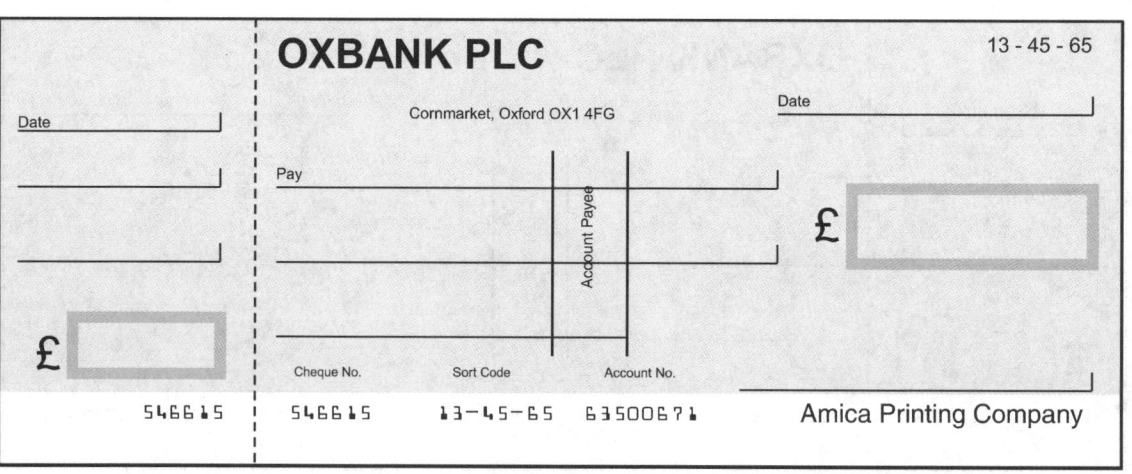

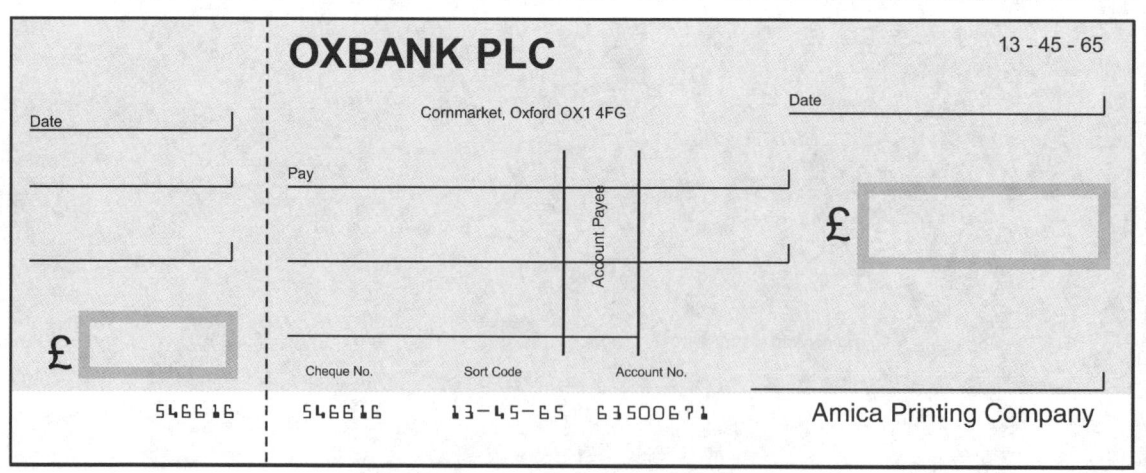

OXBANK PLC 13 - 45 - 65
Cornmarket, Oxford OX1 4FG

Date

Pay

Account Payee

£

Cheque No.   Sort Code   Account No.
546614   546614   13-45-65   63500671

Amica Printing Company

OXBANK PLC 13 - 45 - 65
Cornmarket, Oxford OX1 4FG

Date

Pay

Account Payee

£

Cheque No.   Sort Code   Account No.
546615   546615   13-45-65   63500671

Amica Printing Company

OXBANK PLC 13 - 45 - 65
Cornmarket, Oxford OX1 4FG

Date

Pay

Account Payee

£

Cheque No.   Sort Code   Account No.
546616   546616   13-45-65   63500671

Amica Printing Company

OXBANK PLC

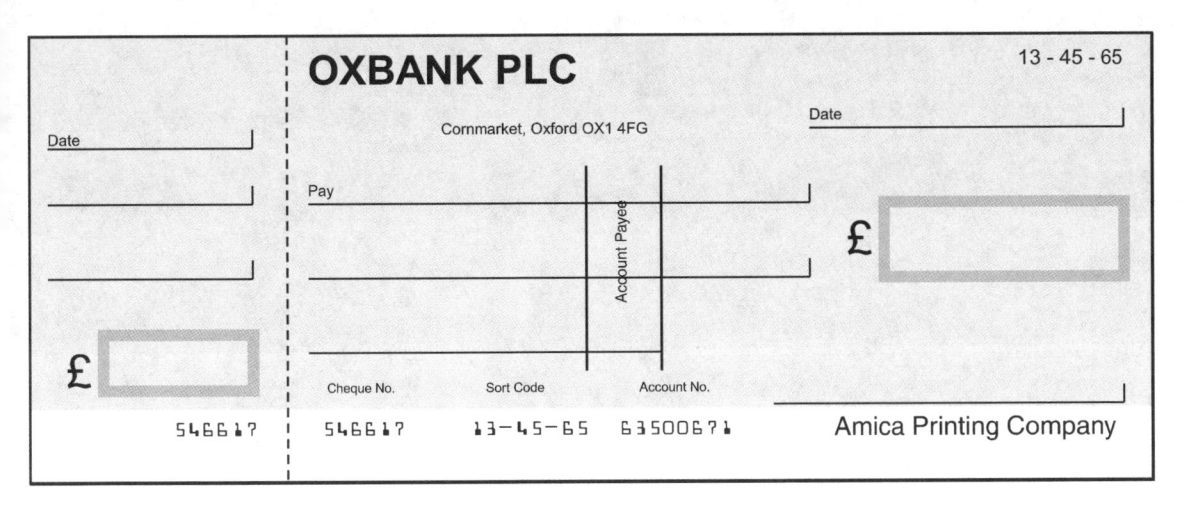

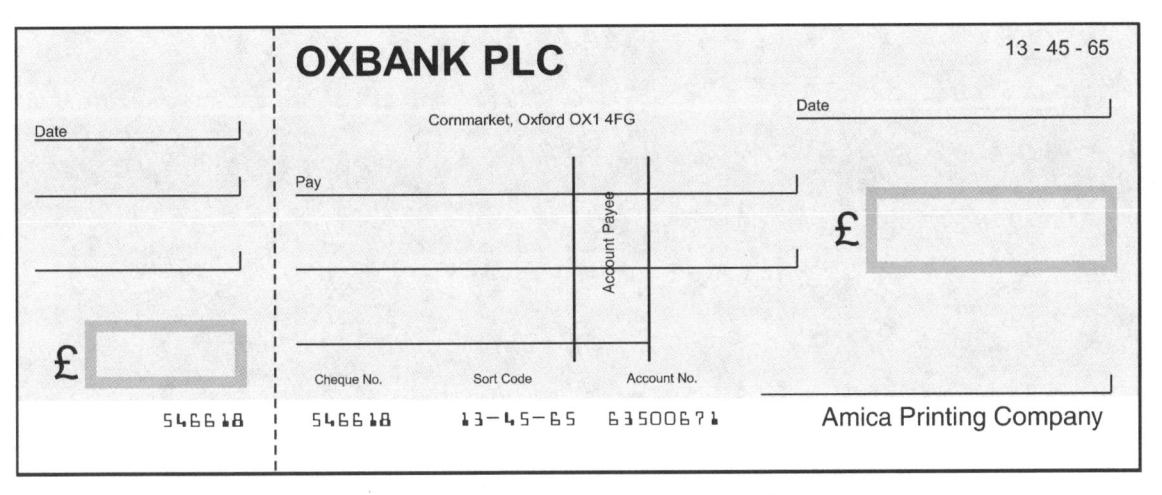

13 - 45 - 65

Cornmarket, Oxford OX1 4FG

Date

Pay

Account Payee

£

Date

Cheque No. 546617 Sort Code 13-45-65 Account No. 63500671

£

546617

Amica Printing Company

OXBANK PLC

13 - 45 - 65

Cornmarket, Oxford OX1 4FG

Date

Pay

Account Payee

£

Date

Cheque No. 546618 Sort Code 13-45-65 Account No. 63500671

£

546618

Amica Printing Company

AAT

SAMPLE SIMULATION
UNIT 3

WEASLEY SUPPLIES LTD

This is the AAT's Sample Simulation for Unit 3. Its purpose is to give you an idea of what an AAT simulation looks like. It is not intended as a definitive guide to the tasks you may be required to perform.

This simulation is in two parts. It is suggested that you spend approximately 90 minutes on each part.

Total time: 3 hours

sample simulation – unit 3

Coverage of performance criteria and range statements

The following performance criteria are covered in this simulation.

Element	PC Coverage
3.1	**Balance bank transactions**
a)	Record details from the relevant **primary documentation** in the **cashbook and ledgers**.
b)	Correctly calculate totals and balances of receipts and payments.
c)	Compare individual items on the bank statement and in the **cashbook** for accuracy.
d)	Identify discrepancies and prepare a bank reconciliation statement.
3.2	**Prepare ledger balances and control accounts**
a)	Make and **record** authorised **adjustments**.
b)	Total relevant accounts in the main ledger.
c)	Reconcile **control accounts** with the totals of the balance in the subsidiary ledger.
d)	Reconcile petty cash control account with the cash in hand and subsidiary records.
e)	Identify **discrepancies** arising from the reconciliation of **control accounts** and either resolve or refer to the appropriate person.
3.3	**Draft an initial trial balance**
a)	Prepare the draft **initial trial balance** in line with the organisation's policies and procedures.
b)	Identify **discrepancies** in the balancing process.
c)	Identify reasons for imbalance and **rectify** them.
d)	Balance the trial balance.

The following performance criterion is **not** covered in this simulation and should be assessed separately.

3.2 f)	Ensure documentation is stored securely and in line with the organisation's confidentiality requirements.

The following range statements are **not** covered in this simulation and should be assessed separately.

Element	Range Statement
3.1	**Cash book and ledgers:** computerised
	Bank reconciliation statement: computerised
3.2	**Record:** computerised
	Control accounts: computerised; non-trade debtors
	Discrepancies: cash in hand not agreeing with subsidiary record and control record
3.3	**Trial balance:** computerised

sample simulation – unit 3

DATA AND TASKS

INSTRUCTIONS

This simulation is designed to let you show your ability to prepare ledger balances and an initial trial balance.

You should read the whole simulation before you start work, so that you are fully aware of what you will have to do.

You are allowed **three hours** to complete your work.

Write your answers in the Answer Booklet provided on pages 313 to 322. If you need more paper for your answers, ask the person in charge.

You should write your answers in blue or black ink, **not** pencil.

You may use correcting fluid, but in moderation. You should cross out your errors neatly and clearly.

You may pull apart and rearrange your booklets if you wish to do so, but you must put them back in their original order before handing them in.

Your work must be accurate, so check your work carefully before handing it in.

You are not allowed to refer to any unauthorised material, such as books or notes, while you are working on the simulation. If you have any such material with you, you must hand it to the person in charge before you start work.

Any instances of misconduct will be reported to the AAT, and disciplinary action may be taken.

Coverage of performance criteria and range statements

It is not always possible to cover all performance criteria and range statements in a single simulation. Any performance criteria and range statements not covered must be assessed by other means by the assessor before a candidate can be considered competent.

Performance criteria and range statement coverage for this simulation is shown on page 300.

sample simulation – unit 3

THE SITUATION

Your name is Kim Wendell. You are a qualified accounting technician working for Weasley Supplies. You report to the manager, Ari Pottle.

All of the company's sales and purchases are on credit terms.

The books of account are maintained in manual form.

Today's date is **Monday 7 July 2006**, and you will be dealing with transactions taking place in **June 2006**.

Ledgers

A sales ledger control account and a purchases ledger control account are maintained in the main (general) ledger. There is a subsidiary (sales) ledger for customers and a subsidiary (purchases) ledger for suppliers.

Bank account and cash book

A bank statement is received monthly. Entries on the bank statement are compared with:

- entries in the cash book:
- a schedule of standing orders, direct debits and credit transfers.

The cash book is updated as appropriate in the light of the bank statement and the schedule of standing orders, direct debits and credit transfers. The main items paid for by standing order, direct debit and credit transfer are:

- business rates;
- insurance and leasing payments;
- staff salaries;
- the company's credit card bill.

These items are analysed as 'Other payments' in the cash book.

sample simulation – unit 3

THE TASKS TO BE COMPLETED

Task 1

Refer to the schedule of standing orders, direct debits and credit transfers on page 305, and the bank statement for June 2006 on page 306 of this book.

- Enter the appropriate details from the schedule in the cash book for June 2006 on page 313 of the Answer Booklet.

- Also enter any other items on the bank statement not so far recorded in the cash book.

Note: You must complete both the total columns and the analysis columns in the cash book.

Task 2

Total all columns of the cash book and bring down a balance as at close of business on 30 June 2006.

Task 3

Prepare a bank reconciliation statement as at 30 June 2006, clearly identifying all discrepancies between the cash book and the bank statement. Use the blank page 314 of the Answer Booklet.

Task 4

Refer to the email from Ari Pottle on page 307 of this book.

- Prepare the journals referred to in the email, including appropriate narrative, using the journal vouchers on page 315 of the Answer Booklet.

Task 5

- Post from the cash book (Task 2) and the journals (Task 4) to the sales ledger control account and the purchases ledger control account on page 316 of the Answer Booklet. (You are not required to make entries in the subsidiary ledgers in respect of these journals.)

- Total the two control accounts and bring down balances as at close of business on 30 June 2006.

303

Task 6

Refer to the list of balances on page 308 of this book, which have been taken from the subsidiary (purchases) ledger on 30 June 2006.

- Total the list of balances and reconcile the total with the balance on the purchases ledger control account.
- Suggest a reason for any discrepancy you observe.

Present your work on the blank page 317 of the Answer Booklet.

Task 7

The petty cash book has been written up for the month of June 2006; see page 318 of the Answer Booklet. On page 319 of the Answer Booklet you will see a list of the notes and coins in the petty cash tin at close of business on 30 June 2006, and a reconciliation schedule.

- Total the petty cash book and bring down a balance at close of business on 30 June 2006.
- Complete the reconciliation schedule, including a note of any discrepancy.

Task 8

Refer to the list of ledger balances prepared by Ari Pottle as at 30 June 2006 (page 308 of this book).

- Enter Ari's balances, and also the control account balances computed in Tasks 2, 5 and 7, onto the trial balance on page 320 of the Answer Booklet. Note that the balance to be entered for cash at bank should reflect the journal entries drafted in Task 4.
- Total the trial balance, and ensure that it balances by entering a suspense account balance.

Task 9

After informing Ari Pottle of the suspense account balance, you have now received the email on page 309 of this book.

- Prepare the journals referred to in the email, including appropriate narrative, using the journal vouchers on page 321 of the Answer Booklet.

Task 10

Enter the journals prepared in Task 9 into the suspense account on page 321 of the Answer Booklet and ensure that the closing balance on this account is zero.

Task 11

Reply to Ari's email explaining how the journals prepared in Task 9 will affect the trial balance and confirming that it will now balance. Use the blank email form on page 322 of the Answer Booklet.

Schedule of standing orders, direct debits and credit transfers (extract)

Standing orders	Amount	When payable
Standing orders		
Medwith Borough Council (business rates)	£600	Monthly from April to January inclusive; no payment in February, March
Safeguard Insurance	£310	Monthly
Finance Leasing plc	£425	March, June, September, December
Direct debits		
Purchasecard plc	Variable	Monthly
Credit transfers		
Staff salaries	Variable	Monthly

STATEMENT

Northern Bank plc
27 High Street, Malliton FR5 6EW   27-76-54

Account: Weasley Supplies   **Statement number:** 226

Account number: 22314561

Date	Details		Payments £	Receipts £	Balance £
2006					
1 June	Balance from previous sheet				5,267.88
6 June	Cash/cheques received	CC		4,776.15	10,044.03
10 June	Cheque 331174		781.03		9,263.00
13 June	Cheque 331175		1,456.91		
13 June	Cash/cheques received	CC		7,715.96	15,522.05
17 June	Safeguard Insurance 30056561	SO	310.00		15,212.05
20 June	Cash/cheques received	CC		15,901.22	31,113.27
23 June	Medwith BC 4412341125	SO	600.00		30,513.27
24 June	Cheque 331176		9,912.75		
24 June	Cash/cheques received	CC		2,816.55	23,417.07
25 June	Cheque 331177		3,901.25		19,515.82
26 June	Bank interest and charges	CHGS	107.33		
26 June	Finance Leasing plc 771233115	SO	425.00		
26 June	Salaries		8,215.50		10,767.99
27 June	Purchasecard plc	CT	2,341.89		8,426.10
30 June	Cash/cheques received	DD		2,451.88	
30 June	Cheque 331179	CC	3,126.99		7,750.99

Key SO Standing order   **CC** Cash and/or cheques   **CT** Credit transfer
O/D Overdrawn   **D/D** Direct Debit   **CHGS** Bank charges

EMAIL

From: Ari Pottle

To: Kim Wendell

CC:

Subject: Journal entries

Date: 7 July 2006

Message:

Hi Kim

Please could you draw up two journal entries for me please?

The first concerns our cheque number 331179. This has been logged in the cash book at an amount of £3,216.99, but in fact was for £3,126.99. The wrong amount has also been posted to the purchases ledger control account.

The second concerns our customer Driftway Limited. They owe us £1,233.75, but have gone into liquidation so we have no chance of recovering the debt. Later on we may be able to recover the VAT included in this amount, but for the moment please write off the whole balance and ignore VAT.

Both of these matters should be dealt with by means of journals dated 30 June 2006.

Thanks

Ari

CREDITORS' BALANCES AT 30 JUNE 2006

	£
Earley and Partners	3,990.65
Horsfall Limited	2,561.22
James Ross	4,016.73
Peters Limited	2,351.67
Pickard Newton (debit balance)	(90.00)
Stainton and Co	3,109.81
Other creditors	5,667.54

MAIN (GENERAL) LEDGER: BALANCES AT 30 JUNE 2006

	£
Administration expenses	3,276.88
Bad debts	2,010.76
Bank	Own figure
Business rates	1,800.00
Capital	46,745.76
Fixed assets	25,219.05
HMRC	4,003.51
Insurance	930.00
Leasing costs	1,275.00
Petty cash	Own figure
Purchases	64,016.83
Purchases ledger control	Own figure
Purchases returns	1,125.31
Salaries expense	35,211.81
Sales	96,558.43
Sales and distribution expenses	2,006.81
Sales ledger control	Own figure
Sales returns	1,327.44
Stock	7,270.00
VAT control (credit balance)	3,995.20

EMAIL

From: Ari Pottle

To: Kim Wendell

CC:

Subject: Correcting the trial balance

Date: 7 July 2006

Message:

Hi Kim

I've looked into the discrepancy on the initial trial balance, and I've found two items that cause the problem.

First, we returned goods to a supplier to the value of £200. We correctly entered this in the subsidiary (purchases) ledger, and in the purchases ledger control account.

However, in the purchases returns account we mistakenly entered it as a debit.

Second, we received a cheque for £3,000 which was correctly debited to the bank account. However, no credit entry was made. The double entry should have been completed in the capital account.

Please could you draft journals dated 30 June 2006 to deal with both of these items, and then let me have a reply to this message confirming that the trial balance will now balance.

Thanks

Ari

ANSWER BOOKLET

ANSWERS (Tasks 1 and 2)

RECEIPTS						CB 241 PAYMENTS			
Sales ledger £	Other receipts £	Total £	Date 2006	Details	Cheque number	Total £	Purchases ledger £	Other payments £
		4,486.85	1 June	Balance b/f				
4,776.15		4,776.15	5 June	Metrix plc				
7,715.96		7,715.96	6 June	Horsfall Limited	331175	1,456.91	1,456.91	
			12 June	Plympton Limited	331176	9,912.75	9,912.75	
			16 June	Stainton and Co	331177	3,901.25		3,901.25
			16 June	HMRC				
15,901.22		15,901.22	19 June	Maidstone plc				
2,816.55		2,816.55	23 June	Earley and Partners	331178	3,341.20	3,341.20	
			23 June	Stenshaw Limited				
			25 June	Pickard Newton	331179	3,216.99	3,216.99	
2,451.88		2,451.88	29 June	Fitzroy Limited				
1926.34		1,926.34	30 June	Dove Ambleside				

313

ANSWERS (Task 3)

ANSWERS (Task 4)

	JOURNAL		
Date 2006	Account names and narratives	Debit £	Credit £

ANSWERS (Task 5)

MAIN (GENERAL) LEDGER

Account Sales ledger control account

Date 2006	Details	Amount £	Date 2006	Details	Amount £
1 June	Balance b/f	30,914.66			
30 June	Invoices in month	32,617.80			

Debit / Credit

Account Purchases ledger control account

Date 2006	Details	Amount £	Date 2006	Details	Amount £
			1 June	Balance b/f	19,334.02
			30 June	Invoices in month	20,201.45

Debit / Credit

ANSWERS (Task 6)

sample simulation – unit 3 – answer booklet

ANSWERS (Task 7)

PETTY CASH BOOK
PCB 52

Receipts £	Date 2006	Details	Voucher number	Total £	VAT £	Postage £	Stationery £	Other expenses £
200.00	1 June	Balance b/f						
	5 June	Postage	358	4.26		4.26		
	9 June	Stationery	359	12.87	1.91		10.96	
	12 June	Tea, coffee etc	360	7.02				7.02
	16 June	Postage	361	3.12		3.12		
	18 June	Stationery	362	13.51	2.01		11.50	
	23 June	Stationery	363	6.58	0.98		5.60	
	26 June	Stationery	364	5.73	0.85		4.88	
	27 June	Postage	365	5.90		5.90		
	30 June	Tea, coffee etc	366	6.50				6.50

ANSWERS (Task 7, continued)

Notes and coin in the petty cash tin, 30 June 2006

Value	Number	Total value £
£20	4	
£10	3	
£5	2	
£1	8	
50p	8	
20p	8	
10p	8	
5p	1	
2p	2	
1p	2	

Petty cash reconciliation

Date: _____

£

Balance per petty cash book
Total of notes and coin
Discrepancy (if any)

Explanation of discrepancy (if any)

....

....

ANSWERS (Task 8)

Trial balance at 30 June 2006

DESCRIPTION	Ledger balances	
	Dr £	Cr £
Administration expenses		
Bad debts		
Bank		
Business rates		
Capital		
Fixed assets		
HMRC		
Insurance		
Leasing costs		
Petty cash		
Purchases		
Purchases ledger control		
Purchases returns		
Salaries expense		
Sales		
Sales and distribution expenses		
Sales ledger control		
Sales returns		
Stock		
VAT control		
Totals		

ANSWERS (Tasks 9 and 10)

JOURNAL

Date 2006	Account names and narrative	Dr £	Cr £

Account Suspense

Debit   Credit

Date 2006	Details	Amount £	Date 2006	Details	Amount £

ANSWERS (Task 11)

EMAIL

From: Kim Wendell

To: Ari Pottle

CC:

Subject: Re: Correcting the trial balance

Date: 7 July 2006

Message:

AAT

SAMPLE SIMULATION
UNIT 4

AVONTREE LTD

This is the AAT's Sample Simulation for Unit 4. Its purpose is to give you an idea of what an AAT simulation looks like. It is not intended as a definitive guide to the tasks you may be required to perform.

Total time: 2 hours 30 minutes

sample simulation – unit 4

Coverage of performance criteria and range statements

The following performance criteria are covered in this simulation.

Element	PC Coverage
4.1	**Code and extract information**
a)	Recognise appropriate cost centres and **elements of costs**.
b)	Extract income and expenditure details are from the relevant sources.
c)	Code income and expenditure correctly.
d)	Refer any problems in obtaining the necessary **information** to the appropriate person.
e)	Identify and report **errors** to the appropriate person.
4.2	**Provide comparisons on costs and income**
b)	Compare **information** extracted from a particular source with actual results.
c)	Identify discrepancies.
d)	Provide comparisons to the appropriate person in the required **format**.

The following performance criteria are **not** covered in this simulation and should be assessed separately.

4.2 a)	Clarify **information** requirements with the appropriate person.
4.2 e)	Follow organisational **requirements for confidentiality** strictly.

The following range statements are **not** covered in this simulation and should be assessed separately.

Element	Range Statement
4.1	**Sources:** sales orders
4.2	**Sources:** previous period's data; forecast data; ledgers
	Format: letter; memo; note
	Confidentiality requirements: sharing of information; storage of documents

DATA AND TASKS

INSTRUCTIONS

This simulation is designed to let you show your ability to supply information for management control.

You should read the whole simulation before you start work, so that you are fully aware of what you will have to do.

You are allowed **two hours and 30 minutes** to complete your work.

Write your answers in the Answer Booklet provided on pages 341 to 346. If you need more paper for your answers, ask the person in charge.

You should write your answers in blue or black ink, **not** pencil.

You may use correcting fluid, but in moderation. You should cross out your errors neatly and clearly.

You may pull apart and rearrange your booklets if you wish to do so, but you must put them back in their original order before handing them in.

Your work must be accurate, so check your work carefully before handing it in.

You are not allowed to refer to any unauthorised material, such as books or notes, while you are working on the simulation. If you have any such material with you, you must hand it to the person in charge before you start work.

Any instances of misconduct will be reported to the AAT, and disciplinary action may be taken.

Coverage of performance criteria and range statements

It is not always possible to cover all performance criteria and range statements in a single simulation. Any performance criteria and range statements not covered must be assessed by other means by the assessor before a candidate can be considered competent.

Performance criteria and range statement coverage for this simulation is shown on page 324.

THE SITUATION

Your name is Parfraz Mehdi, and you are an Accounts Assistant working for Avontree Limited, Unit 5, Burberry Business Park, Newfields NF8 2PR. Avontree is a publisher of textbooks used in primary, secondary and higher education. You report to the Accounts Supervisor, Emily Padden.

Coding of original documents

Avontree's accounts are maintained on a simple computerised system. One of your responsibilities is to code original documents for entry onto this system. For example, you code both sales and purchase invoices and enter relevant details onto data input sheets, which are then used for entering data into the computer system. In some cases you delegate the original coding to a colleague.

Payroll is maintained by Emily Padden on a computerised system separate from the accounts system. Each month she provides you with a payroll printout. Your task is to enter the appropriate codes for posting to the accounts system.

When doing your coding, you will need to refer to the company's policy manual; see page 328 of this book for relevant extracts. The purpose of the coding is to allocate costs and revenues to the appropriate cost and revenue centres, and also to distinguish between different types of costs and revenues.

VAT

Coding of VAT is performed automatically by the computerised accounts system, and therefore it is the amount **before** VAT on a purchase invoice that needs to be coded. There is no VAT on Avontree's sales invoices because textbooks are zero-rated.

The date

In this simulation you will be dealing with transactions arising in May and June 2006.

Today's date is 9 June 2006.

THE TASKS TO BE COMPLETED

Task 1

On pages 329-332 of this book you will find eight sales invoices.

- Enter relevant details of the sales invoices, including appropriate codes, on the data input sheet on page 341 of the Answer Booklet. You will need to refer to the extract from the company's policy manual on page 328 of this book.

Task 2

On pages 333-337 of this book you will find purchase invoices received from Avontree's suppliers, and related purchase orders raised by Avontree. The purchase invoices have already been coded by one of your colleagues.

- Check the purchase invoices to ensure that they match the purchase orders, and also check that your colleague has entered the correct codes on the invoices. You will need to refer to the extract from the company's policy manual on page 328 of this book.

- Your checks should reveal discrepancies. Draft an email to Emily Padden describing these discrepancies. Use the blank email on page 342 of the Answer Booklet.

Task 3

The payroll printout for May 2006 is on page 337 of this book.

- Enter the appropriate amounts and codes on the input sheet on page 343 of the Answer Booklet, ready for inputting the payroll details to the accounts system.

Task 4

Refer to the report on page 344 of the Answer Booklet. This has been extracted from the accounts system and shows the year-to-date (YTD) totals for certain revenue and expenditure accounts up to the end of May 2006, along with comparative figures for the previous year.

- In the column headed 'Variance (£)', enter the monetary amount of the variance between this year and last, using the symbol '+' to indicate an increase over last year and the symbol '–' to indicate a decrease compared with last year.

- In the column headed 'Variance (%)' enter each variance as a percentage of last year's total, again using the symbols '+' and '–' and expressing the percentages to one decimal place.

(To guide you, the first line of the schedule has already been completed.)

Task 5

Draft a brief report to Emily Padden, to which you will attach the schedule you prepared in Task 4. Draw her attention to any instances where the calculated variance exceeds 5%. Use page 345 of the Answer Booklet and date your report 9 June 2006.

Policy manual (extracts)

Coding of sales revenue

Each item of sales revenue must be coded with two pieces of information:

- the revenue centre (see below);
- the type of revenue (see below).

The type of revenue is indicated by the product code. Textbooks for primary education have codes beginning with P. Textbooks for secondary education have codes beginning with S. Textbooks for higher education have codes beginning with H.

Only the net goods value is coded (ie the value of goods after deduction of trade discount).

Revenue centres
UK sales	100
Overseas sales	200

Types of revenue
Textbook sales: primary education	300
Textbook sales: secondary education	400
Textbook sales: higher education	500

Coding of expenditure

Each item of expenditure must be coded with two pieces of information:

- the cost centre (see below);
- the type of expenditure (see below).

Cost centres
Typesetting costs	610
Editing costs	620
Printing and binding costs	630
Distribution and despatch costs	640
Marketing costs	650
Establishment costs	660

Types of cost
Materials	710
Expenses	720
Salaries	730

The costs of services performed by external individuals or organisations are classified as 'expenses'. The costs of paying internal staff are classified as 'salaries'. All salaries are classified to the 'establishment costs' cost centre.

SALES INVOICES

INVOICE
Avontree Limited
Unit 5, Burberry Business Park, Newfields NF8 2PR

To: Megabooks Limited
33 High Street
Maidenhead SL6 1PQ

VAT Registration: 225 6712 89
Date/tax point: 5 June 2006
Invoice number: 52711

Titles supplied	Item code	Quantity	List price £	Total £
GCSE Mathematics	S2251	10	12.50	125.00
Intermediate Mathematics	S1201	12	5.50	66.00

Total at list price		191.00
Less trade discount @ 35%		66.85
Net goods value		124.15
VAT @ 0%		0.00
Total due		**124.15**

Terms: net 30 days

INVOICE
Avontree Limited
Unit 5, Burberry Business Park, Newfields NF8 2PR

To: Books Plus
102 Lampard Avenue
Bristol BS3 5EW

VAT Registration: 225 6712 89
Date/tax point: 5 June 2006
Invoice number: 52712

Titles supplied	Item code	Quantity	List price £	Total £
Applications of Electronics	H3141	4	27.00	108.00
Thermodynamics	H2278	2	32.50	65.00

Total at list price		173.00
Less trade discount @ 40%		69.20
Net goods value		103.80
VAT @ 0%		0.00
Total due		**103.80**

Terms: net 30 days

INVOICE

Avontree Limited
Unit 5, Burberry Business Park, Newfields NF8 2PR

To: Empstone Books Ltd
14 Cygnet Street
Holyport SO13 7KK

VAT Registration: 225 6712 89
Date/tax point: 5 June 2006
Invoice number: 52713

Titles supplied	Item code	Quantity	List price £	Total £
The Metres of English Poetry	S1190	3	16.00	48.00
Tudor History for Teenagers	S3124	6	14.00	84.00
The Stuarts: a Brief Survey	S5155	6	14.00	84.00

Total at list price	216.00
Less trade discount @ 32.5%	70.20
Net goods value	145.80
VAT @ 0%	0.00
Total due	**145.80**

Terms: net 30 days

INVOICE

Avontree Limited
Unit 5, Burberry Business Park, Newfields NF8 2PR

To: Win Hong Books
17 Swire Street
Central
HONG KONG

VAT Registration: 225 6712 89
Date/tax point: 5 June 2006
Invoice number: 52714

Titles supplied	Item code	Quantity	List price £	Total £
Daily Life in Ancient Egypt	P9124	20	6.20	124.00
Daily Life in Ancient Rome	P9130	20	6.20	124.00

Total at list price	248.00
Less trade discount @ 35%	86.80
Net goods value	161.20
VAT @ 0%	0.00
Total due	**161.20**

Terms: net 30 days

sample simulation – unit 4

INVOICE

Avontree Limited
Unit 5, Burberry Business Park, Newfields NF8 2PR

To: Tradesales Limited
65 Limetree Avenue
Birkenhead WA12 5TR
UK

VAT Registration: 225 6712 89
Date/tax point: 5 June 2006
Invoice number: 52715

Titles supplied	Item code	Quantity	List price £	Total £
GCSE Mathematics	S2251	4	12.50	50.00
A level Mathematics	S1452	10	15.00	150.00

Total at list price		200.00
Less trade discount @ 40%		80.00
Net goods value		120.00
VAT @ 0%		0.00
Total due		**120.00**

Terms: net 30 days

INVOICE

Avontree Limited
Unit 5, Burberry Business Park, Newfields NF8 2PR

To: Palmer and Company
18 Ambleden Avenue
Rystone
UK

VAT Registration: 225 6712 89
Date/tax point: 5 June 2006
Invoice number: 52716

Titles supplied	Item code	Quantity	List price £	Total £
GCSE French	S4123	20	12.80	256.00
GCSE Spanish	S4145	16	12.80	204.80

Total at list price		460.80
Less trade discount @ 35%		161.28
Net goods value		299.52
VAT @ 0%		0.00
Total due		**299.52**

Terms: net 30 days

INVOICE

Avontree Limited
Unit 5, Burberry Business Park, Newfields NF8 2PR

To: Business Books
18 High Street
Hensham CV28 5AP
UK

VAT Registration: 225 6712 89
Date/tax point: 5 June 2006
Invoice number: 52717

Titles supplied	Item code	Quantity	List price £	Total £
Management Principles and Practice	H3121	8	26.50	212.00

Total at list price	212.00
Less trade discount @ 30%	63.60
Net goods value	148.40
VAT @ 0%	0.00
Total due	148.40

Terms: net 30 days

INVOICE

Avontree Limited
Unit 5, Burberry Business Park, Newfields NF8 2PR

To: Megabooks Limited
33 High Street
Maidenhead SL6 1PQ
UK

VAT Registration: 225 6712 89
Date/tax point: 5 June 2006
Invoice number: 52718

Titles supplied	Item code	Quantity	List price £	Total £
En Avant: French for Beginners	S2234	22	16.00	352.00

Total at list price	352.00
Less trade discount @ 35%	123.20
Net goods value	228.80
VAT @ 0%	0.00
Total due	228.80

Terms: net 30 days

PURCHASE INVOICES

SALES INVOICE

The Boxshop
25 Lyme Street, Taunton, TA2 4RP

To: Avontree Limited
Unit 5
Burberry Business Park
Newfields NF8 2PR

VAT Registration: 254 1781 26
Date/tax point: 5 June 2006
Invoice number: 288712
Your order: 2305

Description of goods/services	Total £
2,000 postal despatch boxes, PDB126	765.00

Amount (£)	Cost centre/revenue centre	Expenditure/revenue type
765.00	640	710

Goods total	765.00
VAT @ 17.5%	133.87
Total due	898.87

Terms: net 30 days

SALES INVOICE

Editype Limited
28 Wakeland Road, Newfields NF4 7LK

To: Avontree Limited
Unit 5
Burberry Business Park
Newfields NF8 2PR

VAT Registration: 267 9912 46
Date/tax point: 5 June 2006
Invoice number: 2511

Description of goods/services	Total £
Editorial work to your specification on Corporate Strategy	400.00

Amount (£)	Cost centre/revenue centre	Expenditure/revenue type
400.00	640	720

Total at list price	400.00
VAT @ 17.5%	70.00
Total due	470.00

Terms: net 30 days

SALES INVOICE

Education Magazine
17 Britton Street, London EC1M 5TP

To: Avontree Limited
Unit 5
Burberry Business Park
Newfields NF8 2PR

VAT Registration: 315 8123 49
Date/tax point: 5 June 2006
Invoice number: 22111098
Your order: 2259

Description of goods/services	Total £
Sales advertisement in June 2005 issue	870.00

Amount (£)	Cost centre/revenue centre	Expenditure/revenue type
870.00	650	720

Total at list price	870.00
VAT @ 17.5%	152.25
Total due	1,022.25

Terms: net 30 days

SALES INVOICE

Litho Printing Limited
Rosina Street, London E8 7RT

To: Avontree Limited
Unit 5
Burberry Business Park
Newfields NF8 2PR

VAT Registration: 412 5512 38
Date/tax point: 5 June 2006
Invoice number: 217765
Your order: 2271

Description of goods/services	Total £
Printing and binding 5,000 copies of The War of the Roses	16,410.00

Amount (£)	Cost centre/revenue centre	Expenditure/revenue type
16,410.00	630	710

Total at list price	16,410.00
VAT: zero-rated	0.00
Total due	16,410.00

Terms: net 30 days

SALES INVOICE

Typetext Limited
21 Ashton Lane, Newfields NF2 7UT

To: Avontree Limited
Unit 5
Burberry Business Park
Newfields NF8 2PR

VAT Registration: 251 7171 34
Date/tax point: 5 June 2006
Invoice number: 276
Your order: 2286

Description of goods/services	Total £
Typesetting of *GCSE Geography* to agreed specification	1,200.00

Amount (£)	Cost centre/revenue centre	Expenditure/revenue type
1,200.00	610	720

Total at list price	1,200.00
VAT @ 17.5%	210.00
Total due	1,410.00

Terms: net 30 days

SALES INVOICE

Decofix Limited
Panton Close, Newfields NF8 2PR

To: Avontree Limited
Unit 5
Burberry Business Park
Newfields NF8 2PR

VAT Registration: 381 5512 60
Date/tax point: 5 June 2006
Invoice number: 198
Your order: 2268

Description of goods/services	Total £
Repainting of accounts office to agreed specification	312.00

Amount (£)	Cost centre/revenue centre	Expenditure/revenue type
312.00	660	710

Total at list price	312.00
VAT @ 17.5%	54.60
Total due	366.60

Terms: net 30 days

sample simulation – unit 4

PURCHASE ORDER

Avontree Limited
Unit 5, Burberry Business Park,
Newfields NF8 2PR

To:
Litho Printing Limited
Rosina Street
London E8 7RT

Date: 13 May 2006
Order no: 2271

Please supply the items/services below on the agreed terms

Quantity	Description	Item code
500	Bound copies of *The War of the Roses*	N/A

On behalf of Avontree Limited *Emily Padden*

PURCHASE ORDER

Avontree Limited
Unit 5, Burberry Business Park,
Newfields NF8 2PR

To:
The Boxshop
25 Lyme Street
Taunton TA2 4RP

Date: 20 May 2006
Order no: 2305

Please supply the items/services below on the agreed terms

Quantity	Description	Item code
2,000	Postal despatch boxes	PDB126

On behalf of Avontree Limited *Emily Padden*

PURCHASE ORDER

Avontree Limited
Unit 5, Burberry Business Park,
Newfields NF8 2PR

To:
Decofix Limited
Panton Close
Newfields NF6 3QT

Date: 12 May 2006
Order no: 2268

Please supply the items/services below on the agreed terms

Quantity	Description	Item code
1	Repainting of accounts office to agreed specification	N/A

On behalf of Avontree Limited *Emily Padden*

PURCHASE ORDER

Avontree Limited
Unit 5, Burberry Business Park,
Newfields NF8 2PR

To:
Typestext Limited
21 Ashton Lane
Newfields NF2 7UT

Date: 16 May 2006
Order no: 2286

Please supply the items/services below on the agreed terms

Quantity	Description	Item code
1	Typesetting of GCSE Geography to agreed specification	N/A

On behalf of Avontree Limited *Emily Padden*

PURCHASE ORDER

Avontree Limited
Unit 5, Burberry Business Park,
Newfields NF8 2PR

To:
Education Magazine
17 Britton Street
London EC1M 5TP

Date: 9 May 2006
Order no: 2259

Please supply the items/services below on the agreed terms

Quantity	Description	Item code
1	Sales advertisement in June 2006 issue	N/A

Salaries summary

Month: May 2006

Employee name	Gross pay (£)	PAYE tax (£)	Employee NIC	Net pay (£)	Employer NIC (£)
James Bailey	850.00	91.00	46.60	712.40	54.99
Laura Drinkwater	3,000.00	572.00	215.00	2,213.00	308.57
Allan Holmes	1,250.00	189.00	86.60	974.40	102.19
Caroline Johnson	1,000.00	139.00	61.40	799.60	72.45
Parfraz Mehdi	1,400.00	225.00	101.40	1,073.60	119.65
Emily Padden	2,300.00	418.00	191.40	1,690.60	225.85
Roland White	1,100.00	157.00	71.40	871.60	84.25
	10,900.00	1,791.00	773.80	8,335.20	967.95

ANSWER BOOKLET

ANSWERS (Task 1)

DATA INPUT SHEET				
Sales invoices		Date:		
			Coding	
Invoice number	Customer	Amount £	Revenue centre	Type of revenue

ANSWERS (Task 2)

EMAIL

From: Parfraz Mehdi

To:

CC:

Subject:

Date: 9 June 2006

Message:

ANSWERS (Task 3)

DATA INPUT SHEET Payroll		Date:	
		Coding	
Detail	Amount £	Cost centre	Type of expenditure

ANSWERS (Task 4)

	AVONTREE LIMITED PROFIT AND LOSS ACCOUNT Date: 31 May 2006				
		YTD			
Account code	Account name	This year	Last year	Variance £	Variance %
100-300	UK sales: primary	75,600	74,100	+1,500	+2.0
100-400	UK sales: secondary	100,900	108,700		
100-500	UK sales: higher	98,700	95,000		
610-720	Typesetting: expenses	15,300	16,000		
620-720	Editing: expenses	16,400	15,700		
630-710	Printing & binding: materials	40,100	36,500		
640-710	Distribution: materials	4,600	6,100		
650-720	Marketing: expenses	16,400	15,900		
660-720	Establishment: expenses	5,600	5,200		
660-730	Establishment: salaries	34,200	33,000		

ANSWERS (Task 5)

REPORT

To:

From:

Subject:

Date:

If using this page, please state clearly which task you are answering.

PRACTICE EXAM 1

FLOWER CHAIN

These tasks were set by the AAT in December 2008.

Time allowed: 3 hours plus 15 minutes' reading time

unit 3 – practice exam 1

INSTRUCTIONS

This exam paper is in TWO sections.

You must show competence in BOTH sections. So, try to complete EVERY task in BOTH sections.

Section 1 contains 6 tasks and Section 2 contains 10 tasks.

You should spend about 90 minutes on each section.

You should include all essential calculations in your answers.

Both Sections 1 and 2 are based on the business described below.

INTRODUCTION

Suki Jones is the owner of The Flower Chain, a business that supplies fresh flowers.

You are employed by the business as a bookkeeper.

The business uses a manual accounting system.

The VAT rate is 17.5%.

Double entry takes place in the main (general) ledger. Individual accounts of debtors and creditors are kept in subsidiary ledgers as memorandum accounts.

Bank payments and receipts are recorded in the cash book, which is part of the double entry system.

Assume today's date is **30 November 2008** unless you are told otherwise.

SECTION 1 PROCESSING EXERCISE (90 minutes)

DATA

The following balances are relevant to you at the start of the day on 30 November 2008:

	£
Subsidiary (purchases) ledger accounts	
Fresh Fields	5,750
Scented Garden	13,215
The Daisy Chain	8,673
Petal Place	4,517
Main ledger accounts	
Fixtures and fittings	15,315
Sales	147,318
Purchases	96,120
Purchases returns	750
Purchases ledger control	37,238
Loan from bank	7,000
Motor expenses	1,213
VAT (credit balance)	8,710

Task 1.1

Enter the opening balances shown above into the accounts on pages 351 - 353.

DATA

The following transactions all took place on 30 November 2008 and have been entered into the relevant books of prime entry as shown below. No entries have yet been made into the ledger system.

Purchases day-book

Date 2008	Details	Invoice number	Total £	VAT £	Net £
30 Nov	Fresh Fields	163	2,585	385	2,200
30 Nov	Scented Garden	3982	1,410	210	1,200
30 Nov	The Daisy Chain	2300	799	119	680
30 Nov	Petal Place	S320	376	56	320
			5,170	770	4,400

Purchases returns day-book

Date 2008	Details	Credit note number	Total £	VAT £	Net £
30 Nov	Scented Garden	CN392	235	35	200
30 Nov	The Daisy Chain	C290	94	14	80
	Totals		329	49	280

Cash-book

Date 2008	Details	VAT £	Bank £	Date 2008	Details	VAT £	Bank £
30 Nov	Balance b/d		16,674	30 Nov	Fixtures and fittings	525	3,525
30 Nov	Cash sales	315	2,115	30 Nov	Motor tax		245
				30 Nov	Loan repayment		500
				30 Nov	Fresh Fields (creditor)		5,000
				30 Nov	Petal Place (creditor)		4,326
					Balance c/d		5,193
		315	18,789			525	18,789
1 Dec	Balance b/d		5,193				

Task 1.2

From the day-books and cash-book shown above, make the relevant entries into the accounts in the subsidiary (purchases) ledger and main ledger shown on pages 351-353.

Task 1.3

Balance the accounts, showing clearly the balances carried down at 30 November (closing balance).

Task 1.4

Now enter the balances brought down at 1 December (opening balance), showing clearly the date and details, as well as the amount.

SUBSIDIARY (PURCHASES) LEDGER

Fresh Fields

Date 2008	Details	Amount £	Date 2008	Details	Amount £

Scented Garden

Date 2008	Details	Amount £	Date 2008	Details	Amount £

The Daisy Chain

Date 2008	Details	Amount £	Date 2008	Details	Amount £

Petal Palace

Date 2008	Details	Amount £	Date 2008	Details	Amount £

MAIN LEDGER

Fixtures and fittings

Date 2008	Details	Amount £	Date 2008	Details	Amount £

Sales

Date 2008	Details	Amount £	Date 2008	Details	Amount £

Purchases

Date 2008	Details	Amount £	Date 2008	Details	Amount £

Purchases returns

Date 2008	Details	Amount £	Date 2008	Details	Amount £

Purchases ledger control

Date 2008	Details	Amount £	Date 2008	Details	Amount £

Loan from bank

Date 2008	Details	Amount £	Date 2008	Details	Amount £

Motor expenses

Date 2008	Details	Amount £	Date 2008	Details	Amount £

VAT

Date 2008	Details	Amount £	Date 2008	Details	Amount £

Task 1.5

Transfer the balances that you calculated in Tasks 1.3 and 1.4, and the bank balance, to the trial balance on the next page.

DATA

Other balances to be transferred to the trial balance:

	£
Motor vehicles	20,000
Petty cash control	50
Sales ledger control	54,250
Capital	43,969
Discount received	608
Bank interest received	117
Bank interest paid	80
Wages	25,320
Office expenses	2,759
Rent and rates	10,500
Heat and light	632
Insurance	1,240
Advertising	225
Legal fees	800
Miscellaneous expenses	532

Task 1.6

Transfer the balances shown above to the trial balance, and total each column.

The Flower Chain
Trial balance as at 30 November 2008

	Dr £	Cr £
Motor vehicles		
Fixtures and fittings		
Bank		
Petty cash control		
Sales ledger control		
Purchases ledger control		
VAT		
Loan from bank		
Capital		
Sales		
Purchases		
Purchases returns		
Discount received		
Bank interest received		
Bank interest paid		
Wages		
Motor expenses		
Office expenses		
Rent and rates		
Heat and light		
Insurance		
Advertising		
Legal fees		
Miscellaneous expenses		
Total		

unit 3 – practice exam 1

SECTION 2 TASKS AND QUESTIONS (90 minutes)

Answer all the questions.

You should show your answers by inserting a tick, words or figures, as appropriate.

Note: You do **not** need to adjust the accounts in Section 1 as part of any of the following tasks.

Task 2.1

The following is an extract from the coding lists used at The Flower Chain

Supplier name	Account code
The Daisy Chain	DAI001
Fresh Fields	FRE001
Growers Corner	GRO001
LBC Ltd	LBC001
Petal Place	PET001
Raven Gardens	RAV001
Renata Flowers	REN002
D Saunders Ltd	SAU001
Scented Garden	SCE002
Shah Displays	SHA003
Shore Flowers	SHO004
Vale Blooms	VAL001
Young and Brown	YOU001

Flower description	Product code
Red daisies in boxes of 10	DAIR10
White carnations in boxes of 15	CARW15
Yellow roses in boxes of 20	ROSY20
Purple asters in boxes of 20	ASTP20

a) What will be the supplier account codes for the new suppliers shown below?

Supplier name	Supplier account code
P Venables Ltd	
RJH Ltd	

b) What will be the product codes for the new flowers shown below?

Flower description	Product code
Orange lilies in boxes of 10	
Blue lupins in boxes of 15	

Task 2.2

On the first day of every month cash is drawn from the bank to restore the petty cash imprest level to £75.

A summary of petty cash transactions during November is shown below:

Opening balance on 1 November	£22
Cash from bank on 1 November	£53
Expenditure during month	£16

a) What will be the amount required to restore the imprest level on 1 December?

£	

b) Will the receipt from the bank on 1 December be a debit or credit entry in the petty cash book?

	✓
Debit	
Credit	

Task 2.3

An invoice from a supplier has been received at The Flower Chain. The invoice has been damaged in the post and the only amount that can be seen is the VAT amount of £63. No discount has been offered.

a) What is the VAT exclusive (net) amount of the invoice?

Net amount: £
Workings:

b) What is the VAT inclusive (gross) amount of the invoice?

Gross amount: £
Workings:

Task 2.4

Suki Jones has been advised to change from a manual to a computerised accounting system. She has been told that integrated accounting software will prevent many errors.

Give THREE types of error that integrated accounting software will prevent.

1._____

2._____

3._____

Task 2.5

A credit customer, ABC Ltd, has ceased trading, owing The Flower Chain £240 plus VAT.

What will be the accounting entries needed in the main ledger to write off the net amount and VAT?

Account name	Debit £	Credit £

Task 2.6

All the accounting records at the Flower Chain are kept on a bookshelf in the reception office. The reception office is often unstaffed and usually unlocked.

Identify THREE risks to the accounting information.

1. _____

2. _____

3. _____

Task 2.7

Show whether each of the following items are capital or revenue expenditure by placing a tick in one column for each item.

	Capital expenditure ✓	Revenue expenditure ✓
Purchase of a delivery van		
Purchase of office stationery		
Cost of redecorating the office		
Repair to delivery van		
Purchase of specialist refrigeration equipment for storing flowers		

Task 2.8

You now have the following information.

a) Sales of £500 have been credited to the sales returns account.

b) Entries to record a bank payment of £125 for office expenses have been reversed.

c) There is a debit balance of £118 in the suspense account. The following two errors have now been discovered.
 – A bank payment of £299 has been entered in the cash book as £29.
 – Discount allowed of £388 has been omitted from the discount allowed account.

Record the journal entries needed in the main ledger to deal with this information.

You do not need to give dates and narratives.

The Journal

Account names	Dr £	Cr £
a)		
b)		
c)		

Task 2.9

This is a summary of transactions with credit customers during November 2008.

	£
Balance of debtors at 1 Nov 2008	48,125
Goods sold on credit	37,008
Money received from credit customers	28,327
Discount allowed	240
Contra entry (set-off against purchases ledger control account)	2,316

a) Prepare a sales ledger control account from the details shown above. Show clearly the balance carried down at 30 November (closing balance) AND brought down at 1 December.

unit 3 – practice exam 1

Sales ledger control

Date 2008	Details	Amount £	Date 2008	Details	Amount £

The following balances were in the subsidiary (sales) ledger on 1 December.

	£
J Hicks Ltd	3,298
Parks and Gardens	4,109
Greener Grass	18,250
TTL Ltd	18,106
Reeves and Wright	10,400

b) Reconcile the balances shown above with the sales ledger control account balance you have calculated in part a).

£

Sales ledger control account balance as at 1 December 2008
Total of subsidiary (sales) ledger accounts as at 1 December 2008 _____
Difference _____

c) Because of an error in the subsidiary (sales) ledger, there is a difference. What might have caused the difference? Tick TWO reasons only.

✓

VAT has been overstated on an invoice.	
VAT has been understated on an invoice.	
A sales invoice has been entered in the subsidiary ledger twice.	
A sales credit note has been entered in the subsidiary ledger twice.	
A receipt from a customer has been omitted from the subsidiary ledger.	
A receipt from a customer has been entered in the subsidiary ledger twice.	

Task 2.10

On 28 November The Flower Chain received the following bank statement as at 25 November:

High Street Bank plc
The Concourse, Badley, B72 5DG

To: The Flower Chain   Account no: 28710191   Date: 25 November 2008

STATEMENT OF ACCOUNT

Date 2008	Details	Paid out £	Paid in £	Balance £
03 Nov	Balance b/f			9,136 C
07 Nov	Cheque 110870	6,250		2,886 C
17 Nov	Cheque 110872	2,250		636 C
21 Nov	Cheque 110865	3,670		3,034 D
	Direct Debit – Insurance Ensured	500		3,534 D
21 Nov	Bank Giro Credit – BBT Ltd		10,000	6,466 C
21 Nov	Bank Giro Credit – Petals Ltd		2,555	9,021 C
	Direct Debit – Rainbow Ltd	88		8,933 C
25 Nov	Cheque 110871	1,164		7,769 C

D = Debit   C = Credit

The cash book as at 28 November is shown below.

Cash book

Date 2008	Details	Bank £	Date 2008	Cheque no.	Details	Bank £
01 Nov	Balance b/f	5,466	03 Nov	110870	Roberts & Co	6,250
24 Nov	Bevan & Co	1,822	03 Nov	110871	J Jones	1,164
24 Nov	Plant Pots Ltd	7,998	06 Nov	110872	Lake Walks Ltd	2,250
			10 Nov	110873	PH Supplies	275
			17 Nov	110874	Peters & Co	76

a) Check the items on the bank statement against the items in the cash book.

b) Update the cash book as needed.

c) Total the cash book and clearly show the balance carried down at 28 November (closing balance) AND brought down at 29 November (opening balance).

Note: You do not need to adjust the accounts in Section 1.

d) Using the information from the cash book and bank statement, prepare a bank reconciliation statement as at 28 November.

Note: Do not make any entries in the shaded boxes.

Bank reconciliation statement as at 28 November 2008	
Balance per bank statement:	£
Add:	£
Name:	£
Name:	£
Total to add	£
Less:	£
Name:	£
Name:	£
Total to subtract	£
Balance as per cash book	£

PRACTICE EXAM 2

FIRST FASHIONS

These tasks were set by the AAT in June 2008.

Time allowed: 3 hours plus 15 minutes' reading time

unit 3 – practice exam 2

INSTRUCTIONS

This exam paper is in TWO sections.

You must show competence in BOTH sections. So, try to complete EVERY task in BOTH sections.

Section 1 contains 6 tasks and Section 2 contains 10 tasks.

You should spend about 90 minutes on each section.

You should include all essential calculations in your answers.

Both Sections 1 and 2 are based on the business described below.

INTRODUCTION

Ben Mohr is the owner of First Fashions, a clothing warehouse.

You are employed by the business as a bookkeeper.

The business uses a manual accounting system.

The VAT rate is 17.5%.

Double entry takes place in the main (general) ledger. Individual accounts of debtors and creditors are kept in subsidiary ledgers as memorandum accounts.

Payments and receipts from the bank current account are recorded in the cash book, which is part of the double entry system.

Assume today's date is **30 June 2008** unless you are told otherwise.

SECTION 1 PROCESSING EXERCISE (90 minutes)

DATA

The following balances are relevant to you at the start of the day on 30 June 2008:

	£
Subsidiary (sales) ledger accounts	
Sharif Clothing	4,963
Andrews & Company	3,210
Linens Ltd	21,695
Denton Designs	5,425
Main ledger accounts	
Motor vehicles	10,110
Bank savings (debit balance)	15,245
Sales	432,148
Sales returns	5,400
Sales ledger control	174,163
Discount allowed	2,650
Hotel expenses	3,994
VAT (debit balance)	13,762

Task 1.1

Enter the opening balances shown above into the accounts on pages 369 – 371.

DATA

The following transactions all took place on 30 June 2008 and have been entered into the relevant books of prime entry as shown below. No entries have yet been made into the ledger system.

Sales day book

Date 2008	Details	Invoice number	Total £	VAT £	Net £
30 June	Sharif Clothing	4871	3,055	455	2,600
30 June	Andrews & Company	4872	423	63	360
30 June	Linens Ltd	4873	9,964	1,484	8,480
30 June	Denton Designs	4874	2,115	315	1,800
	Totals		15,557	2,317	13,240

Sales returns day book

Date 2008	Details	Credit note number	Total £	VAT £	Net £
30 June	Sharif Clothing	287	188	28	160
30 June	Denton Designs	288	1,739	259	1,480
	Totals		1,927	287	1,640

Cash book

Date 2008	Details	Discount allowed	Bank £	Date 2008	Details	Bank £
30 June	Balance b/f		12,426	30 June	Transfers to bank savings account	2,500
30 June	Linens Ltd	250	12,426	30 June	Motor vehicles (ignore VAT)	28,600
30 June	VAT refund		18,653	30 June	Hotel expenses	175
				30 June	Balance c/d	6,249
		250	37,524			37,524
1 July	Balance b/d		6,249			

Task 1.2

From the day books and cash book shown above, make the relevant entries into the accounts in the subsidiary (sales) ledger and main ledger shown on pages 369-371.

Task 1.3

Balance the accounts, showing clearly the balances carried down at 30 June (closing balance).

Task 1.4

Now enter the balances brought down at 1 July (opening balance), showing clearly the date and details, as well as the amount.

SUBSIDIARY (SALES) LEDGER

Sharif Clothing

Date 2008	Details	Amount £	Date 2008	Details	Amount £

Andrews & Company

Date 2008	Details	Amount £	Date 2008	Details	Amount £

Linens Ltd

Date 2008	Details	Amount £	Date 2008	Details	Amount £

Denton Designs					
Date 2008	Details	Amount £	Date 2008	Details	Amount £

MAIN LEDGER

Motor vehicles					
Date 2008	Details	Amount £	Date 2008	Details	Amount £

Bank savings					
Date 2008	Details	Amount £	Date 2008	Details	Amount £

Sales					
Date 2008	Details	Amount £	Date 2008	Details	Amount £

Sales returns					
Date 2008	Details	Amount £	Date 2008	Details	Amount £

Sales ledger control					
Date 2008	Details	Amount £	Date 2008	Details	Amount £

Discount allowed					
Date 2008	Details	Amount £	Date 2008	Details	Amount £

Hotel expenses					
Date 2008	Details	Amount £	Date 2008	Details	Amount £

VAT					
Date 2008	Details	Amount £	Date 2008	Details	Amount £

Task 1.5

Transfer the balances that you calculated in Tasks 1.3 and 1.4, and the bank balance, to the trial balance on the next page.

DATA

Other balances to be transferred to the trial balance:

	£
Stock	18,754
Petty cash control	75
Purchases ledger control	90,218
Capital	68,781
Purchases	278,100
Purchases returns	15,350
Discount received	1,907
Wages	45,426
Motor expenses	3,276
Office expenses	5,382
Rent and rates	18,000
Subscriptions	450
Professional fees	1,263
Miscellaneous expenses	648
Suspense account (credit balance)	720

Task 1.6

Transfer the balances shown above to the trial balance, and total each column.

First Fashions
Trial balance as at 30 June 2008

	Dr £	Cr £
Motor vehicles		
Stock		
Bank current account		
Bank savings account		
Petty cash control		
Sales ledger control		
Purchases ledger control		
VAT		
Capital		
Sales		
Sales returns		
Purchases		
Purchases returns		
Discount received		
Discount allowed		
Wages		
Motor expenses		
Office expenses		
Rent and rates		
Hotel expenses		
Subscriptions		
Professional fees		
Miscellaneous expenses		
Suspense account		
Totals		

SECTION 2 TASKS AND QUESTIONS (90 minutes)

Answer all the questions.

You should show your answers by inserting a tick, words or figures, as appropriate.

Note: You do not need to adjust the accounts in Section 1 as part of any of the following tasks.

Task 2.1

You have been asked to reconcile the petty cash control account balance (£75.00) with the cash in hand. The following notes and coins are in the petty cash tin:

Notes and coins

2	£10
2	£5
5	£2
20	£1
9	50p
10	50p
100	1p

a) **Complete the following reconciliation.**

Petty cash reconciliation	£	p
Balance of petty cash control account		
Cash in hand		
Difference		

b) **Suggest THREE possible reasons for the difference.**

1. _____

2. _____

3. _____

Task 2.2

At the end of the last VAT period, the VAT account showed that a refund was due from HM Revenue & Customs.

a) **State ONE reason that would cause a refund to be due to First Fashions.**

1. _____

2. _____

3. _____

Sales in June totalled £129,250 including VAT

b) **What is the VAT amount?**

£
Workings:

Task 2.3

A customer has offered to pay for goods by a banker's draft.

What is a banker's draft?

_____

_____

_____

Task 2.4

Ben Mohr is considering computerising the accounting system.

a) **Name TWO items of hardware that Ben will need.**

1. _____

2. _____

b)   **Name TWO advantages of computerising the accounting system.**

1. _____

_____

2. _____

_____

Task 2.5

On 30 June, the suspense account has a credit balance of £720.

On 1 July, the following errors were discovered:

- A bank payment of £225 has been omitted from the rent and rates account.
- A bad debt expense of £945 has been credited correctly to the sales ledger control account, but debited to both the bad debt account and the sales account (ignore VAT).

a)   **Enter the opening balance in the suspense account below.**

b)   **Make the necessary entries to clear the suspense account.**

Suspense account					
Date 2008	Details	Amount £	Date 2008	Details	Amount £

Task 2.6

In what circumstances would First Fashions use a non trade debtors' control account?

_____

_____

_____

_____

_____

Task 2.7

Some accounting errors cause the trial balance totals to disagree.

Show what effect the errors below will have on the trial balance, by placing a tick in the relevant column for each error.

Error	The trial balance will balance ✓	The trial balance will NOT balance ✓
The entries in the main ledger to record a sales invoice were duplicated.		
The entries to record payment of an electricity bill have been reversed.		
The motor expenses account has been added up incorrectly.		
A purchase invoice was entered correctly in the purchases ledger control account but incorrectly in the purchases account.		
A customer did not take the discount offered.		

Task 2.8

Note:

Remember that you do not need to adjust, or refer to, the accounts in Section 1 or in the previous tasks in Section 2.

You now have the following information.

a) £50 has been debited to the discount received account instead of the discount allowed account.

b) A payment of £200 for office expenses has been credited to the bank savings account instead of the bank current account.

c) A credit customer, Kit & Company, has ceased trading, owing First Fashions £2,800 plus VAT. The net amount and VAT must be written off in the main ledger.

Record the journal entries needed in the main ledger to deal with this information.

You do not need to give dates and narratives.

Journal

Account names	Dr £	Cr £
a)		
b)		
c)		

Task 2.9

This is a summary of transactions with credit suppliers during June 2008.

	£
Balance of creditors at 1 June 2008	85,299
Goods bought on credit	39,300
Payments made to credit suppliers	33,106
Discount received	1,000
Goods returned to credit suppliers	275

a) Prepare a purchases ledger control account from the details shown above. Show clearly the balance carried down at 30 June (closing balance) AND brought down at 1 July (opening balance).

Purchases ledger control					
Date 2008	Details	Amount £	Date 2008	Details	Amount £

The following balances were in the subsidiary (purchases) ledger on 1 July.

	£
B & M Ltd	23,000
Bright Stuff	15,394
Rail Trail	11,249
FGT Ltd	28,429
Walton & Company	12,140

b) Reconcile the balances shown above with the purchases ledger control account balance you have calculated in part a).

	£
Purchases ledger control account balance as at 1 July 2008	
Total of subsidiary (purchases) ledger accounts as at 1 July 2008	
Difference	

c) The purchases ledger control account and subsidiary (purchases) ledger do not agree.

Which ONE of the following errors might have caused the difference?

	✓
One of the accounts in the subsidiary ledger has been understated.	
One of the accounts in the subsidiary ledger has been overstated.	
One supplier has offered a discount.	
First Fashions has underpaid a supplier.	
First Fashions has overpaid a supplier.	

Task 2.10

On 21 June, First Fashions received the following bank statement as at 20 June.

Middle Bank plc
Cornbow House, Romsleigh, R45 2LD

To: First Fashions   Account no: 18274653   Date: 20 June 2008

STATEMENT OF ACCOUNT

Date 2008	Details	Paid out £	Paid in £	Balance £
02 June	Balance b/f			12,100 C
06 June	Cheque 136409	500		11,600 C
10 June	Cheque 136410	6,425		5,175 C
10 June	Cheque 136402	50		5,125 C
14 June	Cheque 136411	348		4,777 C
16 June	Bank Giro Credit – DVM Ltd		850	5,627 C
16 June	Cheque 136408	629		4,998 C
20 June	Bank Giro Credit – Remnants Ltd		3,400	8,398 C
	Direct Debit – Property Maintenance	725		7,673 C
	Direct Debit – LDM Ltd	100		7,573 C
20 June	Bank charges	15		7,558 C
20 June	Bank interest		20	7,578 C

D = Debit C = Credit

The cash book as at 21 June is shown below.

Date 2008	Details	Bank £	Date 2008	Cheque no.	Details	Bank £
01 June	Balance b/f	12,050	02 June	136408	Stone & Company	629
20 June	Laura Laing	5,210	02 June	136409	Barker Ltd	500
20 June	DVM Ltd	850	06 June	136410	Belt and Braces	6,425
21 June	Matthew Mann	624	10 June	136411	DRL Ltd	348
			16 June	136412	Philip Gee	175
			17 June	136413	David Kay	216

a) Check the items on the bank statement against the items in the cash book.

b) Update the cash book as needed.

c) Total the cash book and clearly show the balance carried down at 21 June (closing balance) AND brought down at 22 June (opening balance).

Note: You do not need to adjust the accounts in Section 1.

d) Using the information on the bank statement and cash book prepare a bank reconciliation statement as at 21 June.

Note: Do not make any entries in the shaded boxes.

Bank reconciliation statement as at 28 June 2008	
Balance per bank statement:	£
Add:	£
Name:	£
Name:	£
Total to add	£
Less:	£
Name:	£
Name:	£
Total to subtract	£
Balance as per cash book	£

PRACTICE EXAM 3

PARKER PAINTS

These tasks were set by the AAT in December 2007.

Time allowed: 3 hours plus 15 minutes' reading time

INSTRUCTIONS

This exam paper is in TWO sections.

You must show competence in BOTH sections. So, try to complete EVERY task in BOTH sections.

Section 1 contains 6 tasks and Section 2 contains 10 tasks.

You should spend about 90 minutes on each section.

You should include all essential calculations in your answers.

Both Sections 1 and 2 are based on the business described below.

INTRODUCTION

Paula Parker is the owner of Parker Paints, a business that supplies a range of paints.

You are employed by the business as a bookkeeper.

The business uses a manual accounting system.

Double entry takes place in the main (general) ledger. Individual accounts of debtors and creditors are kept in subsidiary ledgers as memorandum accounts.

Bank payments and receipts are recorded in a

    Bank receipts cash-book and a
    Bank payments cash-book.

The cash-book totals are posted to the Cash at Bank account, which is part of the double entry system.

Assume today's date is **30 November 2007** unless you are told otherwise.

SECTION 1 PROCESSING EXERCISE (90 minutes)

DATA

The following opening balances are relevant to you at the start of the day on 30 November 2007:

	£
Subsidiary (sales) ledger accounts	
High Gloss Ltd	12,564
The Paint Shop	2,398
Decorators World	2,309
Homes of Class	15,091
Main ledger accounts	
Office equipment	20,168
Sales	302,975
Sales returns	13,657
Sales ledger control	125,775
Discount allowed	1,350
Repairs and renewals	6,000
Stationery	134
VAT (credit balance)	22,535

Task 1.1

Enter the above balances into the accounts given on pages 387 to 390.

DATA

The following transactions all took place on 30 November 2007 and have been entered into the relevant books of prime entry as shown below. No entries have yet been made into the ledger system. The VAT rate is 17.5%.

Sales day book

Date 2007	Details	Invoice number	Total £	VAT £	Net £
30 Nov	High Gloss Ltd	1349	893	133	760
30 Nov	The Paint Shop	1350	2,585	385	2,200
30 Nov	Decorators World	1351	1,175	175	1,000
30 Nov	Homes of Class	1352	14,100	2,100	12,000
	Totals		18,753	2,793	15,960

Sales returns day book

Date 2007	Details	Credit note number	Total £	VAT £	Net £
30 Nov	The Paint Shop	176	188	28	160
30 Nov	Decorators World	177	705	105	600
	Totals		893	133	760

Bank receipts cash book

Date 2007	Details	Discount allowed £	Bank £
30 Nov	High Gloss	300	10,150
30 Nov	Homes of Class		2,520

Journal

Account name	Dr £	Cr £
Office equipment	1,500	
Repairs and renewals		1,450
Stationery		50
To correct posting error		

Task 1.2

From the day books, bank receipts cash book and journal shown above, make the relevant entries into the accounts in the subsidiary (sales) ledger and main ledger.

Task 1.3

Balance the accounts, showing clearly the balances carried down at 30 November (closing balance).

Task 1.4

Enter the balances brought down at 1 December (opening balance), showing clearly the date, details, and amount.

SUBSIDIARY (SALES) LEDGER

High Gloss Ltd

Date 2007	Details	Amount £	Date 2007	Details	Amount £

The Paint Shop

Date 2007	Details	Amount £	Date 2007	Details	Amount £

Decorators World

Date 2007	Details	Amount £	Date 2007	Details	Amount £

Homes of Class

Date 2007	Details	Amount £	Date 2007	Details	Amount £

MAIN LEDGER

Office equipment

Date 2007	Details	Amount £	Date 2007	Details	Amount £

Sales

Date 2007	Details	Amount £	Date 2007	Details	Amount £

Sales returns

Date 2007	Details	Amount £	Date 2007	Details	Amount £

Sales ledger control

Date 2007	Details	Amount £	Date 2007	Details	Amount £

Discount allowed

Date 2007	Details	Amount £	Date 2007	Details	Amount £

Repairs and renewals

Date 2007	Details	Amount £	Date 2007	Details	Amount £

Stationery

Date 2007	Details	Amount £	Date 2007	Details	Amount £

VAT

Date 2007	Details	Amount £	Date 2007	Details	Amount £

Task 1.5

Transfer the balances that you calculated in Tasks 1.3 and 1.4 to the trial balance on page 392.

Task 1.6

Other balances to be transferred to the trial balance:

	£
Motor vehicles	18,000
Stock	4,950
Cash at bank (debit balance)	5,762
Petty cash control	100
Purchases ledger control	34,918
Capital	72,502
Loan from bank	15,000
Purchases	198,540
Purchases returns	564
Discount received	337
Wages	56,320
Heat and light	2,984
Motor expenses	3,871
Hotel expenses	2,577
Miscellaneous expenses	1,313

a) Transfer the balances shown above to the trial balance.

b) Total the debit and credit columns of the trial balance.

Parker Paints
Trial balance as at 30 November 2007

	Dr £	Cr £
Motor vehicles		
Office equipment		
Stock		
Cash at bank (debit balance)		
Petty cash control		
Sales ledger control		
Purchases ledger control		
VAT		
Capital		
Loan from bank		
Sales		
Sales returns		
Purchases		
Purchases returns		
Discount received		
Discount allowed		
Repairs and renewals		
Stationery		
Wages		
Heat and light		
Motor expenses		
Hotel expenses		
Miscellaneous expenses		
Totals		

SECTION 2 TASKS AND QUESTIONS (90 minutes)

Answer all the questions.

You should show your answers by inserting a tick, words or figures, or circling the correct answer as appropriate.

Note: You do **not** need to adjust the accounts in Section 1 as part of any of the following tasks.

Task 2.1

Parker Paints has received the following BACS remittance advice:

BACS Remittance Advice

To: Parker Paints   From: Handyman Tools Ltd

Your invoice number 1214 dated 15 October for £2,350 has been paid by BACS credit transfer and will arrive in your bank account on 1 December 2007.

---

a) What is the earliest date these funds will be available to Parker Paints?

b) Give ONE advantage to Parker Paints of being paid in this way?

c) Is Handyman Tools Ltd a debtor or creditor in Parker Paints' accounting records?

Task 2.2

Parker Paints currently files copies of all sales invoices in invoice number order.

a) Give ONE disadvantage of filing sales invoices in this way.

b) Give ONE other method of filing the sales invoices that would be more appropriate.

Task 2.3

The petty cash book has been partially completed for November, as shown below.

Date 2007	Details	Amount £	Date 2007	Details	Total £	Stationery £	Postage £	Motor fuel £
1 Nov	Bal b/f	100	7 Nov	Postage stamps	20			
			15 Nov	Pens and pencils	18			
			22 Nov	Petrol	10			
			30 Nov	Envelopes	15			
	Total			Total				

a) Complete the analysis columns for the four items purchased from petty cash (ignore VAT).

b) Total and balance the account, showing clearly the balance carried down at 30 November.

c) Enter the balance brought down at 1 December, showing clearly the date, details, and amount. You do NOT need to restore the imprest amount.

Task 2.4

At the end of the last VAT quarter, Parker Paints was due a refund from HM Revenue and Customs.

a) Would the balance on the VAT account be an asset or a liability in the accounting records of Parker Paints?

Asset/Liability

b) When the refund is received, will it be a debit or credit to the VAT account?

Debit/Credit

c) When the refund is received, will it be a debit or credit to the Cash at bank (debit balance) account?

Debit/Credit

Task 2.5

Parker Paints gives each customer a 'customer account code' for the subsidiary (sales ledger). Examples are as follows:

Customer name	Customer account code
Spencer Ltd	SPL
Marks Ltd	MAL
Brown Brothers	BRB

What will be the customer account code for Case Ltd?

Task 2.6

Paula Parker wants to make the accounting process faster and is considering changing from a manual to a computerised accounting system.

Give THREE reasons why a computerised accounting system will be faster than a manual accounting system.

1) _____

2) _____

3) _____

Task 2.7

Complete the following sentences by inserting the relevant banking terms.

a) A .... would be set up to repay a bank loan in equal monthly instalments.

b) A .... would be set up to repay a bank loan by variable amounts each month.

c) A bank .... would be arranged when short-term borrowing is needed.

Task 2.8

You have the following information:

a) a bank payment of £200 for heat and light has not been recorded

b) entries to record a bank payment of £800 for hotel expenses have been reversed

c) there is a credit balance of £735 in the suspense account. You have now discovered the following two errors:
   – a payment of £50 has been recorded as £500 in the miscellaneous expenses account
   – a receipt from a customer of £285 has been omitted from the sales ledger control account

Record the journal entries needed in the main ledger to deal with this information. You do not need to give dates and narratives.

JOURNAL

Details	Debit £	Credit £
a)		
b)		
c)		

Task 2.9

This is a summary of transactions with suppliers during November 2007:

Balance of creditors at 1 November 2007	£40,550
Goods bought on credit	£18,365
Payments made to credit suppliers	£21,342
Discounts received	£128
Goods returned to credit supplier	£2,527

a) Prepare a purchases ledger control account from the details shown above. Show clearly the balance carried down at 30 November (closing balance) AND brought down at 1 December (opening balance).

Purchase ledger control

Date 2007	Details	Amount £	Date 2007	Details	Amount £

The following opening balances were in the subsidiary (purchases) ledger on 1 December:

	£
Paint Partners	20,876 credit
Colour Coordinates	9,321 credit
JBM Ltd	3,243 credit
Barker & Co	325 debit
Interior Moods	1,153 debit

b) Reconcile the balances shown above with the purchases ledger control account balance you calculated in part a).

£

Purchases ledger control account balance as at 1 December 2007
Total of subsidiary (purchases) ledger accounts as at 1 December 2007   _____
Difference   _____

c) What may have caused the difference you calculated in part b)?

_____

_____

_____

Task 2.10

On 26 November, Parker Paints received the following bank statement as at 23 November:

Centralside Bank plc
High Street, Wellborough, W42 43BQ

To: Parker Paints   Account No 23872619   23 November 2007

STATEMENT OF ACCOUNT

Date 2007	Details	Paid out £	Paid in £	Balance £
1 Nov	Balance b/f			4,320 C
5 Nov	Bank Giro Credit – Colour King Ltd		7,930	12,250 C
10 Nov	Cheque 01872	450		11,800 C
13 Nov	Cheque 01873	321		11,479 C
14 Nov	Direct Debit – Wellborough DC	876		10,603 C
16 Nov	Cheque 01874	1,098		9,505 C
20 Nov	Bank Giro Credit – LBG Ltd		4,000	13,505 C
21 Nov	Direct Debit – Lewis & Lane	290		13,215 C
22 Nov	Cheque 01876	998		12,217 C
23 Nov	Bank charges	27		12,190 C
23 Nov	Bank interest		25	12,215 C

D = Debit C = Credit

The bank receipts cash book and bank payments cash book as at 23 November are summarised below:

Cash book

Date 2007	Details	Bank £	Date 2007	Cheque number	Details	Bank £
1 Nov	Balance b/f	4,320	1 Nov	01872	Colourways Ltd	450
20 Nov	LBG Ltd	4,000	1 Nov	01873	Barker Boards	321
21 Nov	Reeves & Co	3,674	7 Nov	01874	CHG Ltd	1,098
22 Nov	Cool Designs	2,350	8 Nov	01875	Paint It Ltd	2,963
			15 Nov	01876	G Smith Ltd	998
			22 Nov	01877	C Coombs	362

a) Check the items on the bank statement against the items in the cash book.

b) Update the cash book as needed.

c) Total the cash book and clearly show the balance carried down at 23 November (closing balance) and brought down at 24 November (opening balance).

Note: You do not need to adjust the accounts in Section 1.

d) Using the information on the previous page, prepare a bank reconciliation statement as at 23 November.

Note: Do not make any entries in the shaded boxes.

Bank reconciliation statement as at 23 November 2007	
Balance per bank statement:	£
Add:	£
Name:	£
Name:	£
Total to add	£
Less:	£
Name:	£
Name:	£
Total to subtract	£
Balance as per cash book	£

PRACTICE EXAM 4

THE STUDIO

These tasks were set by the AAT in June 2007.

Time allowed: 3 hours plus 15 minutes' reading time

INSTRUCTIONS

This exam paper is in TWO sections.

You must show competence in BOTH sections. So, try to complete EVERY task in BOTH sections.

Section 1 contains 6 tasks and Section 2 contains 10 tasks.

You should spend about 90 minutes on each section.

You should include all essential calculations in your answers.

Both Sections 1 and 2 are based on the business described below.

INTRODUCTION

Desmond Wood is the owner of The Studio, a business that supplies photographic equipment.

You are employed by the business as a bookkeeper.

The business uses a manual accounting system.

Double entry takes place in the main (general) ledger. Individual accounts of debtors and creditors are kept in subsidiary ledgers as memorandum accounts.

Bank payments and receipts are recorded in the cash book, which is part of the double entry system.

Assume today's date is **30 June 2007** unless you are told otherwise.

SECTION 1 PROCESSING EXERCISE (90 minutes)

DATA

The following opening balances are relevant to you at the start of the day on 30 June 2007:

	£
Subsidiary (purchases) ledger accounts	
Snap It	2,600
DND Ltd	5,594
Camco Ltd	4,325
Field Films	10,326
Main ledger accounts	
Fixtures and fittings	9,750
Purchases	224,750
Purchases returns	1,382
Purchases ledger control	31,534
Loan from bank	250
Discount received	2,400
Insurance	1,825
VAT (credit balance)	17,239

Task 1.1

Enter the above opening balances into the accounts given on pages 404 to 407.

DATA

The following transactions all took place on 30 June 2007 and have been entered into the relevant books of prime entry as shown below. No entries have yet been made into the ledger system. The VAT rate is 17.5%.

Purchases day book

Date 2007	Details	Invoice number	Total £	VAT £	Net £
30 June	Snap It	184	17,625	2,625	15,000
30 June	DND Ltd	4322	611	91	520
30 June	Camco Ltd	3619	1,551	231	1,320
30 June	Field Films	L2156	9,400	1,400	8,000
	Totals		29,187	4,347	24,840

Purchases returns day book

Date 2007	Details	Credit note number	Total £	VAT £	Net £
30 June	Camco Ltd	391	1,363	203	1,160
30 June	Field Films	109	987	147	840
	Totals		2,350	350	2,000

Cash book

Date 2007	Details	Bank £	Date 2007	Details	Discount received	Bank £
30 June	Loan from bank	15,000	30 June	Balance b/f		187
30 June	Balance c/d	4,812	30 June	Fixtures and fittings (ignore VAT)		12,000
			30 June	Insurance		2,750
			30 June	DND Ltd (creditor)	125	4,875
		19,812			125	19,812
			1 July	Balance b/d		4,812

Task 1.2

From the day books and cash book shown above, make the relevant entries into the accounts in the subsidiary (purchases) ledger and main ledger.

Task 1.3

Balance the accounts, showing clearly the balances carried down at 30 June (closing balance).

Task 1.4

Enter the balances brought down at 1 July (opening balance), showing clearly the date and details, as well as the amount.

SUBSIDIARY (PURCHASES) LEDGER

Snap It

Date 2007	Details	Amount £	Date 2007	Details	Amount £

Snap It

Date 2007	Details	Amount £	Date 2007	Details	Amount £

Camco Ltd

Date 2007	Details	Amount £	Date 2007	Details	Amount £

Field Films

Date 2007	Details	Amount £	Date 2007	Details	Amount £

MAIN LEDGER

Fixtures and fittings

Date 2007	Details	Amount £	Date 2007	Details	Amount £

Purchases

Date 2007	Details	Amount £	Date 2007	Details	Amount £

Purchases returns

Date 2007	Details	Amount £	Date 2007	Details	Amount £

Purchases ledger control

Date 2007	Details	Amount £	Date 2007	Details	Amount £

Loan from bank

Date 2007	Details	Amount £	Date 2007	Details	Amount £

Discount received

Date 2007	Details	Amount £	Date 2007	Details	Amount £

Insurance

Date 2007	Details	Amount £	Date 2007	Details	Amount £

VAT

Date 2007	Details	Amount £	Date 2007	Details	Amount £

DATA

Other balances to be transferred to the trial balance:

	£
Motor vehicles	13,625
Stock	7,113
Bank savings account	1,000
Petty cash control	100
Sales ledger control	86,421
Capital	32,174
Sales	305,029
Sales returns	3,444
Wages	32,650
Heat and light	1,762
Motor expenses	1,985
Repairs and renewals	328
Office expenses	2,614
Advertising	1,800
Miscellaneous expenses	1,028

Task 1.5

Transfer the balances that you calculated in Tasks 1.3 and 1.4, and the bank balance, to the trial balance on the next page.

Task 1.6

Transfer the remaining balances shown above to the trial balance, and total each column.

The Studio
Trial balance as at 30 June 2007

	Dr £	Cr £
Motor vehicles		
Fixtures and fittings		
Stock		
Bank current account		
Bank savings account		
Petty cash control		
Sales ledger control		
Purchases ledger control		
VAT		
Loan from bank		
Capital		
Sales		
Sales returns		
Purchases		
Purchases returns		
Discount received		
Wages		
Heat and light		
Motor expenses		
Insurance		
Repairs and renewals		
Office expenses		
Advertising		
Miscellaneous expenses		
Totals		

SECTION 2 TASKS AND QUESTIONS (90 minutes)

Answer all the questions.

You should show your answers by inserting a tick, text or figures, as appropriate.

Note: You do **not** need to adjust the accounts in Section 1 for any of the following tasks.

Task 2.1

You have been asked to calculate the sales invoice amount for goods delivered to a credit customer. The price of the goods is £1,200.00 before applying discount and VAT. The customer is entitled to the following discounts:

- trade discount of 10%
- settlement discount of 5% for payment within 7 days.

Complete the following calculation:

INVOICE CALCULATION	£	p
Price of goods		
Trade discount of 10%		
Net invoice total		
VAT		
Invoice total		
Workings		

Task 2.2

The Studio paid several cheques into the bank today but the funds will not be available for several days.

What is the reason for the delay?

_____
_____
_____

Task 2.3

A cheque has been received for £60 plus VAT from D G Black, a customer without a credit account.

What accounts will be used to record this cash sale?

Tick **a**, **b**, **c**, or **d**.

	Accounts	✓
A	Sales VAT Debtors control	
B	D G Black Sales VAT	
C	Sales VAT Bank	✓
D	D G Black VAT Bank	

Task 2.4

Desmond Wood would like to buy a computerised accounting system. The system would automatically produce reports or documents to be sent to customers and suppliers, as well as managers at The Studio.

Show who the report or document would be sent to, by ticking one column for each.

Report or document	To a customer	To a supplier	To a manager
Statement of account	✓		
Aged debtors analysis			✓
Remittance advice		✓	
VAT report			✓
Delivery note	✓		

Task 2.5

The Studio keeps a small amount of petty cash in the office to purchase miscellaneous items during the month. The imprest level is £100. The following purchases were made during June:

			£
17 June	Taxi fare		12
20 June	Coffee and tea		17
29 June	Postage stamps		30

a) Enter each petty cash purchase in the petty cash control account.

b) Total the account showing clearly the balance carried down at 30 June (closing balance) AND brought down at 1 July (opening balance).

c) Restore the imprest level on 1 July.

Petty cash control

Date 2007	Details	Amount £	Date 2007	Details	Amount £
1 June	Bal b/f	100			
	Total			Total	

Task 2.6

The Studio has recently purchased a new delivery van (capital expenditure), and motor insurance for the delivery van (revenue expenditure).

Briefly explain capital and revenue expenditure.

Capital expenditure

___

___

___

Revenue expenditure

___

___

___

Task 2.7

There is a debit balance of £230 in the suspense account. The following two errors have now been discovered:

- a payment of £100 has been recorded as £10 in the travel expenses account
- a payment of £140 has been omitted from the heat and light account

What entries are needed to correct the errors and clear the suspense account?

Account name	£ Debit	£ Credit
_____	_____	_____
_____	_____	_____
_____	_____	_____

Task 2.8

Note: Remember that you do **not** need to adjust, or refer to, the accounts in Section 1 or in the previous tasks in Section 2.

The following information has become available:

a) entries to record a bank payment of £300 for motor expenses have been reversed

b) a bank payment of £75 for electricity has been recorded as a petty cash payment

c) a credit customer, Photo Gem, has ceased trading, owing The Studio £400 plus VAT. The net amount and VAT must be written off in the main ledger

Record the journal entries needed in the main ledger to deal with this information.

You do **not** need to give dates and narratives.

JOURNAL

Details	Debit £	Credit £
a)		
b)		
c)		

Task 2.9

This is a summary of transactions with customers during the month of June 2007.

	£
Balance of debtors at 1 June 2007	73,154
Goods sold on credit	21,726
Money received from credit customers	5,410
Discount allowed	252
Goods returned by credit customers	2,797

a) Prepare a sales ledger control account from the above details. Show clearly the balance carried down at 30 June (closing balance) AND brought down at 1 July (opening balance).

Sales ledger control

Date 2007	Details	Amount £	Date 2007	Details	Amount £

The following balances were in the subsidiary (sales) ledger on 1 July.

	£
L M Trent	24,325
Better Plates	10,943
TML Ltd	8,657
Shutter Box	32,641
Gray & Co	9,800

b) Reconcile the balances shown above with the sales ledger control account balance you have calculated in part a).

	£
Sales ledger control account balance as at 30 July 2007	_____
Total of subsidiary (sales) ledger accounts as at 30 July 2007	_____
Difference	_____

c) The sales ledger control account and subsidiary (sales) ledger do not agree. Name TWO actions you would take in order to trace the difference.

1) _____

2) _____

Task 2.10

On 25 June The Studio received the following bank statement as at 22 June:

Baker Street Bank plc
Hampton House, Hampton, H32 4LQ

To: The Studio   Account no: 18472677   Date: 22 June 2007

STATEMENT OF ACCOUNT

Date 2007	Details	Paid out £	Paid in £	Balance £
01 June	Balance b/f			385 D
07 June	Bank Giro Credit - PKL Ltd		4,000	3,615 C
09 June	Cheque 007313	250		3,365 C
09 June	Cheque 007315	483		2,882 C
14 June	Cheque 007316	2,165		717 C
17 June	Cheque 007317	1,233		516 D
20 June	Direct Debit - Hampton CC	135		651 D
20 June	Direct Debit - Motor Mania	177		828 D
21 June	Bank Giro Credit - Bissell & Co.		2,500	1,672 C
22 June	Bank charges	44		1,628 C
22 June	Bank interest	3		1,631 C

D = Debit C = Credit

The cash book as at 22 June is shown below.

Cash book

Date 2007	Details	Bank £	Date 2007	Cheque number	Details	Bank £
15 June	PKL Ltd	4,000	01 June		1 June balance b/f	635
20 June	Beaker plc	3,245	01 June	07315	Abby Photos	483
21 June	Bissell & Co	2,500	06 June	07316	LTL Ltd	2,165
22 June	Gilchrist Ltd	2,416	06 June	07317	Retro Frames	1,233
			22 June	07318	Tonks & Co	1,020
			22 June	07319	Taylor Agencies	547

a) Check the items on the bank statement against the items in the cash book.

b) Update the cash book as needed.

c) Total the cash book and clearly show the balance carried down at 22 June (closing balance) AND brought down at 23 June (opening balance).

Note: You do not need to adjust the accounts in Section 1.

d) Using the information on the previous page, prepare a bank reconciliation statement as at 22 June.

Note: Do not make any entries in the shaded boxes.

Bank reconciliation statement as at 22 June 2007	
Balance per bank statement:	£
Add:	£
Name:	£
Name:	£
Total to add	£
Less:	£
Name:	£
Name:	£
Total to subtract	£
Balance as per cash book	£

ANSWERS

answers to chapter 1: INTRODUCTION TO BUSINESS

1
- ownership and management
  - a sole trader and the partners in a partnership are the owners of the business and usually the managers as well
  - the owners of a limited company are the shareholders whilst the directors manage the company, often the shareholders are not directors
- liability for debts
  - a sole trader and the partners in a partnership are liable for all of the debts of the business
  - the shareholders in a company have limited liability and therefore cannot be asked for any more monies than the amount paid for their shares
- methods of taking out profit
  - sole traders and partners in a partnership will take money out of the business when they wish, known as drawings
  - the shareholders in a limited company will be paid a dividend normally twice a year

2

		Cash or credit?
i)	purchase of goods for £200 payable by cash in one week's time	Credit
ii)	writing a cheque for the purchase of a new computer	Cash
iii)	sale of goods to a customer where the invoice accompanies the goods	Credit
iv)	receipt of a cheque from a customer for goods purchased today	Cash
v)	purchase of goods where payment is due in three weeks' time	Credit

3			**Capital or revenue?**
i)	purchase of a new computer paid for by cheque	Capital
ii)	purchase of computer disks by cheque	Revenue
iii)	purchase of a new business car on credit	Capital
iv)	payment of road tax on a new business car	Revenue
v)	payment of rent for the business premises	Revenue

4 A profit and loss account shows the historic picture of how the business has performed during the last accounting period. It shows the income and the expenses for the business for the period.

A balance sheet is a list of the assets and liabilities of the business on the last day of the accounting period.

answers to chapter 2: BUSINESS DOCUMENTS – SALES

1

		List price total	Trade discount	Net total
	i)	£416.70	£62.51	£354.19
	ii)	£105.82	£15.87	£89.95
	iii)	£96.45	£14.47	£81.98
	iv)	£263.46	£39.52	£223.94
	v)	£350.90	£52.64	£298.26

2

		Net total	VAT	Invoice total
	i)	£258.94	£45.31	£304.25
	ii)	£316.78	£55.43	£372.21
	iii)	£82.60	£14.45	£97.05
	iv)	£152.99	£26.77	£179.76
	v)	£451.28	£78.97	£530.25

3

		Net total	VAT	Invoice total
	i)	£258.94	£43.95	£302.89
	ii)	£316.78	£53.77	£370.55
	iii)	£82.60	£14.02	£96.62
	iv)	£152.99	£25.97	£178.96
	v)	£451.28	£76.60	£527.88

INVOICE

Southfield Electrical
Industrial Estate
Benham DR6 2FF
Tel 0303379 Fax 0303152
VAT Reg 0264 2274 49

To: Whitehill Superstores
28, Whitehill Park
Benham

Invoice number: 57104

Date/tax point: 8 January 2006

Order number: 32431

Account number: SL 44

Quantity	Description	Stock code	Unit amount £	Total £
8	Hosch Tumble Dryer	6060	300.00	2,400.00
2	Zanpoint Dishwasher	4425	200.00	400.00
				2,800.00
	Trade Discount			280.00
	Net total			2,520.00
	VAT			423.36
	Invoice total			2,943.36

Terms
4% Settlement discount for payment within 10 days, otherwise 30 days net

INVOICE

Southfield Electrical
Industrial Estate
Benham DR6 2FF
Tel 0303379 Fax 0303152
VAT Reg 0264 2274 49

To: Quinn Ltd
High Rocks Estate
Drenchley DR22 6PQ

Invoice number: 57105

Date/tax point: 8 January 2006

Order number: 24316

Account number: SL 04

Quantity	Description	Stock code	Unit amount £	Total £
14	Temax Mixer	3170	35.00	490.00
6	Temax Mixer	3174	46.00	276.00
				766.00
	Trade Discount			114.90
			Net total	651.10
			VAT	113.94
			Invoice total	765.04

Terms
Net 30 days
E & OE

INVOICE

Southfield Electrical
Industrial Estate
Benham DR6 2FF
Tel 0303379 Fax 0303152
VAT Reg 0264 2274 49

To: Harper and Sons
30/34 High Street
Benham DR6 4ST

Invoice number: 57106

Date/tax point: 8 January 2006

Order number: 04367

Account number: SL 26

Quantity	Description	Stock code	Unit amount £	Total £
3	Hosch Washing machine	6150	260.00	780.00
	Trade Discount			78.00
			Net total	702.00
			VAT	119.16
			Invoice total	821.16

Terms
3% settlement discount for payment within 14 days, otherwise 30 days net
E & OE

5	**Weller Enterprises**	–	the invoice number, tax point, order number and account number have not been entered
		–	the terms do not mention the settlement discount that should be offered
		–	the VAT calculation has not taken account of the settlement discount offered – the VAT should be £453.60
	QQ Stores	–	either the wrong stock code or wrong unit price has been used for the food processor as the list price of the 3162 processor is £120.00
		–	the calculation of the total of the food processor is incorrect it should be £980 not £890
		–	the trade discount has been incorrectly calculated – a figure of 15% has been used rather than 12%

answers to chapter 3: DOUBLE ENTRY BOOKKEEPING

1 i) James paid £20,000 into a business bank account in order to start the business;

Effect 1	Effect 2
Increase in cash	Capital of business set up

ii) He paid an initial rental of £2,500 by cheque for the shop that he is to trade from;

Effect 1	Effect 2
Decrease in cash	Rent expense incurred

iii) He purchased a van by cheque for £7,400;

Effect 1	Effect 2
Decrease in cash	Increase in asset – the van

iv) He purchases £6,000 of goods for resale on credit;

Effect 1	Effect 2
Increase in purchases	Increase in creditors

v) He sold goods for £1,000 - the customer paid by cheque;

Effect 1	Effect 2
Increase in cash	Increase in sales

vi) He sold goods on credit for £4,800;

Effect 1	Effect 2
Increase in debtors	Increase in sales

vii) He paid shop assistant's wages by cheque totalling £2,100;

Effect 1	Effect 2
Decrease in cash	Wages expense incurred

double entry bookkeeping – answers

viii) He made further sales on credit for £3,900;

Effect 1

Increase in debtors

Effect 2

Increase in sales

ix) He purchases a further £1,400 of goods for resale by cheque;

Effect 1

Decrease in cash

Effect 2

Increase in purchases

x) £3,700 was received from credit customers;

Effect 1

Increase in cash

Effect 2

Decrease in debtors

xi) He paid £3,300 to credit suppliers;

Effect 1

Decrease in cash

Effect 2

Decrease in creditors

xii) He withdrew £800 from the business for living expenses.

Effect 1

Decrease in cash

Effect 2

Increase in drawings

2

Bank account

	£		£
Capital (i)	20,000	Rent (ii)	2,500
Sales (v)	1,000	Van (iii)	7,400
Debtors (x)	3,700	Wages (vii)	2,100
		Purchases (ix)	1,400
		Creditors (xi)	3,300
		Drawings (xii)	800

Capital account

	£		£
		Bank (i)	20,000

double entry bookkeeping – answers

Rent account

	£		£
Bank (ii)	2,500		

Van account

	£		£
Bank (iii)	7,400		

Purchases account

	£		£
Creditors (iv)	6,000		
Bank (ix)	1,400		

Creditors account

	£		£
Bank (xi)	3,300	Purchases (iv)	6,000

Sales account

	£		£
		Bank (v)	1,000
		Debtors (vi)	4,800
		Debtors (viii)	3,900

Debtors account

	£		£
Sales (vi)	4,800	Bank (x)	3,700
Sales (viii)	3,900		

Wages account

	£		£
Bank (vii)	2,100		

Drawings account

	£		£
Bank (xii)	800		

3

Bank account

	£		£
Capital (i)	20,000	Rent (ii)	2,500
Sales (v)	1,000	Van (iii)	7,400
Debtors (x)	3,700	Wages (vii)	2,100
		Purchases (ix)	1,400
		Creditors (xi)	3,300
		Drawings (xii)	800
		Balance c/d	7,200
	24,700		24,700
Balance b/d	7,200		

Capital account

	£		£
		Bank (i)	20,000

Rent account

	£		£
Bank (ii)	2,500		

Van account

	£		£
Bank (iii)	7,400		

Purchases account

	£		£
Creditors (iv)	6,000		
Bank (ix)	1,400	Balance c/d	7,400
	7,400		7,400
Balance b/d	7,400		

432

Creditors account

	£		£
Bank (xi)	3,300	Purchases (iv)	6,000
Balance c/d	2,700		
	6,000		6,000
		Balance b/d	2,700

Sales account

	£		£
		Bank (v)	1,000
		Debtors (vi)	4,800
Balance c/d	9,700	Debtors (viii)	3,900
	9,700		9,700
		Balance b/d	9,700

Debtors account

	£		£
Sales (vi)	4,800	Bank (x)	3,700
Sales (viii)	3,900	Balance c/d	5,000
	8,700		8,700
Balance b/d	5,000		

Wages account

	£		£
Bank (vii)	2,100		

Drawings account

	£		£
Bank (xii)	800		

Trial balance

	Debits £	Credits £
Bank	7,200	
Capital		20,000
Rent	2,500	
Van	7,400	
Purchases	7,400	
Creditors		2,700
Sales		9,700
Debtors	5,000	
Wages	2,100	
Drawings	800	
	32,400	32,400

4   In the main ledger accounts the total sales on credit and receipts from credit customers have been entered into the debtors account, sales account and bank account. However, this gives no information about how much is owed by each individual debtor. Therefore in many accounting systems a separate ledger is kept known as a subsidiary ledger in which the details of each debtor are kept in the form of a separate ledger account for each debtor. This subsidiary ledger is known as the sales ledger and is kept as well as the total figures in the main ledger. The debtors account in the main ledger, in such a system, tends to be known as the debtors control account.

Similarly with purchases on credit as well as recording the total credit purchases and payments to suppliers in the main ledger a subsidiary ledger is set up for creditors. This will have a ledger account for each individual credit supplier showing each invoice received and each payment made. The subsidiary ledger is known as the purchases ledger and the creditors account in the main ledger is known as the creditors control account.

5 Main ledger

Sales ledger control account

	£		£
Sales – H Simms	1,800	Bank – H Simms	900
Sales – P Good	3,000	Bank – P Good	1,400
Sales – K Mitchell	910	Bank – K Mitchell	910
Sales – C Brown	2,990	Bank – C Brown	490

Sales account

	£		£
		Sales ledger control	1,800
		Sales ledger control	3,000
		Sales ledger control	910
		Sales ledger control	2,990

Subsidiary ledger

H Simms account

	£		£
Sales	1,800	Bank	900

P Good account

	£		£
Sales	3,000	Bank	1,400

K Mitchell account

	£		£
Sales	910	Bank	910

C Brown account

	£		£
Sales	2,990	Bank	490

answers to chapter 4:
ACCOUNTING FOR CREDIT SALES

1 a) and b)

Sales day book

Date	Customer	Invoice number	Gross £	VAT £	Net £
2 Jan	Hoppers Ltd	6237	642.72	95.72	547.00
5 Jan	Body Perfect	6238	728.50	108.50	620.00
6 Jan	Esporta Leisure	6239	406.55	60.55	346.00
9 Jan	Langans Beauty	6240	267.90	39.90	228.00
12 Jan	Body Perfect	6241	643.90	95.90	548.00
16 Jan	Superior Products	6242	259.67	38.67	221.00
18 Jan	Esporta Leisure	6243	488.80	72.80	416.00
23 Jan	Hoppers Ltd	6244	279.65	41.65	238.00
26 Jan	Langans Beauty	6245	321.95	47.95	274.00
			4,039.64	601.64	3,438.00

Cross-cast check:

	£
Net	3,438.00
VAT	601.64
Gross	4,039.64

c) **Main ledger**

Sales ledger control account

	£		£
31 Jan SDB	4,039.64		

VAT account

	£		£
		31 Jan SDB	601.64

Sales account

	£		£
		31 Jan SDB	3,438.00

d) **Subsidiary ledger**

Hoppers Ltd account

	£		£
2 Jan SDB – 6237	642.72		
23 Jan SDB – 6244	279.65		

Body Perfect account

	£		£
5 Jan SDB – 6238	728.50		
12 Jan SDB – 6241	643.90		

Esporta Leisure account

	£		£
6 Jan SDB – 6239	406.55		
18 Jan SDB – 6243	488.80		

Langans Beauty account

	£		£
9 Jan SDB – 6240	267.90		
26 Jan SDB – 6245	321.95		

Superior Products account

	£		£
16 Jan SDB – 6242	259.67		

accounting for credit sales – answers

2   a) and b)

Sales day book

Date	Customer	Invoice number	SL Ref	Gross £	VAT £	Net £
5 Jan	Rocks Garden Supp	08663	22	687.14	102.34	584.80
7 Jan	Eridge Nurseries	08664	07	420.35	62.60	357.75
7 Jan	Abergaven G C	08665	16	904.16	134.66	769.50
9 Jan	Rother Nurseries	08666	13	740.25	110.25	630.00
				2,751.90	409.85	2,342.05

Cross-cast check:

	£
Net	2,342.05
VAT	409.85
Gross	2,751.90

c)   **Main ledger**

Sales ledger control account

	£		£
9 Jan SDB	2,751.90		

VAT account

	£		£
		9 Jan SDB	409.85

Sales account

	£		£
		9 Jan SDB	2,342.05

439

Subsidiary ledger

	Eridge Nurseries		SL 07
	£		£
7 Jan SDB – 08664	420.35		

	Rother Nurseries		SL 13
	£		£
9 Jan SDB – 08666	740.25		

	Abergaven Garden Centre		SL 16
	£		£
7 Jan SDB – 08665	904.16		

	Rocks Garden Supplies		SL 22
	£		£
5 Jan SDB – 08663	687.14		

3 a) and b)

Sales returns day book

Date	Customer	Credit note number	Gross £	VAT £	Net £
17 Jan	Hoppers Ltd	1476	80.72	12.02	68.70
23 Jan	Esporta Ltd	1477	104.84	15.61	89.23
30 Jan	Superior Products	1478	13.80	2.05	11.75
			199.36	29.68	169.68

Cross-cast check:

	£
Net	169.68
VAT	29.68
Gross	199.36

c) **Main ledger**

Sales ledger control account

	£		£
31 Jan SDB	4,039.64	31 Jan SRDB	199.36

VAT account

	£		£
31 Jan SRDB	29.68	31 Jan SDB	601.64

Sales returns account

	£		£
31 Jan SRDB	169.68		

Subsidiary ledger

Hoppers Ltd account

	£		£
2 Jan SDB – 6237	642.72	17 Jan SRDB – 1476	80.72
23 Jan SDB – 6244	279.65		

Body Perfect account

	£		£
5 Jan SDB – 6238	728.50		
12 Jan SDB – 6241	643.90		

Esporta Leisure account

	£		£
6 Jan SDB – 6239	406.55	23 Jan SRDB – 1477	104.84
18 Jan SDB – 6243	488.80		

Langans Beauty account

	£		£
9 Jan SDB – 6240	267.90		
26 Jan SDB – 6245	321.95		

	Superior Products account		
	£		£
16 Jan SDB – 6242	259.67	30 Jan SRDB – 1478	13.80

4 a) and b)

Sales day book

Date	Customer	Invoice number	SL Ref	Gross £	VAT £	Net £
5 Jan	Rocks Garden Supp	08663	22	687.14	102.34	584.80
7 Jan	Eridge Nurseries	08664	07	420.35	62.60	357.75
7 Jan	Abergaven G C	08665	16	904.16	134.66	769.50
9 Jan	Rother Nurseries	08666	13	740.25	110.25	630.00
9 Jan	Rocks Garden Supp	1468	22	(343.57)	(51.17)	(292.40)
				2,408.33	358.68	2,049.65

Cross-cast check:

	£
Net	2,049.65
VAT	358.68
Gross	2,408.33

c) **Main ledger**

Sales ledger control account

	£		£
9 Jan SDB	2,408.33		

VAT account

	£		£
		9 Jan SDB	358.68

Sales account

	£		£
		9 Jan SDB	2,049.65

Subsidiary ledger

Eridge Nurseries   SL 07

	£		£
7 Jan SDB – 08664	420.35		

Rother Nurseries   SL 13

	£		£
9 Jan SDB - 08666	740.25		

Abergaven Garden Centre   SL 16

	£		£
7 Jan SDB – 08665	904.16		

Rocks Garden Supplies   SL 22

	£		£
5 Jan SDB – 08663	687.14	9 Jan SDB – 1468	343.57

answers to chapter 5: RECEIVING MONEY

1 Who is the drawee? – First National Bank

Who is the payee? – J Peterson

Who is the drawer? – F Ronald

2

	Comments
Cheque from B B Berry Ltd	Words and figures differ
Cheque from Q Q Stores	Unsigned
Cheque from Dagwell Enterprises	Payee name is incorrect – Electronics instead of Electrical
Cheque from Weller Enterprises	Dated 6 January 2005 instead of 2006 – this cheque is therefore out of date

3 The cheque is valid but it has a special crossing which means that it can only be paid into the Drenchley branch of the Northern Bank.

4

	Comment and action
Cheque from T M Spence	The cheque guarantee card expired on 31 December 2005. Therefore this cheque cannot be accepted
Cheque from B Withers	The cheque guarantee card is for a different account from the account that the cheque is being written on. The customer is asked for the guarantee card for this account and if it is not available the cheque cannot be accepted
Cheques from C J Long	A cheque guarantee card can only be used to guarantee one cheque for each transaction. As the transaction exceeds the guarantee card limit the cheques cannot be accepted

5

	Comments
Payment from Rocks Garden Supplies	The remittance advice has been wrongly added up – the total should be £864.75
Payment from Eridge Nurseries	The cheque is invalid as the words and figures differ
Payment from Abergaven Garden Centre	This is perfectly acceptable and valid
Payment from Rother Nurseries	On the remittance advice Rother Nurseries has recorded invoice 08674 as £114.78 rather than £214.78 – therefore the amount of the payment is wrong

answers to chapter 6: RECORDING RECEIPTS

1

		VAT	Net amount
i)	£145.28	£21.63	£123.65
ii)	£68.90	£10.26	£58.64
iii)	£258.73	£38.53	£220.20
iv)	£35.82	£5.33	£30.49
v)	£125.60	£18.70	£106.90

2 Cash receipts book

Date	Details	Total	VAT	Cash sales	Sales ledger	Sundry	Discounts allowed
		£	£	£	£	£	£
23 Jan	Hoppers Ltd	545.14			545.14		16.86
23 Jan	Superior Products	116.70			116.70		
24 Jan	Cash sales	128.46	19.13	109.33			
24 Jan	Esporta Leisure	367.20			367.20		11.36
25 Jan	Cash sales	86.75	12.92	73.83			
27 Jan	Body Perfect	706.64			706.64		21.86
27 Jan	Cash sales	58.90	8.77	50.13			
27 Jan	Langans Beauty	267.90			267.90		
		2,277.69	40.82	233.29	2,003.58	–	50.08

Cross-cast check:

	£
Sales ledger	2,003.58
Cash sales	233.29
VAT	40.82
Total	2,277.69

3   Double entry for discounts allowed:

DR   Discounts allowed account
CR   Sales ledger control account

4   Main ledger

Sales ledger control account

	£		£
20 Jan SDB	3,438.04	20 Jan SRDB	80.72
		27 Jan CRB	2,003.58
		27 Jan CRB – discount	50.08

VAT account

	£		£
20 Jan SRDB	12.02	20 Jan SDB	512.04
		27 Jan CRB	40.82

Sales account

	£		£
		20 Jan SDB	2,926.00
		27 Jan CRB	233.29

Discount allowed account

	£		£
27 Jan CRB	50.08		

Subsidiary ledger

Hoppers Ltd account

	£		£
27 Jan SDB – 6237	642.72	17 Jan SRDB – 1476	80.72
		23 Jan CRB	545.14
		23 Jan CRB – discount	16.86

Body Perfect account

	£		£
5 Jan SDB – 6238	728.50	27 Jan CRB	706.64
12 Jan SDB – 6241	643.90	27 Jan CRB – discount	21.86

Esporta Leisure account

	£		£
6 Jan SDB – 6239	406.55	24 Jan CRB	367.20
18 Jan SDB - 6243	488.80	24 Jan CRB – discount	11.36

Langans Beauty account

	£		£
9 Jan SDB – 6240	267.90	27 Jan CRB	267.90

Superior Products account

	£		£
16 Jan SDB – 6242	259.67	23 Jan CRB	116.70

answers to chapter 7:
THE BANKING SYSTEM

1 **Day 1**

The Benham branch of First National sends the cheque to the First National clearing department in London.

Day 2

The First National clearing department sorts all of the cheques received by bank.

The cheque from Hoppers Ltd is sent to the Central Clearing House together with the other cheques received by First National which have been written on Central bank.

The cheque is then sent to the clearing department of Central bank which sends the cheque to the Drenchley branch of Central bank.

Day 3

Provided the cheque is valid and correct it is then paid out of Hoppers Ltd's account and credited to Natural Production's account.

2

Notes/coins	Number	Total £
£50	3	150.00
£20	17	340.00
£10	26	260.00
£5	35	175.00
£2	7	14.00
£1	18	18.00
50p	15	7.50
20p	36	7.20
10p	47	4.70
5p	23	1.15
2p	41	0.82
1p	63	0.63
		979.00

the banking system – answers

3 Calculation of cash to be paid into the bank:

Cash in till Notes/coins	Number	Float required	Paid into bank	Total £
£20	5	–	5	100.00
£10	12	2	10	100.00
£5	13	2	11	55.00
£2	1	–	1	2.00
£1	17	5	12	12.00
50p	9	2	7	3.50
20p	4	–	4	0.80
10p	15	10	5	0.50
5p	12	10	2	0.10
2p	16	10	6	0.12
1p	19	10	9	0.09
				274.11

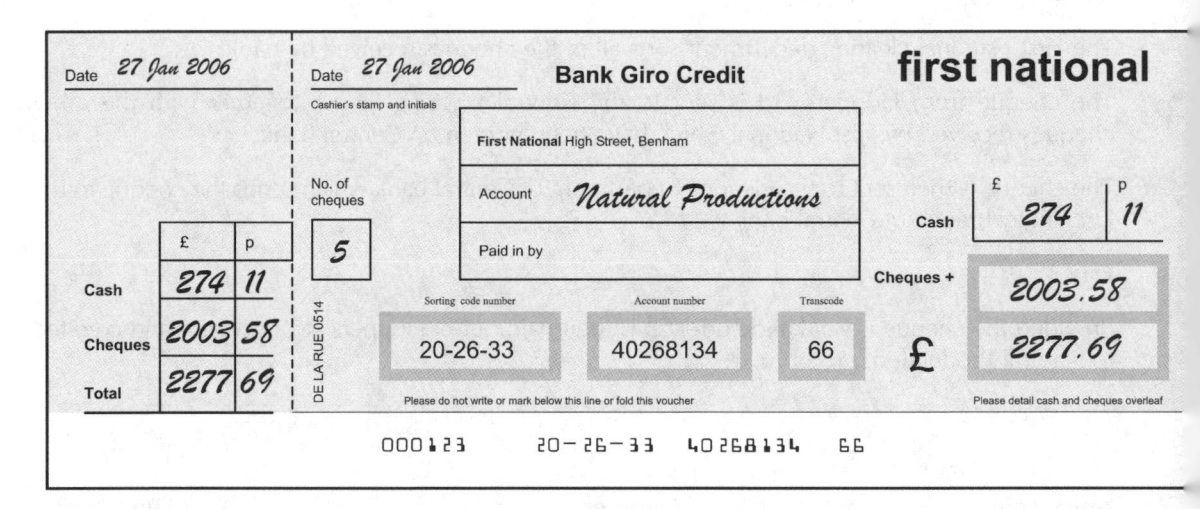

first national

Date: 27 Jan 2006

	£	p
Cash	274	11
Cheques	2003	58
Total	2277	69

Bank Giro Credit

Date: 27 Jan 2006

Cashier's stamp and initials

No. of cheques: 5

First National High Street, Benham

Account: *Natural Productions*

Paid in by:

Sorting code number: 20-26-33
Account number: 40268134
Transcode: 66

	£	p
Cash	274	11
Cheques +	2003	58
£	2277	69

000123 20-26-33 40268134 66

Cash	£	p		Cheques	£	p	
£50 notes	–	–			545	14	Hoppers Ltd CD-16-86
£20 notes	100	00			116	70	Superior Products
£10 notes	100	00			367	20	Esporta Leisure CD-11-36
£5 notes	55	00			706	64	Body Perfect CD-21-26
£2 coins	2	00			267	90	Langans Beauty
£1 coins	12	00					
Other coins	5	11					
Total	274	11		Total	2003	58	

answers to chapter 8: COMMUNICATION WITH CUSTOMERS

1

	T N Designs		
	£		£
1 May Opening balance	2,643.56	8 May CRB	1,473.28
11 May SDB – 27491	828.40	24 May SRDB CN0381	253.89
18 May SDB – 27513	1,083.65	31 May Closing balance	2,828.44
	4,555.61		4,555.61

	Harold & partners		
	£		£
1 May Opening balance	1,367.83	7 May CRB	635.78
5 May SDB – 27465	998.20	7 May CRB – discount	33.46
12 May SDB – 27499	478.92	15 May SRDB – CN0364	106.34
20 May SDB – 27524	258.29	30 May CRB	663.66
		30 May CRB – discount	34.93
		31 May Closing balance	1,629.07
	3,103.24		3,103.24

2

Debtor	Comment
Sunshine Sales	Only just within the credit limit. The major part of the debt is outside the credit terms of 30 days - Sunshine might be encouraged to pay up within the 30 day credit limit. However if this has always been the pattern then there is probably no problem here.
Groom Nurseries	No problems.
Bridge DIY	Although all of the debt is current it is over the credit limit for the customer so no more credit should be given without either payment received or management approval.
Erfield Gardens	The debt is over 30 days old and there has been no current activity on the account. This is a worrying situation and should be followed up.
Lye Nursery	The majority of the debt is current with only a small amount over 30 days. The concern however is the £89.32 due over 90 days. This must be investigated as it may be a disputed amount that will never be paid.

3

SHORT FURNITURE
ERIDGE ESTATE
BENHAM DR6 4QQ
Tel 0303312 Fax 0303300
VAT Reg 0361 3282 60

5 February 2006

Our ref: EG11/01/01

Purchase ledger manager
Erfield Gardens
Erfield House
Erfield Park
Benham DR6 6GL

Dear Sir

Overdue account

It would appear from our records that an amount of £435.77 has been owing from you for more than 60 days. We have enclosed a current statement showing all amounts outstanding and would be grateful if this amount can be settled by return of post.

We look forward to receiving your cheque.

Yours faithfully

Jane Trump

Sales ledger manager

answers to chapter 9:
BUSINESS DOCUMENTS – PURCHASES

1

GOODS RECEIVED NOTE

Whitehill Superstores

Supplier: Southfield Electrical	GRN number: 04884
	Date: 14 Jan 2006
	Order number: 32581

Quantity	Description	Stock code
3	Zanpoint Fridge Freezer	4075
1	Zanpoint Tumble Dryer	4120
1	Hosch Washing Machine	6140

Received by: *Charlie Rubble*

Checked by: *Jim Davids*

Comments: *1 Zanpoint tumble dryer returned due to scratching*

2

DEBIT NOTE

WHITEHILL SUPERSTORES
28 Whitehill Park
Benham DR6 5LM
Tel 0303446 Fax 0303447

To: Southfield Electrical
Industrial Estate
Benham
DR6 2FF

Debit note number: 0613
Date/tax point: 15 Jan 2006
Order number: 32581
Delivery note number: 34976

Quantity	Description	Stock code	Unit amount £	Total £
1	Zanpoint Tumble Dryer	4120	190.00	190.00

Reason: ....

Authorised by: .... **Date:** ....

3

Supplier	Comment
A1 Wood Supplies	The invoice is for 50m of Oak but the delivery note and GRN show that only 45m was delivered. A credit note should be requested by sending out a debit note for the remaining 5m.
Polish People	The invoice is for the cherry polish at a price of £3.16 per litre whereas the purchase order shows a price of £2.99 per litre. A debit note should be issued requesting a credit note for the difference.
Woodwards Woods	The invoice is for 110m of teak but the delivery note has been amended to show that only 95m were actually received and this is confirmed by the GRN. A debit note should be issued requesting a credit note for the difference.

answers to chapter 10: ACCOUNTING FOR CREDIT PURCHASES

1

Purchases day book

Date	Supplier	Invoice number	Gross £	VAT £	Purchases £	Stationery £	Packaging £
4 Jan	P J Phillips	03576	419.47	62.47	357.00		
6 Jan	Trenter Ltd	18435	502.90	74.90	428.00		
9 Jan	W J Jones	43654	246.75	36.75		210.00	
12 Jan	P J Phillips	03598	485.27	72.27	413.00		
16 Jan	Packing Supp	28423	314.90	46.90			268.00
19 Jan	Supp	18478	612.17	91.17	521.00		
20 Jan	Trenter Ltd	84335	733.20	109.20	624.00		
24 Jan	O & P Ltd	28444	192.70	28.70			164.00
28 Jan	Packing	18491	432.40	64.40	368.00		
31 Jan	Supp	43681	122.20	18.20		104.00	
			4,061.96	604.96	2,711.00	314.00	432.00

Cross-cast check:

	£
Packaging	432.00
Stationery	314.00
Materials	2,711.00
VAT	604.96
Gross	4,061.96

Main ledger

Purchases ledger control account

	£		£
		31 Jan PDB	4,061.96

VAT account

	£		£
31 Jan PDB	604.96		

Purchases account

	£		£
31 Jan PDB	2,711.00		

Stationery account

	£		£
31 Jan PDB	314.00		

Packaging account

	£		£
31 Jan PDB	432.00		

Subsidiary ledger

P J Phillips account

	£		£
		4 Jan PDB 03576	419.47
		12 Jan PDB 03598	485.27

Trenter Ltd account

	£		£
		6 Jan PDB 18435	502.90
		19 Jan PDB 18478	612.17
		28 Jan PDB 18491	432.40

W J Jones account

	£		£
		9 Jan PDB 43654	246.75
		31 Jan PDB 43681	122.20

Packing Supplies account

£		£
	16 Jan PDB 28423	314.90
	24 Jan PDB 28444	192.70

O & P Ltd account

£		£
	20 Jan PDB 84335	733.20

2 Purchases day book

Date	Supplier	Invoice number	Ref	Gross £	VAT £	Wood Purchases £	Polish/ varnish purchases £	Other purchases £	Sundry £
27 Jan	Ephraim Supp	09642	PL39	340.39	49.39	291.00			
27 Jan	Cavendish Woods	06932	PL14	828.45	123.38	705.07			
27 Jan	Calverley Bros	67671	PL03	171.08	25.48		145.60		
27 Jan	Culverden & Co	36004	PL23	67.24	9.84			57.40	
				1,407.16	208.09	996.07	145.60	57.40	

Cross-cast check:

	£
Other purchases	57.40
Polish purchases	145.60
Wood purchases	996.07
VAT	208.09
Gross	1,407.16

Main ledger

Purchases ledger control account

£		£
	27 Jan PDB	1,407.16

VAT account

	£		£
27 Jan PDB	208.09		

	Wood purchases account	
	£	£
27 Jan PDB	996.07	

	Polish/varnish purchases account	
	£	£
27 Jan PDB	145.60	

	Other purchases account	
	£	£
27 Jan PDB	57.40	

Subsidiary ledger

Calverley Bros account		PL 03
£		£
	27 Jan PDB 67671	171.08

Cavendish Woods account		PL 14
£		£
	27 Jan PDB 06932	828.45

Culverden & Co account		PL 23
£		£
	27 Jan PDB 36004	67.24

Ephraim Supplies account		PL 39
£		£
	27 Jan PDB 09642	340.39

3 Purchases returns day book

Date	Supplier	Credit note No	Gross £	VAT £	Purchases £	Stationery £	Packaging £
10 Jan	P J Phillips	04216	115.15	17.15	98.00		
16 Jan	W J Jones	CN0643	65.80	9.80		56.00	
30 Jan	O & P Ltd	CN1102	145.70	21.70	124.00		
			326.65	48.65	222.00	56.00	–

Cross-cast check:

	£
Stationery	56.00
Purchases	222.00
VAT	48.65
Gross	326.65

Main ledger

Purchases ledger control account

	£		£
31 Jan PRDB	326.65	31 Jan PDB	4,061.96

VAT account

	£		£
31 Jan PDB	604.96	31 Jan PRDB	48.65

Purchases account

	£		£
31 Jan PDB	2,711.00	31 Jan PRDB	222.00

Stationery account

	£		£
31 Jan PDB	314.00	31 Jan PRDB	56.00

Packaging account

	£		£
31 Jan PDB	432.00		

Subsidiary ledger

P J Phillips account

	£		£
10 Jan PRDB 04216	115.15	4 Jan PDB 03576	419.47
		12 Jan PDB 03598	485.27

W J Jones account

	£		£
16 Jan PRDB CN0643	65.80	9 Jan PDB 43654	246.75
		31 Jan PDB 43681	122.20

O & P Ltd account

	£		£
30 Jan PRDB CN1102	145.70	20 Jan PDB 84335	733.20

answers to chapter 11: MAKING PAYMENTS TO CREDIT SUPPLIERS

1

Invoice No	Payment date	Amount £
i)	6 February	437.66
ii)	17 January	315.82 (Working 1)
iii)	7 February	733.89
iv)	7 February	198.45
v)	19 January	600.64 (Working 2)
vi)	23 January	540.01 (Working 3)

Working 1

	£
Net	275.68
Less: discount	6.89
	268.79
Add: VAT £268.79 x 17.5%	47.03
	315.82

Working 2

	£
Net	527.00
Less: discount	15.81
	511.19
Add: VAT £511.19 x 17.5%	89.45
	600.64

Working 3

	£
Net	473.80
Less: discount	14.21
	459.59
Add: VAT £459.59 x 17.5%	80.42
	540.01

making payments to credit suppliers – answers

2

Invoice		Payment date	Amount of cheque
5 Jan	Henson Press	27 Jan	£329.00
8 Jan	GH Publications	3 Feb	£133.95
12 Jan	Ely Instruments	27 Jan	£640.00 – (2% x 640) + 109.76 £736.96
15 Jan	Hams Instruments	10 Feb	£362.89
19 Jan	CD Supplies	10 Feb	£135.22
22 Jan	Jester Press	27 Jan	£127.60 – (3.5% x 127.60) + 21.54 £144.67
22 Jan	Henson Press	17 Feb	£299.62
23 Jan	CD Supplies	27 Jan	£65.40 – (3% x 65.40) + 11.10 £74.54
25 Jan	Jester Press	27 Jan	£39.50 – (3.5% x 39.50) + 6.67 £44.79
25 Jan	Buser Ltd	27 Jan	£245.00 – (5% x 245.00) + 40.73 £273.48

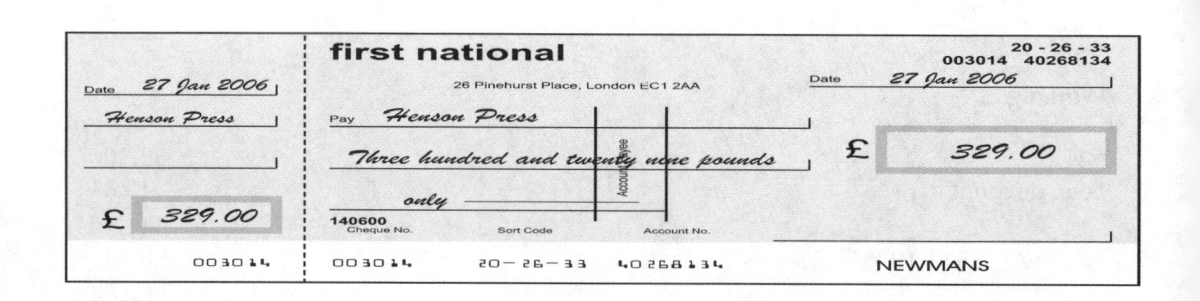

3

	first national	20 - 26 - 33
	26 Pinehurst Place, London EC1 2AA	003014 40268134
Date 27 Jan 2006		Date 27 Jan 2006
Henson Press	Pay Henson Press	
	Three hundred and twenty nine pounds	£ 329.00
£ 329.00	only	
	140600 Cheque No. Sort Code Account No.	
003014	003014 20—26—33 40268134	NEWMANS

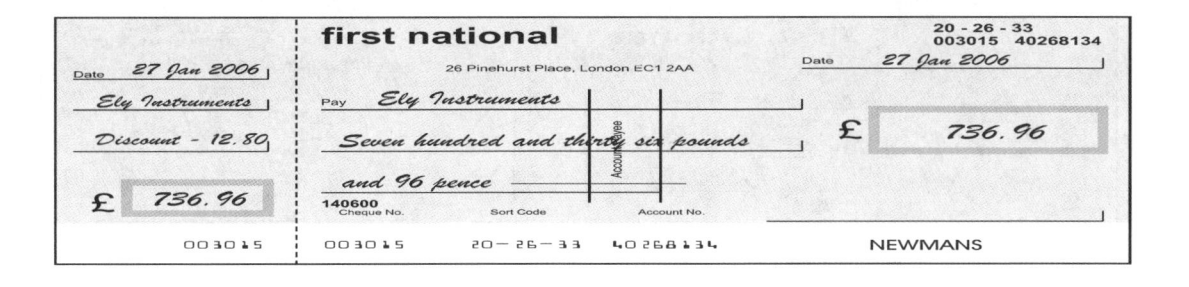

making payments to credit suppliers – answers

Cheque 003015

Date: 27 Jan 2006
Ely Instruments
Discount – 12.80
£ 736.96

Pay Ely Instruments
Seven hundred and thirty six pounds and 96 pence
£ 736.96
Date: 27 Jan 2006
Cheque No. 140600
Sort Code 20-26-33
Account No. 40268134
NEWMANS

Cheque 003016

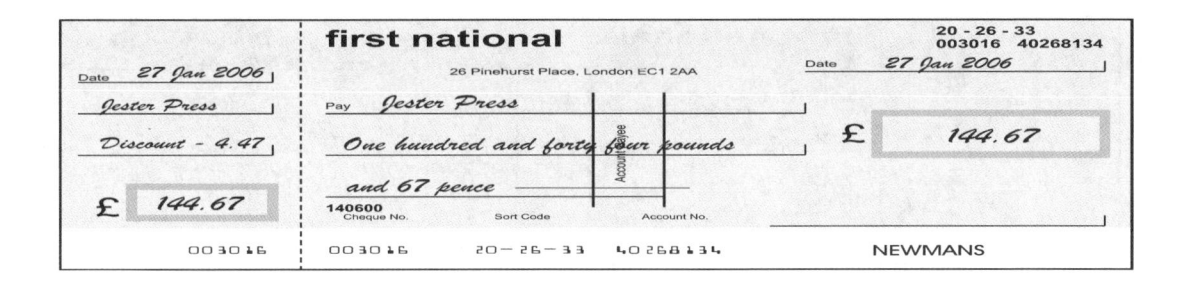

Date: 27 Jan 2006
Jester Press
Discount – 4.47
£ 144.67

Pay Jester Press
One hundred and forty four pounds and 67 pence
£ 144.67
Date: 27 Jan 2006
Cheque No. 140600
Sort Code 20-26-33
Account No. 40268134
NEWMANS

Cheque 003017

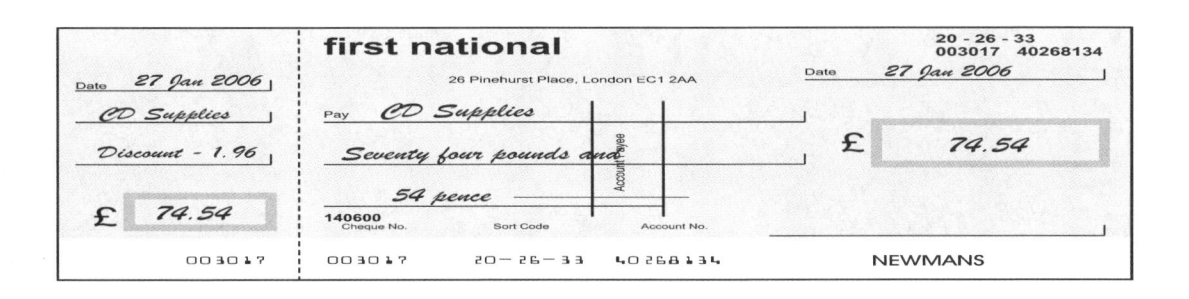

Date: 27 Jan 2006
CD Supplies
Discount – 1.96
£ 74.54

Pay CD Supplies
Seventy four pounds and 54 pence
£ 74.54
Date: 27 Jan 2006
Cheque No. 140600
Sort Code 20-26-33
Account No. 40268134
NEWMANS

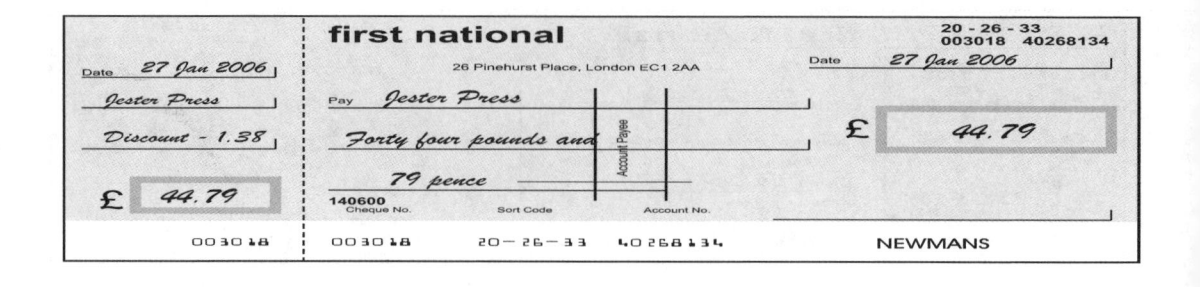

making payments to credit suppliers – answers

Cheque 003018 (stub and cheque)

Stub:
- Date: 27 Jan 2006
- Jester Press
- Discount – 1.38
- £ 44.79

Cheque:
- first national, 26 Pinehurst Place, London EC1 2AA
- Date: 27 Jan 2006
- Pay: Jester Press
- Forty four pounds and 79 pence
- £ 44.79
- Cheque No. 003018 Sort Code 20-26-33 Account No. 40268134
- NEWMANS

Cheque 003019 (stub and cheque)

Stub:
- Date: 27 Jan 2006
- Buser Ltd
- Discount – 12.25
- £ 273.48

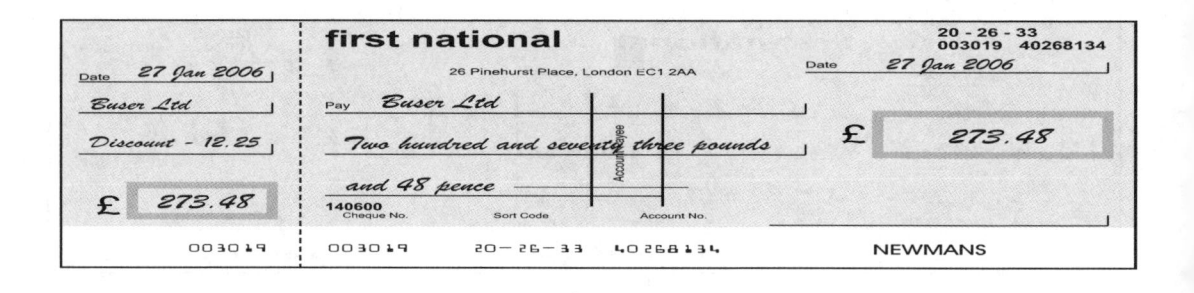

Cheque:
- first national, 26 Pinehurst Place, London EC1 2AA
- Date: 27 Jan 2006
- Pay: Buser Ltd
- Two hundred and seventy three pounds and 48 pence
- £ 273.48
- Cheque No. 003019 Sort Code 20-26-33 Account No. 40268134
- NEWMANS

4

REMITTANCE ADVICE

To: P.T. Supplies
28 Farm Court Road
Drenchley DR22 4XT

From: Edgehill Designs

Date: 7 February 2006

Reference	Amount £	Paid (✓)
20671	107.22	✓
20692	157.63	✓
CN 04722	(28.41)	✓
20718	120.48	
20734	106.18	
CN 04786	(16.15)	

CHEQUE ENCLOSED	**£236.44**

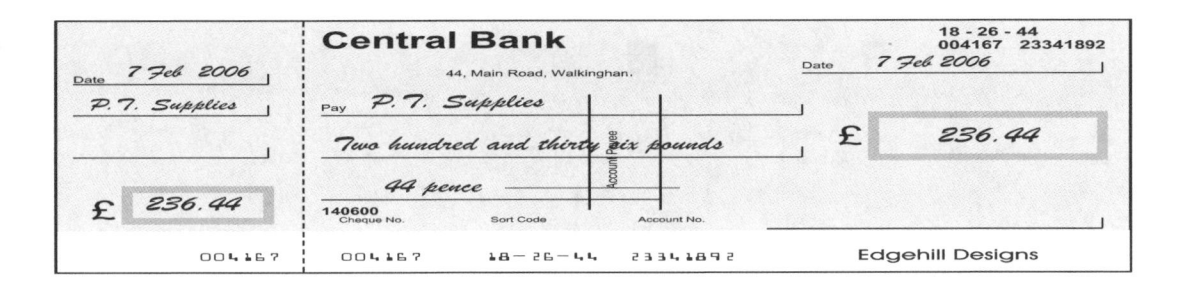

Central Bank
44, Main Road, Walkingham.

Date: 7 Feb 2006
Pay P.T. Supplies
Two hundred and thirty six pounds 44 pence

18-26-44
004167   23341892
Date 7 Feb 2006

£ 236.44

Cheque No. 140600
Sort Code 18-26-44
Account No. 23341892

004167

Edgehill Designs

Date 7 Feb 2006
P.T. Supplies
£ 236.44
004167

answers to chapter 12: RECORDING PAYMENTS

1

		VAT	Net amount
i)	£254.68	£37.93	£216.75
ii)	£159.28	£23.72	£135.56
iii)	£ 49.69	£7.40	£42.29
iv)	£104.28	£15.53	£ 88.75
v)	£ 62.48	£9.30	£53.18
vi)	£823.55	£122.65	£700.90

2 DR Purchases ledger control account   £367.48
    CR Cash   £367.48

    DR Purchases ledger control account   £12.50
    CR Discount received   £12.50

recording payments – answers

3

Date	Details	Cheque No	Total £	VAT £	Cash purchases £	Purchases ledger £	Sundry £	Discounts received £
23 Jan	Trenter Ltd	002144	1,110.09			1,110.09		28.47
23 Jan	Cash purchase	002145	105.79	15.75	90.04			
24 Jan	W J Jones	002146	246.75			246.75		
24 Jan	P J Phillips	002147	789.60			789.60		
24 Jan	Cash purchase	002148	125.68	18.71	106.97			
25 Jan	Packing Supp	002149	305.45			305.45		8.04
26 Jan	O & P Ltd	002150	703.87			703.87		18.72
27 Jan	Cash purchase	002151	95.00	14.14	80.86			
			3,482.23	48.60	277.87	3,155.76	–	55.23

Cross-cast check:

	£
Purchases ledger	3,155.76
Cash purchases	277.87
VAT	48.60
Total	3,482.23

Main ledger

Purchases ledger control account

	£		£
31 Jan PRDB	326.65	31 Jan PDB	4,061.96
27 Jan CPB	3,155.76		
27 Jan CPB – discounts	55.23		

VAT account

	£		£
31 Jan PDB	604.96	31 Jan PRDB	48.65
27 Jan CPB	48.60		

Purchases account

	£		£
31 Jan PDB	2,711.00	31 Jan PRDB	222.00
27 Jan CPB	277.87		

Discounts received account

	£		£
		27 Jan CPB	55.23

Subsidiary ledger

P J Phillips account

	£		£
10 Jan PRDB 04216	115.15	4 Jan PDB 03576	419.47
24 Jan CPB 002147	789.60	12 Jan PDB 03598	485.27

W J Jones account

	£		£
16 Jan PRDB CN0643	65.80	9 Jan PDB 43654	246.75
24 Jan CPB 002146	246.75	31 Jan PDB 43681	122.20

O & P Ltd account

	£		£
30 Jan PRDB CN1102	145.70	20 Jan PDB 84335	733.20
27 Jan CPB 002150	703.87		
27 Jan CPB discount	18.72		

Trenter Ltd account

	£		£
23 Jan CPB 002144	1,110.09	6 Jan PDB 18435	502.90
23 Jan CPB discount	28.47	28 Jan PDB 18491	432.40

Packing Supplies account

	£		£
25 Jan CPB 002149	305.45	16 Jan PDB 28423	314.90
25 Jan CPB discount	8.04	24 Jan PDB 28444	192.70

4 Cash payments book

Date	Details	Cheque No	Total £	VAT £	Purchases ledger £	Rent & rates £	Sundry £	Discounts received £
27 Jan	Henson Press	003014	329.00		329.00			
27 Jan	Ely Instr	003015	736.96		736.96			12.80
27 Jan	Jester Press	003016	144.67		144.67			4.47
27 Jan	CD Supplies	003017	74.54		74.54			1.96
27 Jan	Jester Press	003018	44.79		44.79			1.38
27 Jan	Buser Ltd	003019	273.48		273.48			12.25
27 Jan	Rates	SO	255.00			255.00		
27 Jan	Rent	DD	500.00			500.00		
			2,358.44	–	1,603.44	755.00	–	32.86

Cross-cast check:

	£
Rent & rates	755.00
Purchases ledger	1,603.44
Total	2,358.44

Main ledger

Purchases ledger control account

	£		£
27 Jan CPB	1,603.44		
27 Jan CPB - discounts	32.86		

Rent and rates account

	£		£
27 Jan CPB	755.00		

Discounts received

	£		£
		27 Jan CPB	32.86

Subsidiary ledger

Buser Ltd

	£		£
27 Jan CPB 003019	273.48		
27 Jan CPB discount	12.25		

CD Supplies

	£		£
27 Jan CPB 003017	74.54		
27 Jan CPB discount	1.96		

Ely Instruments

	£		£
27 Jan CPB 003015	736.96		
27 Jan CPB discount	12.80		

Henson Press

	£		£
27 Jan CPB 003014	329.00		

Jester Press

	£		£
27 Jan CPB 003016	144.67		
27 Jan CPB – discount	4.47		
27 Jan CPB 003018	44.79		
27 Jan CPB – discount	1.38		

5 Dear Sir

We have just received an invoice from yourselves for goods with a list price of £1,000 plus VAT giving an invoice total of £1,175. However we note that your normal practice is to grant our company a 20% trade discount as we have been regular customers of your business for a number of years. If the discount is given then the invoice total will be £940 (£1,000 x 20%) x 1.175). Therefore, if our company is still to receive a trade discount from you, please send a credit note for £235 and we will then pay the revised total.

Yours faithfully

A N Accountant

answers to chapter 13: PETTY CASH PROCEDURES

1 £68.34

2

RECEIPTS			PAYMENTS							
Date	Details	Amount £	Date	Details	Voucher number	Total £	VAT £	Travel £	Post £	Stationery £	Office supplies £
16 Jan	Bal b/f	120.00	23 Jan	Coffee	0721	3.99					3.99
			23 Jan	Stamps	0722	24.00			24.00		
			24 Jan	Taxi fare	0723	10.50	1.56	8.94			
			24 Jan	Paper	0724	6.97	1.03			5.94	
			26 Jan	Train fare	0725	13.60		13.60			
			27 Jan	Disks	0726	10.98	1.63				9.35
						70.04	4.22	22.54	24.00	5.94	13.34

Cross-cast check:

	£
Office supplies	13.34
Stationery	5.94
Postage	24.00
Travel	22.54
VAT	4.22
	70.04

Main ledger

VAT account

	£		£
27 Jan PCB	4.22		

Travel expenses account

	£		£
27 Jan PCB	22.54		

Postage account

	£		£
27 Jan PCB	24.00		

Stationery account

	£		£
27 Jan PCB	5.94		

Office supplies account

	£		£
27 Jan PCB	13.34		

answers to chapter 14: PAYROLL ACCOUNTING PROCEDURES

1 a)

	£
Gross wage	440.00
PAYE	(77.76)
Employee's NIC	(43.18)
Pension contribution (440.00 x 5%)	(22.00)
Net pay	297.06

b) £297.06 will be paid to Peter
£22.00 will be paid into the pension fund on his behalf
£170.29 (£77.76 + £43.18 + £49.35) will be paid to HM Revenue and Customs

c)

Wages expense account

	£		£
Gross wages control	440.00		
Gross wages control - employer's NIC	49.35		

Gross wages control account

	£		£
CPB – net pay	297.06	Wages expense	440.00
PAYE/NIC – PAYE	77.76	Wages expense – employer's NIC	49.35
PAYE/NIC – employee's NIC	43.18		
Pension contribution	22.00		
PAYE/NIC – employer's NIC	49.35		

PAYE/NIC creditor account

	£		£
		Gross wages control	77.76
		Gross wages control	43.18
		Gross wages control	49.35

Pension contribution account

	£		£
		Gross wages control	22.00

2

Employee	Gross annual salary £	Taxable annual salary £	Income tax @ 10% £	Income tax @ 22% £	NIC £	Net annual salary £
J Short	30,000	25,700	150	5,324	2,640	21,886
P Nielson	24,000	19,700	150	4,004	2,040	17,806
J Taylor	17,400	13,100	150	2,552	1,380	13,318
M Harris	15,500	11,200	150	2,134	1,190	12,026
J Philpott	14,600	10,300	150	1,936	1,100	11,414

answers to chapter 15:
BANK RECONCILIATION STATEMENT

1

	Transaction	Debit or credit?
i)	£470.47 paid into the bank	Credit
ii)	standing order of £26.79	Debit
iii)	cheque payment of £157.48	Debit
iv)	interest earned on the bank balance	Credit
v)	BACS payment for wages	Debit

2 Cash receipts book

Date	Details	Total £	VAT £	Sales ledger £	Music sales £	Instrument sales £	CD sales £	Discounts allowed £	Sundry £
27 Jan	Tunfield DC	594.69 ✓		594.69					
27 Jan	Tunshire CO	468.29 ✓		468.29				14.48	
27 Jan	Cash sales	478.90 ✓			478.90				
27 Jan	Tunfield BB	1,059.72 ✓		1,059.72				33.03	
27 Jan	Cash sales	736.58 ✓	109.70			626.88			
27 Jan	Cash sales	251.67	37.48				214.19		
27 Jan	Bank interest*	3.68							3.68
27 Jan	Tunfield AOS*	108.51		108.51					
		3,702.04	147.18	2,231.21	478.90	626.88	214.19	47.51	3.68

* Note: these items and the ticks relate to later activities in this chapter.

bank reconciliation statement – answers

3

Unmatched item	Action to be taken
Bank Giro Credit Tunfield AOS	This must be checked to any supporting documentation such as any remittance advice from Tunfield AOS or the original invoice - when it has been checked the amount should be entered into the cash receipts book
Standing order to British Elec	The standing order schedule should be checked to ensure that this is correct and it should then be entered into the cash payments book
Bank interest received	This should be entered into the cash receipts book
Cash sales from CDs	The £251.67 cash sales from CDs do not appear on the bank statement. This is a reconciling item
Cheques	Cheque numbers 003016, 003018 and 003019 are all unpresented cheques and will appear in the bank reconciliation statement

4 Cash payments book

Date	Cheque no	Details	Total £	VAT £	Purchases ledger £	Rent & rates £	Sundry £	Discount received £
27 Jan	003014	Henson Press	329.00 ✓		329.00			
27 Jan	003015	Ely Instr	736.96 ✓		736.96			12.80
27 Jan	003016	Jester Press	144.67		144.67			4.47
27 Jan	003017	CD Supplies	74.54 ✓		74.54			1.96
27 Jan	003018	Jester Press	44.79		44.79			1.38
27 Jan	003019	Buser Ltd	273.48		273.48			12.25
27 Jan	SO	Rates	255.00 ✓			255.00		
27 Jan	DD	Rent	500.00 ✓			500.00		
27 Jan	SO	British Elec	212.00 ✓				212.00	
			2,570.44		1,603.44	755.00	212.00	32.86

	£
Opening balance	379.22
Receipts	3,702.04
Payments	(2,570.44)
Amended cash book balance	1,510.82

bank reconciliations statement – answers

5 Bank reconciliation statement as at 27 January 2006

	£	£
Balance per bank statement		1,722.09
Outstanding lodgement		251.67
		1,973.76
Unpresented cheques		
003016	144.67	
003018	44.79	
003019	273.48	
		(462.94)
Amended cash book balance		1,510.82

6 **B** Outstanding lodgements and unpresented cheques.

7 **B** £(565)o/d – £92 dishonoured cheque = £(657) o/d

8 **D** The question refers to the figure to be shown in the balance sheet

	£	£
Balance per cash book		5,675
Reversal – Standing order entered twice	125	
Adjustment – Dishonoured cheque (450 x 2)		900
Entered in error as a debit		
Bank overdraft	6,450	
Amended cash book balance	6,575	6,575

9 **B**

	£
Cash book balance	2,490
Adjustment re charges	(50)
Adjustment re dishonoured cheque	(140)
	2,300

10 **B**

	£	£
Bank statement balance b/d	13,400	
Dishonoured cheque	300	
Bank charges not in cash book	50	
Unpresented cheques		2,400
Uncleared banking	1,000	
Adjustment re error (2 x 195)		390
Cash book balance c/d		11,960
	14,750	14,750
Cash book balance b/d		11,960

bank reconciliation statement – answers

Alternative approach:

	£	£
Cash book balance b/d	11,960	
Dishonoured cheque		300
Bank charges not in cash book		50
Unpresented cheques	2,400	
Uncleared banking		1,000
Adjustment re error (2 x 195)	390	
Bank statement balance c/d		13,400
	14,750	14,750
Bank statement balance b/d	13,400	

11 A

	£	£
Cash book (the cash book has a credit balance)		1,240
Unpresented cheques	450	
Uncleared deposit		140
Bank charges		75
Bank overdraft	1,005	
	1,455	1,455

12 D Provided that the cash receipts have been correctly posted to the cash book, then the fact that they have incorrectly been posted to creditors instead of cash sales and debtors will not affect the bank reconciliation.

13 D All the other options would have the bank account £250 less than the cash book.

14 B

	£	£
Cash book		500
Unpresented cheques	6,000	
Uncleared deposit		5,000
Bank balance		500
	6,000	6,000

15 A bank reconciliation is needed to identify **errors** either in the cash book of the business or made by the **bank itself**.

16

	£
Balance per cash book	2,490
Less: bank charges	(50)
Less: dishonoured cheque	(140)
	2,300

answers to chapter 16: CONTROL ACCOUNT RECONCILIATIONS

1

Sales ledger control account

	£		£
Opening balance	12,589	Opening balance	900
Credit sales	12,758	Sales returns	1,582
Returned cheque	722	Cash received	11,563
		Discount allowed	738
		Bad debt written off	389
		Closing balance	10,897
	26,069		26,069

2

Purchases ledger contol account

	£		£
Purchases returns	728	Opening balance	8,347
Cash paid	8,837	Credit purchases	9,203
Discounts received	382		
Closing balance	7,603		
	17,550		17,550

control account reconciliations – answers

3

		Control account	List of balances	Both
i)	Invoice entered into the sales day book as £980 instead of £890			✓
ii)	Purchase day book overcast by £1,000	✓		
iii)	Discounts allowed of £20 not entered into the cash receipts book			✓
iv)	An invoice taken as £340 instead of £440 when being posted to the subsidiary ledger		✓	
v)	Incorrect balancing of a subsidiary ledger account		✓	
vi)	A purchase return not entered into the purchases returns day book			✓

4 Main ledger

Sales ledger control account

	£		£
Opening balance	5,000	Cash receipts (2,400 + 3,600 +1,100 + 4,800)	11,900
Sales (2,000 + 2,700 + 1,100 + 3,800)	9,600	Balanced c/d	2,700
	14,600		14,600
Balance b/d	2,700		

Subsidiary ledger

H Simms account

	£		£
Opening balance	900	Cash receipts	2,400
Sales	2,000	Balanced c/d	500
	2,900		2,900
Balance b/d	500		

P Good account

	£		£
Opening balance	1,600	Cash receipts	3,600
Sales	2,700	Balanced c/d	700
	4,300		4,300
Balance b/d	700		

K Mitchell account

	£		£
Sales	1,100	Cash receipt	1,100

C Brown account

	£		£
Opening balance	2,500	Cash receipts	4,800
Sales	3,800	Balanced c/d	1,500
	6,300		6,300
Balance b/d	1,500		

Reconciliation of subsidiary ledger balances with control account balance

	£
H Simms	500
P Good	700
K Mitchell	–
C Brown	1,500
Sales ledger control account	2,700

5 Main ledger

Purchases ledger control account

	£		£
Cash payment		Opening balance	2,700
(1,700 + 3,200 + 3,000)	7,900	Purchases	
Balance c/d	2,100	(1,600 + 2,500 + 3,200)	7,300
	10,000		10,000
		Balance b/d	2,100

Subsidiary ledger

J Peters account

	£		£
Cash payment	1,700	Opening balance	300
Balance c/d	200	Purchases	1,600
	1,900		1,900
		Balance b/d	200

control account reconciliations – answers

T Sands account

	£		£
Cash payment	3,200	Opening balance	1,700
Balance c/d	1,000	Purchases	2,500
	4,200		4,200
		Balance b/d	1,000

L Farmer account

	£		£
Cash payment	3,000	Opening balance	700
Balanced c/d	900	Purchases	3,200
	3,900		3,900
		Balance b/d	900

Reconciliation of subsidiary ledger balances with control account balance

	£
J Peters	200
T Sands	1,000
L Farmer	900
Purchases ledger control account	2,100

6

Sales ledger control account

	£		£
Balance b/d	13,452	Sales returns	100
		Bad debt	200
		Balance	13,152
	13,452		13,452
Balance b/d	13,152		

	£
Subsidiary ledger list of balances	12,614
Over statement of receipt	180
Balance omitted	358
Amended total	13,152

control account reconciliations – answers

7

Purchases ledger control account

	£		£
Discounts received (2 x 256)	512	Balance d/d	26,677
Balanced c/d	27,165	Purchases	1,000
	27,677		677
		Balance b/d	27,165

	£
Subsidiary list of balances	27,469
Discount omitted	(64)
Debit balance (2 x 120)	(240)
Amended total	27,165

8 a)

		Voucher Total
		£
0473		12.60
0474		15.00
0475		19.75
0476		9.65
0477		10.00
0478		13.84
0479		4.26
0480		16.40
		101.50

Petty cash value

		£
£10 note	1	10.00
£5 note	4	20.00
£2 coin	3	6.00
£1 coin	7	7.00
50p coin	5	2.50
20p coin	8	1.60
10p coin	9	0.90
5p coin	4	0.20
2p coin	11	0.22
1p coin	8	0.08
		48.50

	£
Voucher total	101.50
Petty cash	48.50
Imprest amount	150.00

b) The petty cash control account in the main ledger is given below:

Petty cash control

		£			£
1 Jan	Balance b/d	150.00	31 Jan	Petty cash book	101.50
			31 Jan	Balance c/d	48.50
		150.00			150.00
1 Feb	Balance b/d	48.50			

Cash in the petty cash box   £48.50

9   **A**   Y is a creditor of X.

10 **B**   All other options would lead to a higher balance in the supplier's records.

11 **C**   Debits total £32,750 + £125,000 + £1,300 = £159,050. Credits total £1,275 + £122,550 + £550 = £124,325. ∴ Net balance = £34,725 debit.

12 **A**   £8,500 − (2 × £400) = £7,700.

13 **A**

	£
Opening balance	34,500
Credit purchases	78,400
Discounts	(1,200)
Payments	(68,900)
Purchase returns	(4,700)
	38,100

14 A control account is an account in the nominal ledger in which a record is kept of the **total value of a number of similar but individual items**.

15 Control accounts are useful chiefly for **debtors** and **creditors**.

16 The control account and the list of balances.

17 £46,538.

18 To confirm the accuracy of postings to the sales ledger control account and subsidiary sales ledger accounts.

19 £75,355

	£
Balance per listing	81,649
Less: Invoice posted twice	(4,688)
Less: payment omitted	(1,606)
	75,355
Balance per control account	76,961
Less: payment omitted	(1,606)
	75,355

answers to chapter 17: PREPARING AN INITIAL TRIAL BALANCE

1

Sales ledger control account

	£		£
Opening balance	16,387	Cash receipts	15,388
Sales	17,385	Discounts allowed	734
		Sales returns	1,297
		Bad debt written off	479
		Balance c/d	15,874
	33,772		33,772
Balance b/d	15,874		

Purchases ledger control account

	£		£
Cash payments	10,756	Opening balance	11,529
Discounts received	529	Purchases	10,487
Purchases returns	926		
Balance c/d	9,805		
	22,016		22,016
		Balance b/d	9,805

preparing an initial trial balance – answers

2

Ledger account	Balance	Debit or credit?
Sales	625,679	Credit
Telephone	1,295	Debit
Debtors	52,375	Debit
Wages	104,288	Debit
Purchases returns	8,229	Credit
Bank overdraft	17,339	Credit
Purchases	372,589	Debit
Drawings	38,438	Debit
Sales returns	32,800	Debit
Motor car	14,700	Debit
Creditors	31,570	Credit

3

	£	£
Motor vehicles	76,800	
Office equipment	36,440	
Sales		285,600
Purchases	196,800	
Bank overdraft		2,016
Petty cash	36	
Capital		90,000
Sales returns	5,640	
Purchases returns		4,320
Sales ledger control	42,960	
Purchases ledger control		36,120
VAT (credit balance)		15,540
Stock	12,040	
Telephone	1,920	
Electricity	3,360	
Wages	74,520	
Loan		36,000
Discounts allowed	7,680	
Discounts received		4,680
Rent	14,400	
Bad debts written off	1,680	
	474,276	474,276

4   **C**   DR Assets and expenses/CR Liabilities, capital and revenues.

5   **D**   A liability or a revenue.

6   **D**   Bank overdraft.

7   **B**

8   **D**

9   The **trial balance** lists all the balances in every account in the nominal ledger at the end of a period.

answers to chapter 18: ERRORS AND THE TRIAL BALANCE

1

Sales ledger control account

	£		£
Balance b/d	1,683	Cash received	14,228
Sales	15,899	Discounts allowed	900
		Bad debts written off	245
		Sales returns	1,467
		Balance c/d	742
	17,582		17,582

VAT account

	£		£
VAT on purchases	1,985	Balance b/d	2,576
		VAT on sales	2,368
Balance c/d	3,074	VAT on purchases returns	115
	5,059		5,059

2

	£	£
Motor vehicle	18,720	
Stock	2,520	
Bank (debit balance)	10,956	
Sales ledger control	5,280	
Purchases ledger control		3,840
Capital		48,000
Sales		78,000
Sales returns	6,000	
Purchases	50,400	
Purchases returns		3,240
Bank charges	120	
Discounts allowed	1,080	
Discounts received		720
Wages and salaries	26,160	
Rent and rates	7,440	
Telephone	1,224	
Electricity	3,060	
Bad debts written off	840	
	133,800	133,800

errors and the trial balance – answers

3 **a)** Journal entries

			£	£
i)	Debit	Sales ledger control	1,000	
	Credit	Sales		1,000
ii)	Debit	Electricity (in the TB)	1,642	
	Credit	Suspense		1,642
iii)	Debit	Discounts allowed (2 x £865)	1,730	
	Credit	Suspense		1,730
iv)	Debit	Sales ledger control	360	
	Credit	Cash book		360
v)	Debit	Purchases ledger control	120	
	Credit	Discounts received		120

b)

Suspense account

	£		£
Opening balance	3,372	Electricity	1,642
		Discounts allowed	1,730
	3,372		3,372

4 **B** £890 should have been debited to the expense account. Instead, £980 has been debited. To bring this amount down to £890, the expense account should be credited with £90.

5 **B** An error of omission.

6 **C** One side of a transaction has been recorded in the wrong account, and that account is of the same class as the correct account.

7 **A**

Suspense account

	£		£
Balance b/d	210	Gas bill (420 – 240)	180
Giscount received	70	Discount (2 x 50)	100
	280		280

8 **C** A fixed asset has been debited to the wrong class of account (purchases).

errors and the trial balance – answers

9   **B**   The posting is correct, but the wrong amount has been used.

10   **A**   These are the postings that clear the suspense account:

Suspense account

	£		£
Opening balance	1,350	Discounts allowed	7,500
Discount received	6,150		
	7,500		7,500

11   **D**   Debits will exceed credits by 2 × £48 = £96.

12   **A**   The other options would make the credit side total £50 more than the debit side.

13   A trial balance will not disclose the following types of errors:

– Errors of omission

– Errors of commission

– Compensating errors

– Errors of principle

14   Original entry.

15

	Yes	No
Omitting both entries for a transaction		✓
Posting the debit entry for an invoice to an incorrect expense account		✓
Omitting the debit entry for a transaction	✓	
Posting the debit entry for a transaction as a credit entry	✓	

16   £1,800 debit.

17   £157,818.

answers to chapter 19: BUSINESS TRANSACTIONS AND THE LAW

1 i)   Offeror – Short Furniture
         Offeree – Rother Nurseries

   ii) Yes, there has been both offer and acceptance

   iii) No, the stipulation about delivery from Rother Nurseries is a counter-offer that invalidates the original offer. It is now up to Short Furniture to decide whether or not to accept this counter-offer from Rother Nurseries.

2 No. The advertisement is an invitation to treat not an offer. When the customers call Short Furniture, that is the offer which Short Furniture can either accept or reject.

3 No. Acceptance cannot be in the form of silence. Therefore the fact that the customer has not responded means that there is no acceptance.

4 Yes. Acceptance is valid from the date on which it was posted ie, Friday of this week.

business transactions and the law – answers

5 a) The Data Protection Act 1998 affords protection to individuals over personal data that is held about them. The Act applies to records held on computer as well as records held in a manual system. The Act covers personal data which is data relating to an individual and that individual is known as the data subject.

b) The eight principles of good information handling from the Data Protection Act are that information should be:

- fairly and lawfully processed
- processed for limited purposes
- adequate, relevant and not excessive
- accurate
- not held for longer than is necessary
- processed in line with the data subject's rights
- kept securely
- not transferred to countries outside the European Union unless there is adequate protection in those countries

answers to chapter 20: INTRODUCTION TO MANAGEMENT INFORMATION

1   **Management task**   **Management role**

   i)   estimating advertising costs for the following year   Planning
   ii)   comparing this month' sales income to that for last month   Control
   iii) considering the opening of an additional factory   Decision-making
   iv)   determining how many production employees are required
         for the following quarter's production   Planning
   v)   comparing the actual costs for the month to the budgeted costs   Control
   vi)   considering taking out a loan to help fund expansion   Decision-making

2
- amount of production planned
- productivity of production employees
- normal weekly hours of production employees
- number of possible overtime hours
- basic pay rates and overtime rates
- levels of absenteeism amongst production employees

3
- production budget showing quantity of goods to be produced
- materials usage showing the quantity of material required for the production
- materials cost budget showing the cost of the materials that must be purchased

answers to chapter 21: ELEMENTS OF COST

1

	Cost	Classification
i)	advertising costs in local paper	Expense
ii)	cost of imported wood	Materials
iii)	store keeper's wages	Labour
iv)	new blades for saws	Expense
v)	cost of wood polish	Materials
vi)	accountant's salary	Labour
vii)	repair cost of delivery van	Expense
viii)	insurance of the cutting machinery	Expense
ix)	telephone bill	Expense

2

STOCK RECORD CARD

Stock code 02611

Date	In	Out	Balance
2006 1 Jan 2 Jan 5 Jan	45 metres	25 metres	35 metres 10 metres 55 metres

STOCK RECORD CARD

Stock code P4612

Date	In	Out	Balance
2006 1 Jan 4 Jan 5 Jan	20 metres	10 metres	15 metres 5 metres 25 metres

elements of cost – answers

3

Employee	Total hours	Basic hours	Basic pay £	Overtime hours	Overtime pay £	Total gross £	Employers' NIC £
P Knight	38	35	357.00	3	45.90	402.90	39.16
P Anil	35	35	252.00	-	-	252.00	19.84
K Chappatte	39	35	297.50	4	51.00	348.50	32.19
H Dennis	37	35	252.00	2	21.60	273.60	22.60
K Fisher	38	35	227.50	3	29.25	256.75	20.45
J Hunt	40	35	297.50	5	63.75	361.25	33.82
D Jones	38	35	227.50	3	29.25	256.75	20.45
L Minns	41	35	252.00	6	64.80	316.80	28.13
S Percy	35	35	252.00	-	-	252.00	19.84
I Roberts	39	35	297.50	4	51.00	348.50	32.19
G Tracy	35	35	227.50	-	-	227.50	16.70
F Albert	37	35	248.50	2	21.30	269.80	22.12
L Gill	35	35	248.50	-	-	248.50	19.39
J Norman	41	35	248.50	6	63.90	312.40	27.57
T Stevens	38	35	248.50	3	31.95	280.45	23.48

4

	Cutting cost centre £	Assembly cost centre £	Finishing cost centre £	Marketing cost centre £	Admin cost centre £	Total £
Gross wages	2,873.12	5,301.57	4,781.56	3,350.50	1,079.20	17,385.95
Employer's NIC	261.14	480.70	415.70	292.81	92.90	1,543.25
	3,134.26	5,782.27	5,197.26	3,643.31	1,172.10	18,929.20

Workings

Cutting
- gross wages 1,327.55 + 1,008.00 + (1/3 x 1,612.70) = £2,873.12
- employer's NIC 123.94 + 84.00 + (1/3 x 159.59) = £261.14

Assembly
- gross wages 1,008.00 + 1,026.40 + 1,445.00 + 1,284.60 + (1/3 x 1,612.70) = £5,301.57
- employer's NIC 84.00 + 86.30 + 138.63 + 118.58 + (1/3 x 159.59) = £480.70

Finishing
- gross wages 1,026.85 + 1,004.35 + 1,267.20 + 945.60 + (1/3 x 1,612.70) = £4,781.56
- employer's NIC 86.36 + 83.54 + 116.40 + 76.20 + (1/3 x 159.59) = £415.70

Marketing
- gross wages 994.00 + 1,234.70 + 1,121.80 = £3,350.50
- employer's NIC 82.25 + 112.34 + 98.22 = £292.81

answers to chapter 22: CODING

1

INVOICE

Short Furniture
Eridge Estate
Benham DR6 4QQ
Tel 0303312 Fax 0303300
VAT Reg 0361 3282 60

To: Rother Nurseries
Rother Road
Benham

Invoice number: 08721

Date/tax point: 27 Jan 2006

Order number: 06148

Account number: SL 13

Quantity	Description	Stock code	Unit amount £	Total £
2	Coffee Table	CT002	96.00	192.00
6	Dining Chair	DC416	73.00	438.00
			Net total	630.00
			VAT	110.25
			Invoice total	740.25

Terms
Net 30 days
E & OE

coding – answers

INVOICE

Short Furniture
Eridge Estate
Benham DR6 4QQ
Tel 0303312 Fax 0303300
VAT Reg 0361 3282 60

To: Fenband Stores
Victory Shopping Centre
Benham

Invoice number: 08722

Date/tax point: 27 Jan 2006
Order number: 43217

Account number: SL 61

Quantity	Description	Stock code	Unit amount £	Total £
7	Sunlounger	SL642	210.00	1,470.00
1	Bench	B443	110.00	110.00
				1,580.00
	Trade Discount			158.00
	Net total			1,422.00
	VAT			248.85
	Invoice total			1,670.85

£1,323 (123)

£99 (122)

Terms
Net 30 days
E & OE

coding – answers

INVOICE

A1 Wood Supplies
Heath Park
Drenchley DR22 6KL
VAT Reg 4621 3117 04

To: Short Furniture
Eridge Estate
Benham DR6 4QQ

Invoice number: 764989

Date/tax point: 27 Jan 2006

Order number: 46794

Account number: S04

Quantity	Description	Stock code	Unit amount £	Total £
30m	Stripped Pine	P4612	12.38	371.40
40m	Oak	02611	15.87	638.80
				1,010.20
	Trade Discount			151.53
			Net total	858.67
			VAT	145.75
			Invoice total	1,004.42

(211)

Terms
3% settlement discount for payment within 14 days, otherwise net 30 days
E & OE

INVOICE

Polish People
23/25 Main Street
Wakeham DR17 4ZF
Tel 0421666 Fax 0421667
VAT Reg 3692 9417 63

To: Short Furniture
Eridge Estate
Benham DR6 4QQ

Invoice number: 06715

Date/tax point: 27 Jan 2006

Order number: 04701

Account number: SL 13

Quantity	Description	Stock code	Unit amount £	Total £
40 litres	Exterior Wood Polish – cherry	88631	3.16	126.40
20 litres	Exterior Wood Polish – teak	88413	2.83	56.60
			Net total	183.00
			VAT	32.02
			Invoice total	215.02

Terms
Net 30 days
E & OE

INVOICE

J. T. Turner
Black Horse House
Budlett DR4 6TM
VAT Reg 3667 1294 61

To: Short Furniture
Eridge Estate
Benham DR6 4QQ

Invoice number: 06302

Date/tax point: 27 Jan 2006

Order number: 04699

Account number: SL 43

Quantity	Description	Stock code	Unit amount £	Total £
12 dozen	4" cross head 2/8 screws	S428	3.83	45.96
30 dozen	3" cross head 1/8 screws	S318	1.94	58.20
				104.16
	Trade Discount			15.62
			Net total	88.54
			VAT	14.87
			Invoice total	103.14

Terms
4% settlement discount for payment within 10 days, otherwise 30 days net
E & OE

Coding listing – Income and expenditure – January 2006

Code	Balance £	Amendment £	Updated balance £
111	16,387.50	438.00	
112	13,265.95		
113	9,326.20		
114	3,587.90	192.00	
115	1,037.00		
121	10,385.30		
122	7,256.30	99.00	
123	3,646.70	1,323.00	
124	3,027.60		
125	926.40		
211	35,287.74	858.67	
215	-		
216	-		
222	1,285.47	88.54	
223	1,036.80		
225	-		
226	-		
234	8,385.40	183.00	
235	-		
236	-		
245	-		
246	-		
255	-		
256	-		

coding – answers

2

	Cutting cost centre £	Assembly cost centre £	Finishing cost centre £	Marketing cost centre £	Admin cost centre £	Total £
Gross wages	2,873.12	5,301.57	4,781.56	3,350.50	1,079.20	17,385.95
Employer's NIC	261.14	480.70	415.70	292.81	92.90	1,543.25
	3,134.26	5,782.27	5,197.26	3,643.31	1,172.10	18,929.20
	(215)	(225)	(235)	(245)	(255)	

Coding listing – Income and expenditure – January 2006

Code	Balance £	Amendment £	Updated balance £
111	16,387.50	438.00	
112	13,265.95		
113	9,326.20		
114	3,587.90	192.00	
115	1,037.00		
121	10,385.30		
122	7,256.30	99.00	
123	3,646.70	1,323.00	
124	3,027.60		
125	926.40		
211	35,287.74	858.67	
215	-	3,134.26	
216	-		
222	1,285.47	88.54	
223	1,036.80		
225	-	5,782.27	
226	-		
234	8,385.40	183.00	
235	-	5,197.26	
236	-		
245	-	3,643.31	
246	-		
255	-	1,172.10	
256	-		

513

3

Expense	Totals £	Cutting £	Assembly £	Finishing £	Marketing £	Admin £
Blades	340	340				
Electricity 60% x 1,560	1,560	936	156	156	156	156
Advertising	550				550	
Rent 2,100 x 1,000/7,000 2,100 x 3,000/7,000 2,100 x 2,000/7,000 2,100 x 500/7,000	2,100	300	900	600	150	150
Telephone 70% x 420 30% x 420	420				294	126
	4,970	1,576	1,056	756	1,150	432
		(216)	(226)	(236)	(246)	(256)

Coding listing – Income and expenditure – January 2006

Code	Balance £	Amendment £	Updated balance £
111	16,387.50	438.00	
112	13,265.95		
113	9,326.20		
114	3,587.90	192.00	
115	1,037.00		
121	10,385.30		
122	7,256.30	99.00	
123	3,646.70	1,323.00	
124	3,027.60		
125	926.40		
211	35,287.74	858.67	
215	-	3,134.26	
216	-	1,576.00	
222	1,285.47	88.54	
223	1,036.80		
225	-	5,782.27	
226	-	1,056.00	
234	8,385.40	183.00	
235	-	5,197.26	
236	-	756.00	
245	-	3,643.31	
246	-	1,150.00	
255	-	1,172.10	
256	-	432.00	

coding – answers

4   Coding listing – Income and expenditure – January 2006

Code	Balance £	Amendment £	Updated balance £
111	16,387.50	438.00	16,825.50
112	13,265.95		13,265.95
113	9,326.20		9,326.20
114	3,587.90	192.00	3,779.90
115	1,037.00		1,037.00
121	10,385.30		10,385.30
122	7,256.30	99.00	7,355.30
123	3,646.70	1,323.00	4,969.70
124	3,027.60		3,027.60
125	926.40		926.40
211	35,287.74	858.67	36,146.41
215	-	3,134.26	3,134.26
216	-	1,576.00	1,576.00
222	1,285.47	88.54	1,374.01
223	1,036.80		1,036.80
225	-	5,782.27	5,782.27
226	-	1,056.00	1,056.00
234	8,385.40	183.00	8,568.40
235	-	5,197.26	5,197.26
236	-	756.00	756.00
245	-	3,643.31	3,643.31
246	-	1,150.00	1,150.00
255	-	1,172.10	1,172.10
256	-	432.00	432.00

5

	A	B	C	D
1	Cost code	£	£	£
2	10101	28,375	6,234	=B2+C2
3	10102	13,773	3,154	=B3+C3
4	10103	12,356	1,783	=B4+C4
5	10201	17,365	4,254	=B5+C5
6	10202	21,925	4,793	=B6+C6
7	10203	11,482	2,015	=B7+C7

answers to chapter 23: COMPARISON OF COSTS AND INCOME

1

MEMO

To: Phil McKenna

From: Jane Mitchell

Date: 5 January 2007

Subject: Comparison of December 2006 production costs

Comparison of December 2006 costs to November 2006 costs

	December 2006 £	November 2006 £
Raw materials	2,968	5,216
Labour	1,635	2,667
Expenses	372	552
Total	4,975	8,435

It should be noted that production in November is normally greater than that of December in order meet demand for the Christmas market. Therefore the December 2006 costs are also compared to the costs for the same month in the previous year.

Comparison of December 2006 costs to December 2005 costs

	December 2006 £	December 2005 £
Raw materials	2,968	2,537
Labour	1,635	1,367
Expenses	372	350
	4,975	4,254

517

2

NOTE

To: Phil McKenna

From: Jane Mitchell

Date: 5 January 2006

Comparison of December 2006 costs to budget

	December 2006 costs		
	Actual	Forecast	Variance
	£	£	£
Raw materials	2,968	2,700	268 adverse
Labour	1,635	1,650	15 favourable
Expenses	372	420	48 favourable

3

	Month		Year to date	
	Forecast	Actual	Forecast	Actual
	£	£	£	£
July	8,700	8,500	8,700	8,500
August	8,100	8,500	16,800	17,000
September	9,800	9,900	26,600	26,900
October	8,600	9,000	35,200	35,900
November	8,500	8,500	43,700	44,400
December	9,900	9,600	53,600	54,000
January	7,400	7,100	61,000	61,100
February	7,800		68,800	
March	8,400		77,200	
April	8,500		85,700	
May	8,700		94,400	
June	8,800		103,200	

4

	A	B	C	D	E
1	Cost	Actual	Budget	Variance	Percentage
2	Materials	41,705	45,000	C2–B2	=(D2/C2)*100
3	Labour	68,376	60,000	C3–B3	=(D3/C3)*100
4	Expenses	25,357	22,500	C4–B4	=(D4/C4)*100

SAMPLE SIMULATION – UNIT 1

TUBNEY TECHNOLOGY LTD

ANSWERS

Task 1

Note on sale not invoiced

The delivery to Kendrick & Co could not be invoiced because the order asks for 100 PA220 parts, but the delivery note states that 1,000 RL188 parts have been delivered.

Action to be taken

The matter should be passed to Mark Alberts for checking.

Task 1 (continued)

INVOICE

Tubney Technology Ltd
Oxford Business Park
Oxford OX2 8VN
Phone: 01865 444555
Fax 01865 444666

To: Ardington plc

Invoice number: 8950

VAT Registration: 305 034 97 63

Date/tax point: 18 September 2006

Subsidiary (sales) ledger code: 100

Description	Quantity	Price £	Total £
MM936	1,000	0.50	500.00
AD897	2,000	0.35	700.00
	Goods total		1,200.00
	Trade discount @ 0%		0.00
	Sub-total		1,200.00
	VAT @ 17.5%		202.65
	Invoice total		**1,402.65**

Settlement discount: 3.5% for payment in 14 days
(to be deducted when computing VAT)

£42.00

Task 1 (continued)

INVOICE

Tubney Technology Ltd
Oxford Business Park
Oxford OX2 8VN
Phone: 01865 444555
Fax 01865 444666

To: Dreadnought PC Ltd

Invoice number: 8951

VAT Registration: 305 034 97 63

Date/tax point: 18 September 2006

Subsidiary (sales) ledger code: 200

Description	Quantity	Price £	Total £
HighDensity 10 cm SIM cards as per quotation	500	–	1,950.00
	Goods total		1,950.00
	Trade discount @ 5%		97.50
	Sub-total		1,852.50
	VAT @ 17.5%		312.84
	Invoice total		**2,165.34**

Settlement discount: 3.5% for payment in 14 days
(to be deducted when computing VAT)

£64.83

Task 1 (continued)

INVOICE

Tubney Technology Ltd
Oxford Business Park
Oxford OX2 8VN
Phone: 01865 444555
Fax 01865 444666

To: Lineman plc

Invoice number: 8952

VAT Registration: 305 034 97 63

Date/tax point: 18 September 2006

Subsidiary (sales) ledger code: 400

Description	Quantity	Price £	Total £
AD897	3,000	0.35	1,050.00
DF014	200	3.60	720.00
GW208	150	12.80	1,920.00
		Goods total	3,690.00
		Trade discount @ 0%	0.00
		Sub-total	3,690.00
		VAT @ 17.5%	623.14
		Invoice total	**4,313.14**
Settlement discount: 3.5% for payment in 14 days (to be deducted when computing VAT)			£129.15

Task 1 (continued)

INVOICE

Tubney Technology Ltd
Oxford Business Park
Oxford OX2 8VN
Phone: 01865 444555
Fax 01865 444666

To: PrimeTime Mobiles

Invoice number: 8953

VAT Registration: 305 034 97 63

Date/tax point: 18 September 2006

Subsidiary (sales) ledger code: 500

Description	Quantity	Price £	Total £
PA220	250	5.55	1,387.50
MM936	3,000	0.50	1,500.00
		Goods total	2,887.50
		Trade discount @ 5%	144.37
		Sub-total	2,743.13
		VAT @ 17.5%	463.24
		Invoice total	**3,206.37**

Settlement discount: 3.5% for payment in 14 days
(to be deducted when computing VAT)

£96.00

Task 2

CREDIT NOTE

Tubney Technology Ltd
Oxford Business Park
Oxford OX2 8VN
Phone: 01865 444555
Fax 01865 444666

To: Kendrick & Co

Credit note number: 650

VAT Registration: 305 034 97 63

Date/tax point: 18 September 2006

Subsidiary (sales) ledger code: 300

Item	Quantity	Price £	Total £
GW208 (Original invoice 8900 dated 8 Sept)	20	12.80	256.00

Goods total	256.00
Trade discount @ 0%	0.00
Sub-total	256.00
VAT @ 17.5%	43.23
Credit note total	299.23

Task 2 (continued)

CREDIT NOTE

Tubney Technology Ltd
Oxford Business Park
Oxford OX2 8VN
Phone: 01865 444555
Fax 01865 444666

To: Rondar plc

Credit note number: 651

VAT Registration: 305 034 97 63

Date/tax point: 18 September 2006

Subsidiary (sales) ledger code: 600

Item	Quantity	Price £	Total £
PA220 (Original invoice 8905 dated 10 Sept)	15	5.55	83.25
		Goods total	83.25
		Trade discount @ 0%	0.00
		Sub-total	83.25
		VAT @ 17.5%	14.05
		Credit note total	97.30

Tasks 3 and 4

Invoices and credit notes should be authorised before despatch by: the Accounts Manager, Samir Aleffi.

Day's total settlement discount on invoices (to be agreed to discount analysis): £331.98 (42.00 + 64.83 + 129.15 + 96.00)

SALES DAY BOOK							Folio: SDB 38
Date 2006	Customer	Subsidiary (sales) ledger code: DR	Invoice number	Total £	VAT £	Net £	
18-Sept	Ardington plc	100	8950	1,402.65	202.65	1,200.00	
18-Sept	Dreadnought PC Ltd	200	8951	2,165.34	312.84	1,852.50	
18-Sept	Lineman plc	400	8952	4,313.14	623.14	3,690.00	
18-Sept	PrimeTime Mobiles	500	8953	3,206.37	463.24	2,743.13	
						830.00	
	Totals			11,087.50	1,601.87	9,485.63	
Main ledger codes				DR 2000	CR 6000	CR 4000	

Tasks 3 and 4 (continued)

SALES RETURNS DAY BOOK   Folio: SRDB 9

Date 2006	Customer	Subsidiary (sales) ledger code: DR	Credit note number	Total £	VAT £	Net £
18-Sept	Kendrick & Co	300	650	299.23	43.23	256.00
18-Sept	Rondar plc	600	651	97.30	14.05	83.25
	Totals			396.53	57.28	339.25
Main ledger codes				CR 2000	DR 6000	DR 5000

Tasks 4 and 7

MAIN LEDGER

2000 SALES LEDGER CONTROL ACCOUNT

Date 2006	Details	Folio	Amount £	Date 2006	Details	Folio	Amount £
18-Sept	Invoices	SDB 38	11,087.50	18-Sept	Credit notes	SRDB 9	396.53
				18-Sept	Receipts	CB 38	11,413.67
				18-Sept	Discount allowed	CB 38	129.66

3000 DISCOUNT ALLOWED

Date 2006	Details	Folio	Amount £	Date 2006	Details	Folio	Amount £
18-Sept	Receipts	CB 38	29.66				

4000 SALES

Date 2006	Details	Folio	Amount £	Date 2006	Details	Folio	Amount £
				18-Sept	Invoices	SDB 38	9,485.63

5000 SALES RETURNS

Date 2006	Details	Folio	Amount £	Date 2006	Details	Folio	Amount £
18-Sept	Credit notes	SRDB 9	339.25				

6000 VAT

Date 2006	Details	Folio	Amount £	Date 2006	Details	Folio	Amount £
18-Sept	Credit notes	SRDB 9	57.28	18-Sept	Invoices	SDB 38	1,601.87

SUBSIDIARY (SALES) LEDGER

100 ARDINGTON PLC

Date 2006	Details	Folio	Amount £	Date 2006	Details	Folio	Amount £
22-Aug	Inv 8790	SDB 34	512.84	18-Sept	Cheque	CB 38	512.84
18-Sept	Inv 8950	SDB 38	1,402.65				

200 DREADNOUGHT PLC LTD

Date 2006	Details	Folio	Amount £	Date 2006	Details	Folio	Amount £
19-Aug	Inv 8750	SDB 34	9,993.88	18-Sept	Cheque	CB 9	9,939.88
18-Sept	Inv 8951	SDB 38	2,165.34	18-Sept	Balance c/d		2,219.34
			12,159.22	18-Sept	Discount allowed	CB 38	12,159.22

300 KENDRICK & CO

Date 2006	Details	Folio	Amount £	Date 2006	Details	Folio	Amount £
5-Sept	Inv 8890	SDB 36	420.79	18-Sept	CN 650	SRDB 9	299.23
8-Sept	Inv 8900	SDB 37	1,496.16	18-Sept	Cash	CB 38	408.19
				18-Sept	Disc allowed	CB 38	12.60
				18-Sept	Balance c/d		1,196.93
			1,916.95				1,916.95

400 LINEMAN PLC

Date 2006	Details	Folio	Amount £	Date 2006	Details	Folio	Amount £
8-Sept	Inv 8910	SDB 37	569.820	18-Sept	BACS	CB 38	552.76
18-Sept	Inv 8952	SDB 38	4,313.14	18-Sept	Disc allowed	CB 38	17.06

500 PRIMETIME MOBILES

Date 2006	Details	Folio	Amount £	Date 2006	Details	Folio	Amount £
20-Aug	Inv 8765	SDB 34	4,264.05				
18-Sept	Inv 8953	SDB 38	3,206.37				

600 RONDAR PLC

Date 2006	Details	Folio	Amount £	Date 2006	Details	Folio	Amount £
13-May	Inv 6535	SDB 7	169.86	18-Sept	Credit note 651	SRDB 9	97.30
2-Jun	Inv 6590	SDB 10	210.87				

700 SLOMAX & PARTNERS

Date 2006	Details	Folio	Amount £	Date 2006	Details	Folio	Amount £
18-Sept	Balance b/d		3,972.09				

Task 5

Notes

Wrongly completed cheque

The cheque from the PrimeTime Mobiles cannot be paid in as it has not been signed.

Action to be taken

Return the cheque to the customer, requesting a properly completed one.

Disagreement with supporting documentation

The Dreadnought PC Ltd cheque agrees with the customer's supporting documentation, its remittance advice, but both disagree with the subsidiary (sales) ledger account and the discount analysis. This is because there is a transposition error of £54 in the customer's records.

Action to be taken

Pay in the cheque, but write to the customer pointing out that it has made a recording error and so has underpaid by £54, so this amount is still outstanding.

Task 5 (continued)

Contents of envelope handed in by Mark Albert with Kendrick & Co receipt

Value	Number	Total value £
£50	4	200.00
£20	8	160.00
£10	4	40.00
£5	1	5.00
£2	0	0.00
£1	2	2.00
50p	1	0.50
20p	2	0.40
10p	1	0.10
5p	3	0.15
2p	1	0.02
1p	2	0.02
		408.19

Tasks 6 and 8

MAIN LEDGER

1000 CASH BOOK CB 38

RECEIPTS

Date 2006	Details	Ref	Receipt £	Discount allowed £	Customer account £	Subsidiary (sales) ledger code
18-Sept	Kendrick & Co	Cash	408.19	12.60	408.19	300
18-Sept	Ardington plc	Cheque	512.84	0.00	512.84	100
18-Sept	Dreadnought PC Ltd	Cheque	9,939.88	0.00	9,939.88	200
	Paying in total		10,860.91			
17-Sept	Lineman plc	BACS	552.76	17.06	552.76	400
			11,413.67	29.66	11,413.67	
Main ledger codes				DR 3000	CR 2000	
				CR 2000		

sample simulation – unit 1 – answers

Task 7

Date: 18-Sept-06	Paid in by		

Please detail cheques and cash overleaf

	£	p
NOTES £50	200	00
£20	160	00
£10	40	00
£5	5	00
£2	0	00
£1	2	00
50p	0	50
20p, 10p, 5p	0	65
2p, 1p	0	04
TOTAL CASH	408	19
Cheques	10,452	72
£	**10,860**	**91**

Bank giro credit

Bank: Oxford Bank plc
High Street, Oxford, Ox2 7DF

Account: Tubney Technology Ltd

Paid in by: Lynsey Jones

NUMBER OF CHEQUES: 2

Sort code: 25 - 45 - 78
Account number: 98746510

Details of cheques	Amount	
	£	p
Ardington plc	512	84
Dreadnought PC Ltd	9,939	88
Total cheques carried over	**10,452**	**72**

Task 9

STATEMENT

Tubney Technology Ltd
Oxford Business Park
Oxford OX2 8VN

To: Dreadnought PC Ltd

Date: 18 September 2006

Subsidiary (sales) ledger code: 200

Date 2006	Transaction reference	Debit £	Credit £	Amount
19-Aug	Invoice 8750	9,993.88		9,993.88
18-Sept	Invoice 8951	2,165.34		12,159.22
18-Sept	Cheque received		9,939.88	2,219.34

Balance outstanding 2,219.34

Our terms are strictly 30 days, with 3.5% cash settlement discount available for payment within 14 days.

Task 9 (continued)

STATEMENT

Tubney Technology Ltd
Oxford Business Park
Oxford OX2 8VN

To: Kendrick & Co

Date: 18 September 2006

Subsidiary (sales) ledger code: 200

Date 2006	Transaction reference	Debit £	Credit £	Amount
5-Sept	Invoice 8890	420.79		420.79
8-Sept	Invoice 8900	1,496.16		1,916.95
18-Sept	Credit note 650		299.23	1,617.72
18-Sept	Cash received - thank you		408.19	1,209.53
18-Sept	Settlement discount given		12.60	1,196.93

Balance outstanding 1,196.93

Our terms are strictly 30 days, with 3.5% cash settlement discount available for payment within 14 days.

Task 10

Tubney Technology Ltd
Oxford Business Park, Oxford OX2 8VN
Phone: 01865 444555 Fax: 01865 444666

Ms U Ogangwe
Slomax & Partners
Success House
200 Old Kent Road
London SE2 9CV

18 September 2006

Dear Ms Ogangwe

Account 700: Current balance £3,972.09

We recently received your cheque for £2,078.65. Unfortunately the date on this cheque is 16 September 2005, so we were unable to bank it as the bank would reject it as out of date. I enclose the cheque. Please either amend the date or reissue it with correct details.

I would remind you that this substantial portion of your total debt (£2,078.65) is now more than 60 days old, and the remainder (£1,893.44) is also overdue.

Our credit terms are strictly 30 days. Our policy is for any account that becomes more than 60 days old to be automatically put 'on stop' until it is settled in full. I regret to tell you, therefore, that we will not be able to make any further supplies to you until we receive a cheque in settlement of your entire debt.

Once we have received a cheque for £3,972.09 (please ensure that it is dated 2006) we can return to normal trading with you, and will be able to fulfil the order that we received from you yesterday.

If you wish to discuss this matter further, please give me a call.

Yours sincerely

Samir Aleffi

Accounts Manager

Task 10 (continued)

MEMO

To: Mark Alberts, Sales Manager
From: Lynsey Jones, Accounts Assistant
CC: Samir Aleffi, Accounts Manager
Subject: Kendrick & Co payment method
Date: 18 September 2006

As your floor limit is only £100, you would have to call the credit card company to gain authorisation for Mr Kendrick to use his corporate credit card in payment of the firm's debts. In itself this should not be a problem, but it is subject to the credit limit on his card account.

Kendrick & Co's current account balance with us is £1,196.93, so it may not be possible for Mr Kendrick to settle the full balance with the credit card because he may not have sufficient credit on his card. However, he could pay us with cash or a cheque for any excess amount.

If he comes in tomorrow to do this then he will be able to take advantage of the settlement discount that is still available on Invoice 8900.

Lynsey

Task 11

EMAIL

From: lynsey.jones@tubneytech.co.uk

To: samir.aleffi@tubneytech.co.uk

CC:

Subject: Computerisation

Date: 18 September 2006

Message:

Hi Samir

Moving to a fully computerised accounts system does not mean that we have to move to a different sequence of invoice and credit note numbers, or different ledger codes. The computer can be programmed to make use of the same codes as we use manually, so disruption here should not occur.

We currently input invoice, credit note and cash receipts details to the computer.

This then produces the discount analysis and aged debtors analysis. If we computerise further these details could also be used by the system to draw up computerised day books (for sales, sales returns and cash), to post the day books to the main and subsidiary (sales) ledgers, and to prepare customer statements from the subsidiary (sales) ledger.

SAMPLE SIMULATION – UNIT 2

AMICA PRINTING CO.

ANSWERS

sample simulation – unit 2 – answers

Tasks 1 and 3

INVOICE

Abingdon Paper Ltd
Milton Park
Abingdon
Oxon OX13 9AS
T: 01235 412233
F: 01235 412866

To: Amica Printing Company
McLaren Trading Estate
Wantage OX2 8SD

VAT Registration: 9175698745

Date/tax point: 22 September 2006

Quantity	Description	Unit amount £	Total £
5	100gsm Nordic White A1	200.00	1,000.00
4	260gsm Polar Ice A1	350.00	1,400.00
	Good total		2,400.00
	Trade discount @ 5%		120.00
	Sub-total		2,280.00
	VAT @ 17.5%		399.00
	Invoice total		2,679.00

Terms
30 days net
E & OE

Errors or discrepancies: None.

Action to be taken: Record in purchase day book.

Invoice number: 6070

Tasks 1 and 3 (continued)

INVOICE
Feltham Bindery Ltd
Chertsey Road Trading Estate
Feltham
Middlesex TW12 5AB
T/F: 020 8371 5987

To: Amica Printing Company
McLaren Trading Estate
Wantage OX12 8SD

VAT Registration: 6873687344

Date/tax point: 22 September 2006

Description	Rate £	Total £
Consultancy report on installation of fully automated binding line, as per Sam Fisher's purchase order of 2 September 2006, and conversation with Alex Cook	4,250.00	4,250.00
Sub-total		4,250.00
VAT @ 17.5%		743.75
Invoice total		**4,993.75**

Terms: strictly 30 days net

Terms
30 days net
E & OE

Errors or discrepancies:
Amount charged does not agree with Sam Fisher's purchase order of 2 September.

Action to be taken:
Do not record in purchase day book. Talk to Alex Cook.

Invoice number: N/A

Tasks 1 and 3 (continued)

INVOICE

HAMBURG PRINT PLATES LTD
Highgrove Road
Newbury
Berks NY9 4BW
T: 01461 476431
F: 01461 547643

To: Amica Printing Company
McLaren Trading Estate
Wantage OX12 8SD

VAT Registration: 0547351034

Date/tax point: 22 September 2006

Description	Quantity	Rate £	Total £
Myobi 600 press plates	70	37.50	2,625.00
Hamburg 1000 print press plates	50	35.00	1,750.00
Hamburg 250 print press plates	100	25.00	2,500.00
		Goods total	6,875.00
		Trade discount @ 0%	0.00
		Sub-total	6,875.00
		VAT @ 17.5%	1,167.03
		Invoice total	8,042.03
Cash (settlement) discount: 3% for payment in 7 days (to be deducted when computing VAT), otherwise 30 days net			£206.25

Errors or discrepancies: None.

Action to be taken: Record in purchase day book.

Invoice number: 6071

Tasks 1 and 3 (continued)

INVOICE

Ilsley Inks Ltd
Ridgeway House
East Ilsley
Berks NY7 1LS
T: 01461 7576764
F: 01461 343463

To: Amica Printing Company
McLaren Trading Estate
Wantage OX12 8SD

VAT Registration: 0917757537

Date/tax point: 22 September 2006

Description	Quantity	Rate £	Total £
Cyan ink for Hamburg colour presses	15	20.00	300.00
Yellow ink for Myobi presses	20	12.50	250.00
		Goods total	550.00
		Trade discount @ 5%	27.50
		Sub-total	522.50
		VAT @ 17.5%	91.43
		Invoice total	613.93

Terms: strictly 30 days net

Errors or discrepancies:
No evidence that goods have been delivered.

Action to be taken:
Do not record in purchase day book. Check whether Edward Hunt has purchase orders, delivery notes or goods received notes.

Invoice number: N/A

sample simulation – unit 2 – answers

Tasks 1 and 3 (continued)

INVOICE

Sidney Stationers Ltd
40 Market Square
Wantage OX12 5KK
T: 01235 497611
F: 01235 576643

To: Amica Printing Company
McLaren Trading Estate
Wantage OX12 8SD

VAT Registration: 1473658734

Date/tax point: 22 September 2006

Description	Quantity	Price £	Total £
A4 lever arch files – red	200	1.49	298.00
	Goods total		298.00
	Trade discount	0%	0.00
	Sub-total		298.00
	VAT	17.5%	52.15
	Invoice total		350.15

Terms: strictly 30 days net

Errors or discrepancies: None.

Action to be taken: Record in purchase day book.

Invoice number: 6072

Tasks 1 and 3 (continued)

INVOICE

Wantage Engineering Ltd
Grove Road
Wantage OX12 7SM
T: 01235 232155
F: 01235 235698

To: Amica Printing Company
McLaren Trading Estate
Wantage OX12 8SD

VAT Registration: 4654646446

Date/tax point: 22 September 2006

Description	Quantity	Price £	Total £
Print press cleaning fluid	50 litres	6.50	250.00
Machine oil	10 litres	5.00	60.00
Press tester units	25	15.00	475.00
Goods total			785.00
Trade discount		10%	78.00
Sub-total			707.00
VAT		17.5%	123.72
Invoice total			**830.72**

Cash (settlement) discount: 1% for payment in 21 days
(to be deducted when computing VAT), otherwise 30 days net — £7.07

Errors or discrepancies:
- Cross-casts wrong.
- Trade discount correctly stated at 10% but the full 10% has not been deducted.
- Cash (settlement) discount correctly calculated at 1%, but not deducted when computing VAT.

Action to be taken: Do not record. Send letter to supplier.

Invoice number: N/A

Tasks 1 and 2

Notes for conversation with Alex Cook
Re: Invoice from Feltham Bindery Ltd dated 22 September 2006

The amount of £4,250 plus VAT charged for the consultancy report on installing a binding line does not agree with the purchase order, which is for £3,250 plus VAT. The supplier's invoice states that the amount was agreed with Alex. Can she please clarify?

Notes for conversation with Edward Hunt
Re: Invoice from Ilsley Inks Ltd dated 22 September 2006

No documentation can be found to suggest that these inks were either ordered or delivered. Does Edward have the purchase order, delivery note and goods received note?

Task 1

AMICA PRINTING COMPANY

McLaren Trading Estate, Wantage OX12 8SD

Tel: 01235 687465 Fax: 01235 687412

Wantage Engineering
Grove Road
Wantage OX12 7SM

23 September 2006

Dear Sir/Madam

I am returning your invoice to us dated 22 September. I am afraid that we cannot record it as it contains a number of errors:

- while the unit prices stated on the invoice are correct, they have been crosscast incorrectly.

- trade discount of 10% has been correctly stated, but the actual calculation is wrong.

- the cash (settlement) discount of 1% has not been deducted when computing VAT. This means that the amount of VAT is incorrect.

Please send us a corrected invoice as soon as possible.

Yours faithfully

Hei Lam Cheng

Accounts Assistant

sample simulation – unit 2 – answers

Tasks 2 and 3

CREDIT NOTE

HAMBURG PRINT PLATES LTD
Highgrove Road
Newbury
Berks NY9 4BW
T: 01461 476431
F: 01461 547643

To: Amica Printing Company
McLaren Trading Estate
Wantage OX12 8SD

VAT Registration: 0547351034

Date/tax point: 22 September 2006

Description	Quantity	Rate £	Total £
Hamburg 500 print press plates **Reason for credit** Damaged (part of batch delivered and invoiced 15 September 2006)	5	30.00	150.00
Goods total			150.00
Trade discount @ 0%			0.00
Sub-total			150.00
VAT @ 17.5%			25.46
Credit note total			**175.46**

Reduce cash (settlement) discount on original invoice by £4.50

Errors or discrepancies: None.

Action to be taken: Record in purchase returns day book.

Credit note number: 277

Tasks 2 and 3 (continued)

CREDIT NOTE

Ilsley Inks Ltd
Ridgeway House
East Ilsley
Berks NY7 1LS
T: 01461 7576764
F: 01461 343463

To: Amica Printing Company
McLaren Trading Estate
Wantage OX12 8SD

VAT Registration: 0917757537

Date/tax point: 22 September 2006

Description	Unit price £	Total £
Special order pigment 291 – 10 kilos	25.00	250.00
Reason for credit Incorrect pigment delivered and invoiced 15 September 2006		
Goods total		250.00
Trade discount @ 5%		12.50
Sub-total		237.50
VAT @ 17.5%		41.56
Credit note total		279.06

Errors or discrepancies: None.

Action to be taken: Record in purchase returns day book.

Credit note number: 278

Tasks 3 and 4

PURCHASE DAY BOOK							Folio: PDB 30
Invoice number	Supplier	Subsidiary (purchases) ledger code	Date 2006	Total £	VAT £	Purchases £	Stationery £
6070	Abingdon Paper	1101	22 Sept	2,679.00	399.00	2,280.00	
6071	Hamburg Print	1103	22 Sept	8,042.03	1,167.03	6,875.00	
6072	Sidney Stationers	1105	22 Sept	350.15	52.15		298.00
	Total			11,071.18	1,618.18	9,155.00	298.00
Main ledger codes				110 CR	220 DR	190 DR	210 DR

Tasks 3 and 4 (continued)

PURCHASE RETURNS DAY BOOK   Folio: PRDB 6

Credit note number	Supplier	Subsidiary (purchases) ledger code	Date 2006	Total £	VAT £	Purchases Returns £	Stationery £
277	Hamburg Print	1103	22 Sept	175.46	25.46	150.00	
278	Ilsley Inks	1104	22 Sept	279.06	41.56	237.50	
	Total			454.52	67.02	387.50	
Main ledger codes				110 DR	220 CR	200 CR	

sample simulation – unit 2 – answers

Tasks 4 and 10

MAIN LEDGER

090 ADMINISTRATION

Date 2006	Details	Folio	Amount £	Date 2006	Details	Folio	Amount £
23 Sept	Cash book payments	CB 30	300.00				

110 PURCHASE LEDGER CONTROL ACCOUNT

Date 2006	Details	Folio	Amount £	Date 2006	Details	Folio	Amount £
23 Sept	Purchase returns	PRDB6	454.52	22 Sept	Balance b/d		7,186.79
23 Sept	CB payments	CB 30	12,008.65	23 Sept	Purchases	PDB 30	11,071.18
23 Sept	Discount rec'd	CB 30	201.75				
23 Sept	Balance c/d		5,593.05				
			18,257.97				18,257.97
				24 Sept	Balance b/d		5,593.05

120 DISCOUNT RECEIVED

Date 2006	Details	Folio	Amount £	Date 2006	Details	Folio	Amount £
				23 Sept	Discount rec'd	CB 30	201.75

Tasks 4 and 10 (continued)

MAIN LEDGER

130 FACTORY WAGES CONTROL

Date 2006	Details	Folio	Amount £	Date 2006	Details	Folio	Amount £
23 Sept	Net pay	CB 30	4,569.53	23 Sept	Total gross pay	Payroll Month 6	6,198.21
23 Sept	PAYE	Payroll Month 6	1,206.65				
23 Sept	Total ee's NIC	Payroll Month 6	422.03				

140 FACTORY WAGES EXPENSE

Date 2006	Details	Folio	Amount £	Date 2006	Details	Folio	Amount £
23 Sept	Total gross pay	Payroll Month 6	6,198.21				
23 Sept	Total er's NIC	Payroll Month 6	426.55				

150 PAYE/NIC CREDITOR

Date 2006	Details	Folio	Amount £	Date 2006	Details	Folio	Amount £
				23 Sept	PAYE	Payroll Month 6	1,206.65
				23 Sept	Ee's NIC	Payroll Month 6	422.03
				23 Sept	Total er's NIC	Payroll Month 6	426.55

170 POSTAGE

Date 2006	Details	Folio	Amount £	Date 2006	Details	Folio	Amount £

Tasks 4 and 10 (continued)

MAIN LEDGER

180 PRODUCTION EXPENSES

Date 2006	Details	Folio	Amount £	Date 2006	Details	Folio	Amount £
23 Sept	Petty cash	PCB 30	13.61				

190 PURCHASES

Date 2006	Details	Folio	Amount £	Date 2006	Details	Folio	Amount £
23 Sept	Purchases	PDB 30	9,155.00				

200 PURCHASES RETURNS

Date 2006	Details	Folio	Amount £	Date 2006	Details	Folio	Amount £
				23 Sept	Purchase returns	PRDB 6	387.50

210 STATIONERY

Date 2006	Details	Folio	Amount £	Date 2006	Details	Folio	Amount £
23 Sept	Purchases	PDB 30	298.00				
23 Sept	Petty cash	PCB 30	5.95				

Tasks 4 and 10 (continued)

MAIN LEDGER

220 VAT

Date 2006	Details	Folio	Amount £	Date 2006	Details	Folio	Amount £
23 Sept	Purchases	PDB 30	1,618.18	23 Sept	Purchase returns	PRDB 6	67.02
23 Sept	Petty cash	PCB 30	3.42				

SUBSIDIARY (PURCHASES) LEDGER

1101 ABINGDON PAPER LTD

Date 2006	Details	Folio	Amount £	Date 2006	Details	Folio	Amount £
23 Sept	Payment	CB 30	2,511.56	2 Sept	Invoice 5980	PDB27	✓2,511.56
23 Sept	Balance c/d		2,679.00	23 Sept	Invoice 6070	PDB 30	2,679.00
			5,190.56				5,190.56
				24 Sept	Balance b/d		2,679.00

1102 FELTHAM BINDERY LTD

Date 2006	Details	Folio	Amount £	Date 2006	Details	Folio	Amount £

Tasks 4 and 10 (continued)

SUBSIDIARY (PURCHASES) LEDGER

1103 HAMBURG PRINT PLATES LTD

Date 2006	Details	Folio	Amount £	Date 2006	Details	Folio	Amount £
23 Sept	Credit note 277	PRDB 6	✓ 175.46	5 Sept	Invoice 5982	PDB27	✓1,017.68
23 Sept	Payment	CB 30	8,682.50	15 Sept	Invoice 6040	PDB 29	1,754.62
23 Sept	Discount rec'd	CB 30	201.75	23 Sept	Invoice 6071	PDB 30	✓8,042.03
23 Sept	Balance c/d		1,754.62				
			10,814.33				10,814.33
				24 Sept	Balance b/d		1,754.62

1104 ILSLEY INKS LTD

Date 2006	Details	Folio	Amount £	Date 2006	Details	Folio	Amount £
23 Sept	Credit note 278	PRDB 6	279.06	2 Sept	Invoice 5985	PDB27	✓ 726.46
23 Sept	Payment	CB 30	726.46	15 Sept	Invoice 6042	PDB29	1,088.34
23 Sept	Balance c/d		809.28				
			1,814.80				1,814.80
				24 Sept	Balance b/d		809.28

1105 SIDNEY STATIONERS LTD

Date 2006	Details	Folio	Amount £	Date 2006	Details	Folio	Amount £
29 Aug	Credit note 250	PRDB5	✓17.62	28 Aug	Invoice 5965	PDB26	✓105.75
23 Sept	Payment	CB 30	88.13	23 Sept	Invoice 6072	PDB 30	350.15
23 Sept	Balance c/d		350.15				
			455.90				455.90
				24 Sept	Balance b/d		350.15

1106 WANTAGE ENGINEERING LTD

Date 2006	Details	Folio	Amount £	Date 2006	Details	Folio	Amount £

Task 5

STATEMENT

Lam,
Please pay ticked item.
Alex Cook

Abingdon Paper Ltd
Milton Park
Abingdon
Oxon OX13 9AS
T: 01235 412233
F: 01235 412866

To: Amica Printing Company
McLaren Trading Estate
Wantage OX12 8SD

VAT Registration: 9175698745

Date: 22 September 2006

Date	Transaction reference	Amount
1 Sept 2006	Invoice	2,511.56 ✓
22 Sept 2006	Invoice	2,679.00

Balance outstanding 5,190.56

Our terms are strictly net 30 days

Discount to be taken: None

Discrepancies: None

Action to be taken about discrepancies: None

Tasks 5 and 9

STATEMENT

HAMBURG PRINT PLATES LTD
Highgrove Road
Newbury
Berks NY9 4BW
T: 01461 476431
F: 01461 547643

Iam,
Please pay ticked items.
Cash discount of £201.75 to be
taken on invoice and credit note
dated 22 September 06.
Alex Cook

To: Amica Printing Company
McLaren Trading Estate
Wantage OX12 8SD

VAT Registration: 0547351034

Date: 22 September 2006

Date	Transaction reference	Amount
4 Sept 2006	Invoice	1,017.68 ✓
15 Sept 2006	Invoice	1,754.62
22 Sept 2006	Credit note	-175.46 ✓
22 Sept 2006	Invoice	8,042.03 ✓

Balance outstanding 10,638.87

3% settlement (cash) discount is available for payment within 7 days. Otherwise, our terms are strictly net 30 days.

Discount to be taken:
£206.25 on invoice dated 22-Sept-06 less £4.50 on credit note dated 22-Sept-06 = £201.75

Discrepancies:
None

Action to be taken about discrepancies:
None

Task 5 (continued)

STATEMENT

Ilsley Inks Ltd
Ridgeway House
East Ilsley
Berks NY7 1LS
T: 01461 7576764 F: 01461 343463

Lam,
Please pay ticked item.
Alex Cook

To: Amica Printing Company
McLaren Trading Estate
Wantage OX12 8SD

VAT Registration: 0917757537

Date: 22 September 2006

Date	Transaction reference	Amount
1 Sept 2006	Invoice	726.46 ✓
22 Sept 2006	Invoice	1,088.34
22 Sept 2006	Credit note	-279.06

Balance outstanding 1,535.74

Our terms are strictly net 30 days

Discount to be taken: None

Discrepancies: None

Action to be taken about discrepancies: None

sample simulation – unit 2 – answers

Task 5 (continued)

STATEMENT

Lam,
Please pay ticked items.
Alex Cook

Sidney Stationers Ltd
40 Market Square
Wantage
OX12 5KK
T: 01235 497611
F: 01235 576643

To: Amica Printing Company
McLaren Trading Estate
Wantage OX12 8SD

VAT Registration: 1473658734

Date: 22 September 2006

Date	Transaction reference	Amount
27 Aug 2006	Invoice	105.75 ✓
28 Aug 2006	Credit note	-17.62 ✓
22 Sept 2006	Invoice	350.15

Balance outstanding 438.28

Our terms are strictly net 30 days

Discount to be taken: None

Discrepancies: None

Action to be taken about discrepancies: None

Task 5 (continued)

REMITTANCE ADVICE

Amica Printing Company, McLaren Trading Estate, Wantage OX12 8SD
Tel: 01235 687465 Fax: 01235 687412

Supplier: Abingdon Paper Ltd

Subsidiary (purchase) ledger code: 1101

Date	Transaction reference	Amount (£)
2 September	Invoice	2,511.56
23 September	Cheque enclosed	-2,511.56

REMITTANCE ADVICE

Amica Printing Company, McLaren Trading Estate, Wantage OX12 8SD
Tel: 01235 687465 Fax: 01235 687412

Supplier: Hamburg Print Plates Ltd

Subsidiary (purchase) ledger code: 1103

Date	Transaction reference	Amount (£)
5 September	Invoice	1,017.68
23 September	Credit note	-175.46
23 September	Invoice	8,042.03
23 September	Cash discount taken	-201.75
23 September	Payment by BACS	-8,682.50

Task 5 (continued)

REMITTANCE ADVICE

Amica Printing Company, McLaren Trading Estate, Wantage OX12 8SD
Tel: 01235 687465 Fax: 01235 687412

Supplier: Ilsley Inks Ltd

Subsidiary (purchase) ledger code: 1104

Date	Transaction reference	Amount (£)
2 September	Invoice	726.46
23 September	Cheque enclosed	-726.46

REMITTANCE ADVICE

Amica Printing Company, McLaren Trading Estate, Wantage OX12 8SD
Tel: 01235 687465 Fax: 01235 687412

Supplier: Sidney Stationers Ltd

Subsidiary (purchase) ledger code: 1105

Date	Transaction reference	Amount (£)
28 August	Invoice	105.75
29 August	Credit note	-17.62
23 September	Cheque enclosed	-88.13

Task 5 (continued)

Notes re: non-payment of cheque requisition

There is insufficient supporting evidence for the payment of the cheque requisition to Yarnton Estates Ltd. The cheque requisition does not state the nature of the expenditure, so it cannot be analysed. It should therefore be discussed with Alex Cook, who should decide whether payment can be made.

Tasks 5, 6, 9 and 10

MAIN LEDGER

100 CASH BOOK PAYMENTS — CB 30

Date 2006	Details	Cheque number/ BACS ref	Folio	Payment £	Admin £	Factory wages £	Petty cash £	Suppliers £	Discount received £	Subsidiary (purchases) ledger codes
23 Sept	Hamburg Print Plates Ltd	BACS	Remittance	8,682.50				8,682.50	201.75	1103
23 Sept	Abingdon Paper Ltd	Chq 546611	Remittance	2,511.56				2,511.56		1101
23 Sept	Ilsley Inks Ltd	Chq 546612	Remittance	726.46				726.46		1104
23 Sept	Sidney Stationers Ltd	Chq 546613	Remittance	88.13				88.13		1105
23 Sept	Children in Need	Chq 546614	Cheque req	300.00	300.00					
23 Sept	P Allen	Chq 546615	Payroll	732.73		732.73				
23 Sept	U Gupta	Chq 546616	Payroll	175.87		175.87				
23 Sept	Permanent payroll	BACS	Payroll	3,660.93		3,660.93				
23 Sept	Petty cash	Chq 546617	PCB 30	242.10			242.10			
				17,120.28	300.00	4,569.53	242.10	12,008.65	201.75	
			DR		090	130		110		
Main ledger codes			CR						110 120	

Task 6

Amica Printing Company				
Employee: Pippa Allen	Employee no: FT683			
NI No: KS 82 01 92 M	Tax code: 475L	Date: 26 Sept 2006	Tax period: Mth 6	
Pay for FOUR weeks ending: 19 September 2006	Hours	Rate (£)	AMOUNT (£)	YEAR TO DATE (£)
Basic hours	150.00	5.50	825.00	
Time and a half	12.00	8.25	99.00	
Bonus		15.00	15.00	
PAY FOR PERIOD			939.00	4,695.00
PAYE			149.93	899.57
Employees' NI (Employer's NI £61.28)			56.34	
TOTAL DEDUCTIONS			206.27	
NET PAY			732.73	

Errors or discrepancies: None

Action to be taken: None

Task 6 (continued)

Amica Printing Company				
Employee: Usha Gupta	Employee no: FT685			
NI No: WL 29 30 48 P	Tax code: BR		Date: 26 Sept 2006	Tax period: Mth 6
Pay for FOUR weeks ending: 19 September 2006	Hours	Rate (£)	AMOUNT (£)	YEAR TO DATE (£)
Basic hours	37.50	5.50	206.25	
Time and a half	4.00	8.25	33.00	
Bonus		5.00	5.00	
PAY FOR PERIOD			244.25	244.25
PAYE			53.73	53.73
Employees' NI (Employer's NI £17.50)			14.65	
TOTAL DEDUCTIONS			68.38	
NET PAY			175.87	

Errors or discrepancies: None

Action to be taken: None

Tasks 6 and 10

FACTORY PAYROLL MONTH 6

Employee:	Employee number	Pay for period £	PAYE £	Employee's NIC £	Net pay £	Employer's NIC £
Temporary factory payroll total						
Permanent factory payroll total		5,014.96	1,002.99	351.04	3,660.93	347.77
Total factory payroll						
Main ledger codes DR		140	130	130		140
CR		130	150	150		150
Payment by BACS - permanent						
Payment by cheque						

Task 7

EMAIL

To: henrylynch@amica.co.uk

From: heilamcheng@amica.co.uk

CC:

Subject: Larry Haynes

Date: 23 September 2006

Message:

Hi Henry

Thank you for your email regarding Larry Haynes. Sorry, but I could not leave the copy payslips and other details on your desk this morning as the documents are connected to the payroll and hence are highly confidential. I am also concerned about the security aspects of leaving such information on a desk.

To help Mr Haynes, I suggest that he comes to the office here, with you if he chooses, so I can hand the information to him in person.

Task 8

PETTY CASH VOUCHER

Number: *099* Date: 23 Sept 2006

Expenditure   *Amount*

Stationery	Net	5.95
	VAT	1.04
	Gross	6.99

Supporting documentation:
Receipt dated 22 September 2006

Paid to:
Edward Hunt 23 September 2006

PETTY CASH VOUCHER

Number: *100* Date: 23 Sept 2006

Expenditure   *Amount*

Production expenses	Net	13.61
	VAT	2.38
	Gross	15.99

Supporting documentation:
Receipt dated 22 September 2006

Paid to:
Larry Haynes 23 September 2006

Notes on why not all receipts have been paid out

The Post Office receipt, at £50.90, exceeds the authorised limit for claims to be paid out of petty cash. Martha Collins should be advised to submit an expenses claim form.

Task 8 (continued)

PETTY CASH LISTING

Notes and coin in box	In petty cash box as at 22-Sept-06 £	To be paid out 23-Sept-06			In petty cash box as at 23-Sept-06 £
		Voucher number: 099 £	Voucher number: 100 £	Voucher number: £	
£50	0.00				
£20	40.00				40.00
£10	20.00		10.00		10.00
£5	15.00	5.00	5.00		5.00
£2	0.00				
£1	3.00	1.00			2.00
50p	1.50	0.50	0.50		0.50
20p	1.00	0.40	0.40		0.20
10p	0.20				0.20
5p	0.10	0.05	0.05		
2p	0.04	0.04			
1p	0.04		0.04		
Total	80.88	6.99	15.99		57.90

Tasks 8 and 10

160 PETTY CASH BOOK — PCB 30

Date 2006	Details	Receipts £	Date 2006	Voucher number	Payments £	Postage £	Production expenses £	Stationery £	VAT £
22 Sept	Balance b/d	80.88	23 Sept	099	6.99			5.95	1.04
			23 Sept	100	15.99		13.61		2.38
				Totals	22.98		13.61	5.95	3.42
				Interim Balance c/d	57.90				
23 Sept	Balance b/d	80.88			80.88				
23 Sept	Cash	57.90							
		242.10	23 Sept	End of day balance c/d	300.00				
23 Sept		300.00			300.00				
Main ledger codes				**DR**			180	210	220
				CR					

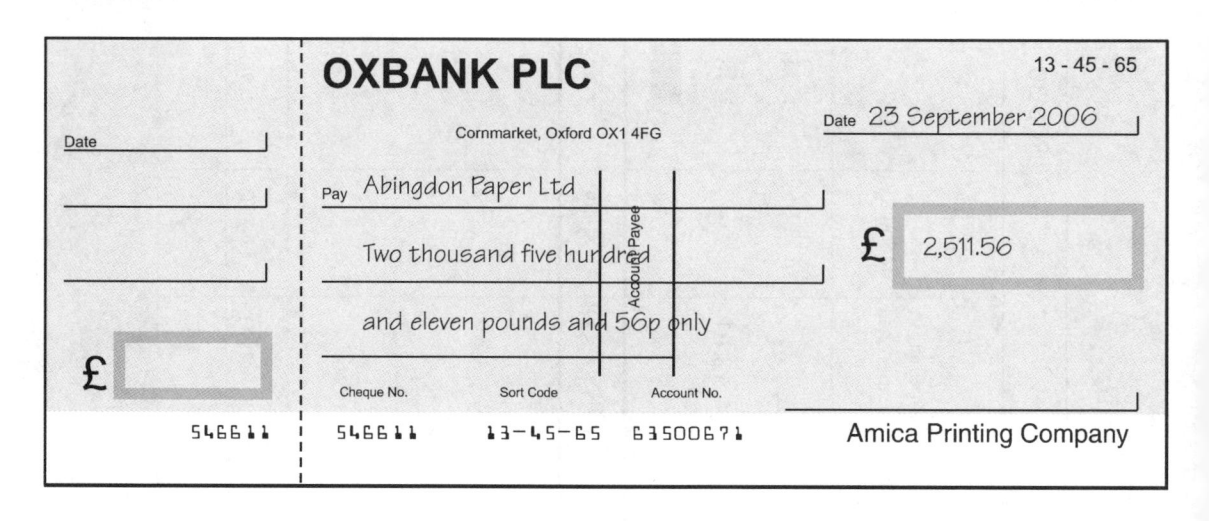

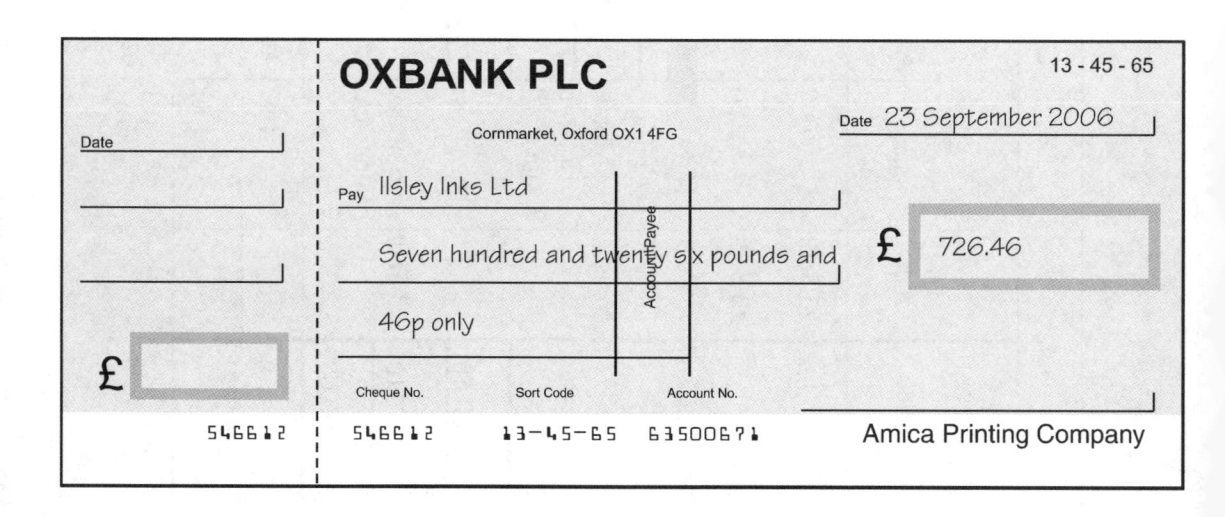

Task 9

OXBANK PLC
Cornmarket, Oxford OX1 4FG
13 - 45 - 65
Date 23 September 2006

Pay Abingdon Paper Ltd

Two thousand five hundred and eleven pounds and 56p only

£ 2,511.56

Cheque No. 546611   Sort Code 13-45-65   Account No. 63500671

Amica Printing Company

OXBANK PLC
Cornmarket, Oxford OX1 4FG
13 - 45 - 65
Date 23 September 2006

Pay Ilsley Inks Ltd

Seven hundred and twenty six pounds and 46p only

£ 726.46

Cheque No. 546612   Sort Code 13-45-65   Account No. 63500671

Amica Printing Company

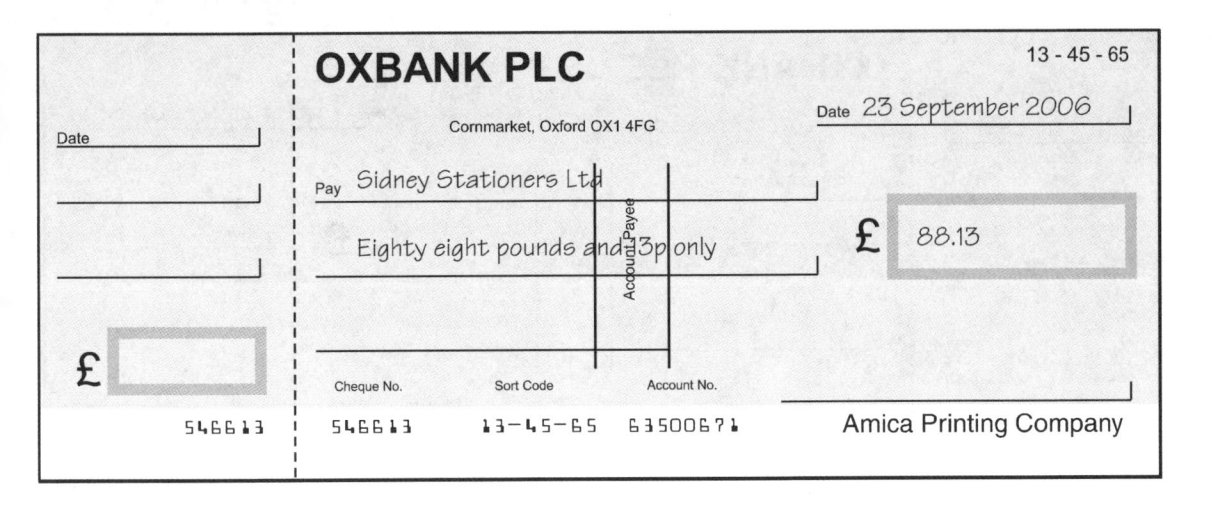

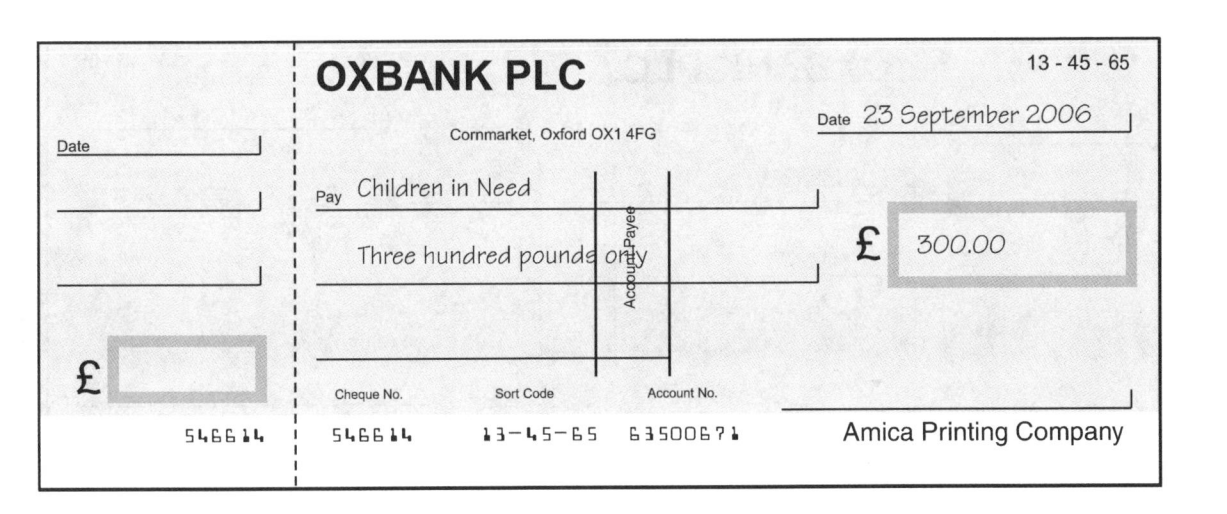

Task 9 (continued)

OXBANK PLC
13 - 45 - 65
Cornmarket, Oxford OX1 4FG
Date 23 September 2006
Pay Sidney Stationers Ltd
Eighty eight pounds and 13p only
£ 88.13
Cheque No. 546613 Sort Code 13-45-65 Account No. 63500671
Amica Printing Company

OXBANK PLC
13 - 45 - 65
Cornmarket, Oxford OX1 4FG
Date 23 September 2006
Pay Children in Need
Three hundred pounds only
£ 300.00
Cheque No. 546614 Sort Code 13-45-65 Account No. 63500671
Amica Printing Company

sample simulation – unit 2 – answers

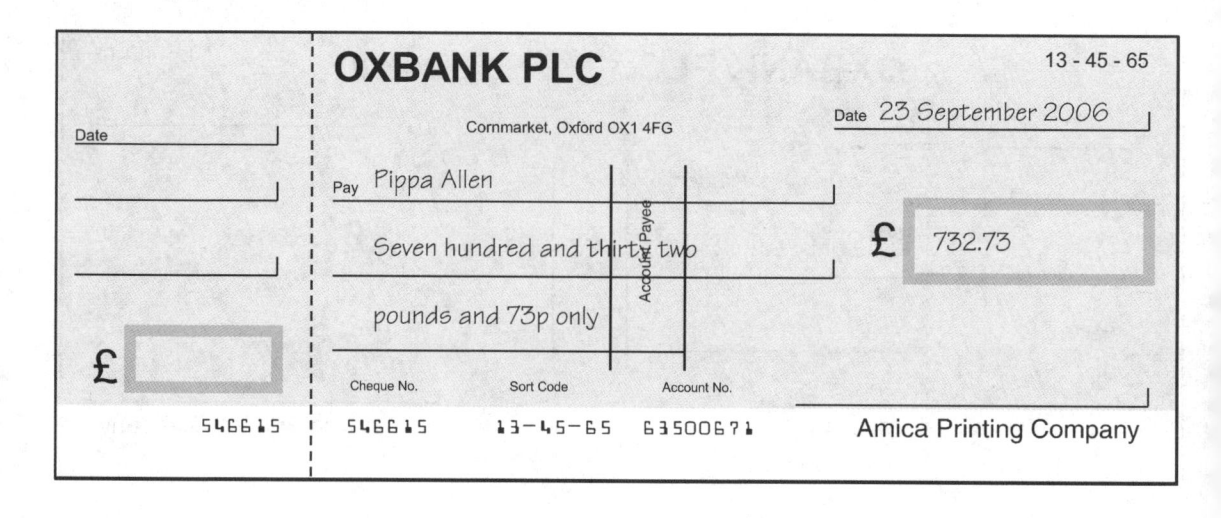

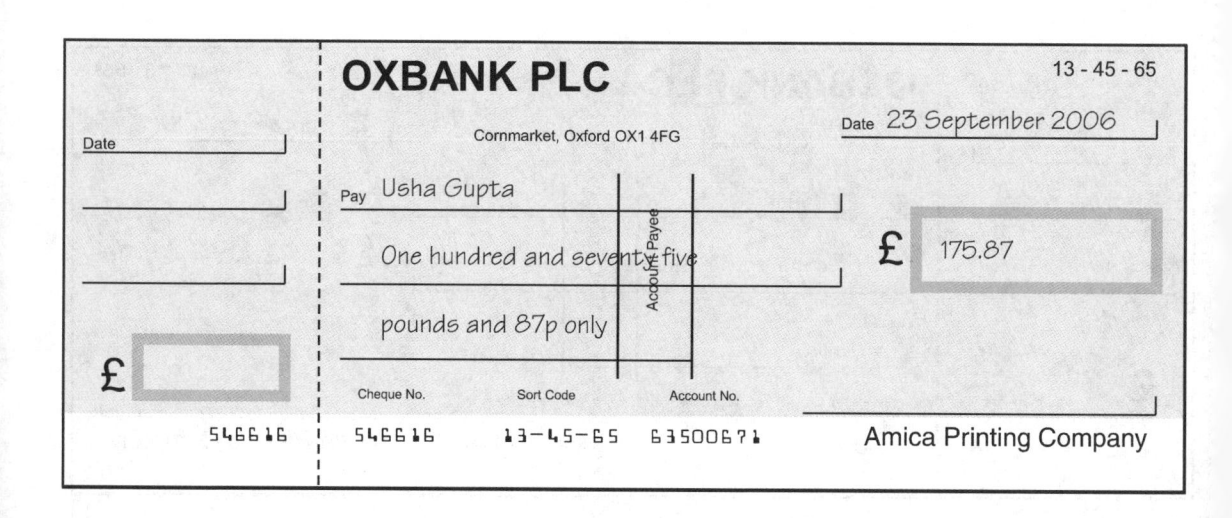

Task 9 (continued)

OXBANK PLC
Cornmarket, Oxford OX1 4FG
13 - 45 - 65
Date 23 September 2006
Pay Pippa Allen
Seven hundred and thirty two pounds and 73p only
£ 732.73
Cheque No. 546615 Sort Code 13-45-65 Account No. 63500671
Amica Printing Company

Date
£
546615

OXBANK PLC
Cornmarket, Oxford OX1 4FG
13 - 45 - 65
Date 23 September 2006
Pay Usha Gupta
One hundred and seventy five pounds and 87p only
£ 175.87
Cheque No. 546616 Sort Code 13-45-65 Account No. 63500671
Amica Printing Company

Date
£
546616

Task 9 (continued)

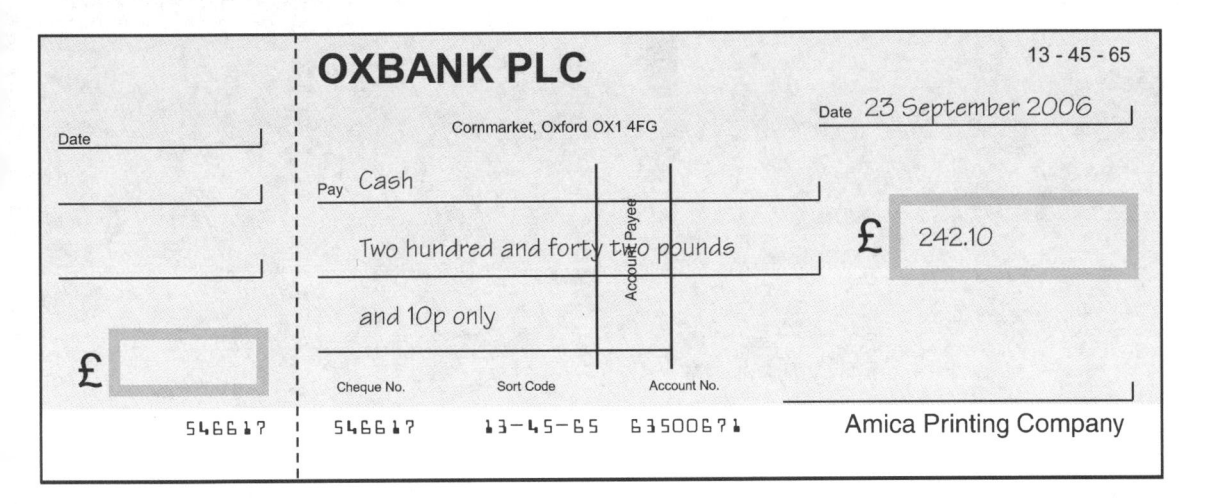

OXBANK PLC 13 - 45 - 65
Cornmarket, Oxford OX1 4FG

Date 23 September 2006

Pay Cash

Two hundred and forty two pounds and 10p only

£ 242.10

Cheque No. 546617 Sort Code 13-45-65 Account No. 63500671

Amica Printing Company

546617

SAMPLE SIMULATION – UNIT 3

WEASLEY SUPPLIES LTD

sample simulation – unit 3 – answers

Tasks 1 and 2

CB 241

RECEIPTS						PAYMENTS			
Sales ledger £	Other receipts £	Total £	Date 2006	Details	Cheque number	Total £	Purchases ledger £	Other payments £	
			1 June	Balance b/f					
4,776.15		4,486.85	5 June	Metrix plc					
		4,776.15	6 June	Horsfall Limited	331175	1,456.91	1,456.91		
7,715.96		7,715.96	12 June	Plympton Limited	331176	9,912.75	9,912.75		
			16 June	Stainton and Co	331177	3,901.25		3,901.25	
			16 June	Inland Revenue					
15,901.22		15,901.22	19 June	Maidstone plc					
			23 June	Earley and Partners	331178	3,341.20	3,341.20		
2,816.55		2,816.55	23 June	Stenshaw Limited					
			25 June	Pickard Newton	331179	3,216.99	3,216.99		
2,451.88		2,451.88	29 June	Fitzroy Limited					
1,926.34		1,926.34	30 June	Dove Ambleside					
				Medwith BC	SO	600.00		600.00	
				Safeguard Insurance	SO	310.00		310.00	
				Finance Leasing plc	SO	425.00		425.00	
				Purchasecard plc	DD	2,341.89		2,341.89	
				Salaries	CT	8,215.50		8,215.50	
				Bank charges	CHGS	107.33		107.33	
			30 June	Balance c/d		6,246.13			
35,588.10		40,074.95				40,074.95	17,927.85	15,900.97	
		6,246.13	1 July	Balance b/d					

Task 3

Bank reconciliation statement at 30 June 2006

	£	£
Balance per bank statement at 30 June		7,750.99
Add: outstanding lodgement		1,926.34
		9,677.33
Deduct: unpresented cheque 331178	3,341.20	
discrepancy on cheque 331179	90.00	
		3,431.20
Balance per cash book at 30 June		6,246.13

Note for assessors: Some candidates may spot the discrepancy on cheque 331179 while performing Tasks 1 and 2, and may alter the cash book to reflect this. Such candidates will not have the £90.00 discrepancy as an item in their bank reconciliation for Task 3 and will not need the first journal in Task 4. This alternative approach is acceptable and should not be penalised.

Task 4

JOURNAL

Date 2006	Account names and narratives	Debit £	Credit £
30 June	Cash at bank	90.00	
	Purchases ledger control account		90.00
	Being correction of mistake in recording cheque 331179		
30 June	Bad debts	1,233.75	
	Sales ledger control account		1,233.75
	Being write-off of balanced owed by Driftway Limited		

sample simulation – unit 3 – answers

Task 5

MAIN (GENERAL) LEDGER

Account Sales ledger control account

Debit | | | Credit | |
--- | --- | --- | --- | --- | ---
Date 2006 | Details | Amount £ | Date 2006 | Details | Amount £
1 June | Balance b/f | 30,914.66 | 30 June | Bank | 35,588.10
30 June | Invoices in month | 32,617.80 | 30 June | Journal: bad debt | 1,233.75
 | | | 30 June | Balance c/d | 26,710.61
 | | 63,532.46 | | | 63,532.46
1 July | Balance b/d | 26,710.61 | | |

Account Purchases ledger control account

Debit | | | Credit | |
--- | --- | --- | --- | --- | ---
Date 2006 | Details | Amount £ | Date 2006 | Details | Amount £
30 June | Bank | 17,927.85 | 1 June | Balance b/f | 19,334.02
30 June | Balance c/d | 21,697.62 | 30 June | Invoices in month | 20,201.45
 | | | 30 June | Journal: cheque misstated | 90.00
 | | 39,625.47 | | | 39,625.47
 | | | 1 July | Balance b/d | 21,697.62

Task 6

Creditors reconciliation at 30 June 2006

	£
Total of balances in subsidiary (purchases) ledger	21,607.62
Balance on control account	21,697.62
Discrepancy	90.00

Explanation of discrepancy

It seems likely that the journal relating to cheque number 331179 has not yet been actioned in the subsidiary ledger. Once this is adjusted for the balance owing to Pickard Newton becomes zero, and the total balances amount to £21,697.62, agreeing with the balance on the control account.

Task 7

PETTY CASH BOOK — PCB 52

Receipts £	Date 2006	Details	Voucher number	Total £	VAT £	Postage £	Stationery £	Other expenses £
200.00	1 June	Balance b/f						
	5 June	Postage	358	4.26		4.26		
	9 June	Stationery	359	12.87	1.91		10.96	
	12 June	Tea, coffee etc	360	7.02				7.02
	16 June	Postage	361	3.12		3.12		
	18 June	Stationery	362	13.51	2.01		11.50	
	23 June	Stationery	363	6.58	0.98		5.60	
	26 June	Stationery	364	5.73	0.85		4.88	
	27 June	Postage	365	5.90		5.90		
	30 June	Tea, coffee etc	366	6.50				6.50
		Totals		65.49	5.75	13.28	32.94	13.52
	30 June	Balance c/d		134.51				
200.00				200.00				

Task 7 (continued)

Notes and coin in the petty cash tin, 30 June 2006

	Number	Total value £
£20	4	80.00
£10	3	30.00
£5	2	10.00
£1	8	8.00
50p	8	4.00
20p	8	1.60
10p	8	0.80
5p	1	0.05
2p	2	0.04
1p	2	0.02
		134.51

Petty cash reconciliation

Date: 14 July 2006

	£
Balance per petty cash book	134.51
Total of notes and coin	134.51
Discrepancy (if any)	NIL

Explanation of difference (if any)

N/A

Task 8

Trial balance at 30 June 2006

DESCRIPTION	Ledger balances	
	Dr £	Cr £
Administration expenses	3,276.88	
Bad debts	2,010.76	
Bank	6,336.13	
Business rates	1,800.00	
Capital		46,745.76
Fixed assets	25,219.05	
HMRC		4,003.51
Insurance	930.00	
Leasing costs	1,275.00	
Petty cash	134.51	
Purchases	64,016.83	
Purchases ledger control		21,697.62
Purchases returns		1,125.31
Salaries expense	35,211.81	
Sales		96,558.43
Sales and distribution expenses	2,006.81	
Sales ledger control	26,710.61	
Sales returns	1,327.44	
Stock	7,270.00	
VAT control		3,995.20
Suspense account		3,400.00
Totals	177,525.83	177,525.83

Tasks 9 and 10

Date 2006	Account names and narrative	Dr £	Cr £
30 June	Suspense account 　　Purchases returns Being purchases returns of £200 wrongly debited to the returns account Suspense account 　　Capital Being cash receipt previously not posted	400.00 3,000.00	 400.00 3,000.00

Account Suspense

Debit			Credit		
Date 2006	Details	Amount £	Date 2006	Details	Amount £
30 June	Jnl: purchase returns Jnl: capital introduced	400.00 3,000.00	30 June	To balance TB	3,400.00
		3,400.00			3,400.00

Task 11

EMAIL

From: Kim Wendell

To: Ari Pottle

CC:

Subject: Re: Correcting the trial balance

Date: 7 July 2006

Message:

Hi Ari

I've made the changes you mentioned in your email. The effects are as follows.

First, the purchases returns figure (a credit balance on the trial balance) will increase by £400.

Second, the capital figure (also a credit balance on the trial balance) will increase by £3,000.

Finally, the £3,400 credit balance on suspense account will vanish, having been replaced by the above.

The net effect is that the trial balance will balance without any suspense account.

Regards, Kim

SAMPLE SIMULATION – UNIT 4

AVONTREE LTD

sample simulation – unit 4 – answers

Task 1

DATA INPUT SHEET				
Sales invoices			Date: 9 June 2006	
			Coding	
Invoice number	Customer	Amount £	Revenue centre	Type of revenue
52711	Megabooks Limited	124.15	100	400
52712	Books Plus	103.80	100	500
52713	Empstone Books Ltd	145.80	100	400
52714	Win Hong Books	161.20	200	300
52715	Tradesales Limited	120.00	100	400
52716	Palmer and Company	299.52	100	400
52717	Business Books	148.40	100	500
52718	Megabooks Limited	228.80	100	400

Task 2

EMAIL

From:	Parfraz Mehdi
To:	Emily Padden
CC:	
Subject:	Checks on purchase invoices
Date:	9 June 2006

Message:

I have just checked a batch of purchase invoices. I have noticed the following discrepancies.

1. We have an invoice for £400 plus VAT from Editype Limited. I can find no purchase order corresponding to this. Please could you let me know if an order was raised.

2. We have an invoice from Litho Printing Ltd in respect of 5,000 copies of The Wars of the Roses. Only 500 copies appear to have been ordered (our order number 2271).

3. We have an invoice from Decofix Ltd for repainting the accounts office. This has been coded 660-710. I think it should be 660-720.

Task 3

DATA INPUT SHEET			
Payroll		Date: 9 June 2006	
		Coding	
Detail	Amount £	Cost centre	Type of expenditure
Gross pay	10,900.00	660	730
Employer NIC	967.95	660	730

Task 4

AVONTREE LIMITED PROFIT AND LOSS ACCOUNT Date: 31 May 2006					
		YTD			
Account code	Account name	This year	Last year	Variance £	Variance %
100-300	UK sales: primary	75,600	74,100	+1,500	+2.0
100-400	UK sales: secondary	100,900	108,700	-7,800	-7.2
100-500	UK sales: higher	98,700	95,000	+3,700	+3.9
610-720	Typesetting: expenses	15,300	16,000	-700	-4.4
620-720	Editing: expenses	16,400	15,700	+700	+4.5
630-710	Printing & binding: materials	40,100	36,500	+3,600	+9.9
640-710	Distribution: materials	4,600	6,100	-1,500	-24.6
650-720	Marketing: expenses	16,400	15,900	+500	+3.1
660-720	Establishment: expenses	5,600	5,200	+400	+7.7
660-730	Establishment: salaries	34,200	33,000	+1,200	+3.6

Task 5

REPORT

To: Emily Padden

From: Parfraz Mehdi

Subject: Variances YTD, May 2006

Date: 9 June 2006

I attach the schedule of variances, showing YTD figures to end of May for both this year and last.

In the following cases the variances exceed 5% of last year's figure.

- Account 100–400: down 7.2% on last year
- Account 630–710: up 9.9% on last year
- Account 640–710: down 24.6% on last year
- Account 660–720: up 7.7% on last year

PRACTICE EXAM 1 – UNIT 3

FLOWER CHAIN

Tasks 1.1– 1.4

SUBISIDIARY (PURCHASES) LEDGER

Fresh Fields

Date 2008	Details	Amount £	Date 2008	Details	Amount £
30 Nov	Bank	5,000	30 Nov	Balance b/f	5,750
30 Nov	Balance c/d	3,335	30 Nov	Purchases	2,585
		8,335			8,335
			1 Dec	Balance b/d	3,335

Scented Garden

Date 2008	Details	Amount £	Date 2008	Details	Amount £
30 Nov	Purchases returns	235	30 Nov	Balance b/f	13,215
30 Nov	Balance c/d	14,390	30 Nov	Purchases	1,410
		14,625			14,625
			1 Dec	Balance b/d	14,390

The Daisy Chain

Date 2008	Details	Amount £	Date 2008	Details	Amount £
30 Nov	Purchases returns	94	30 Nov	Balance b/f	8,673
30 Nov	Balance c/d	9,378	30 Nov	Purchases	799
		9,472			9,472
			1 Dec	Balance b/d	9,378

Petal Palace

Date 2008	Details	Amount £	Date 2008	Details	Amount £
30 Nov	Bank	4,326	30 Nov	Balance b/f	4,517
30 Nov	Balance c/d	567	30 Nov	Purchases	376
		4,893			4,893
			1 Dec	Balance b/d	567

MAIN LEDGER

Fixtures and fittings

Date 2008	Details	Amount £	Date 2008	Details	Amount £
30 Nov	Balance b/f	15,315	30 Nov	Balance c/d	18,315
30 Nov	Bank	3,000			
		18,315			18,315
1 Dec	Balance b/d	18,315			

Sales

Date 2008	Details	Amount £	Date 2008	Details	Amount £
30 Nov	Balance c/d	149,118	30 Nov	Balance b/f	147,318
			30 Nov	Bank	1,800
		149,118			149,118
			1 Dec	Balance b/d	149,118

Purchases

Date 2008	Details	Amount £	Date 2008	Details	Amount £
30 Nov	Balance b/f	96,120	30 Nov	Balance c/d	100,520
30 Nov	Purchases ledger control	4,400			
		100,520			100,520
1 Dec	Balance b/d	100,520			

Purchases returns

Date 2008	Details	Amount £	Date 2008	Details	Amount £
30 Nov	Balance c/d	1,030	30 Nov	Balance b/f	750
			30 Nov	Purchases ledger control	280
		1,030			1,030
			1 Dec	Balance b/d	1,030

Purchases ledger control

Date 2008	Details	Amount £	Date 2008	Details	Amount £
30 Nov	Purchases returns	329	30 Nov	Balance b/f	37,238
30 Nov	Bank	5,000	30 Nov	Purchases	5,170
30 Nov	Bank	4,326			
30 Nov	Balance c/d	32,753			
		42,408			42,408
			1 Dec	Balance b/d	32,753

Loan from bank

Date 2008	Details	Amount £	Date 2008	Details	Amount £
30 Nov	Bank	500	30 Nov	Balance b/f	7,000
30 Nov	Balance c/d	6,500			
		7,000			7,000
			1 Dec	Balance b/d	6,500

Motor expenses

Date 2008	Details	Amount £	Date 2008	Details	Amount £
30 Nov	Balance b/f	1,213	30 Nov	Balance c/d	1,458
30 Nov	Bank	245			
		1,458			1,458
1 Dec	Balance b/d	1,458			

VAT

Date 2008	Details	Amount £	Date 2008	Details	Amount £
30 Nov	Balance b/f	13,762	30 Nov	Sales	2,317
30 Nov	Sales returns	287	30 Nov	Bank	18,653
30 Nov	Balance c/d	6,921			
		20,970			20,970
			1 July	Balance b/d	6,921

The Flower Chain
Trial balance as at 30 November 2008

	Dr £	Cr £
Motor vehicles	20,000	
Fixtures and fittings	18,315	
Bank	5,193	
Petty cash control	50	
Sales ledger control	54,250	
Purchases ledger control		32,753
VAT		7,779
Loan from bank		6,500
Capital		43,969
Sales		149,118
Purchases	100,520	
Purchases returns		1,030
Discount received		608
Bank interest received		117
Bank interest paid	80	
Wages	25,320	
Motor expenses	1,458	
Office expenses	2,759	
Rent and rates	10,500	
Heat and light	632	
Insurance	1,240	
Advertising	225	
Legal fees	800	
Miscellaneous expenses	532	
Totals	241,874	241,874

SECTION 2

Task 2.1

a)
```
VEN002
RJH003
```

Code is the first three letters of supplier's name, ignoring initials and 'the', then a consecutive number starting from 001 of suppliers beginning with that initial letter.

b)
```
LILO10
LUPB15
```

Code is the first three letters of the flower's name; then the first letter of the colour of the flower; and finally the number of flowers in a box.

Tip: Ensure that you are consistent in the make up of codes, do NOT ignore the existing structure.

Task 2.2

a) £16

Working:

	$
Opening balance	22
Cash from bank	53
Less:	
Expenditure during month	(16)
Balance at end of month	59

Therefore 75 − 59 = $16 required to restore the imprest level

b) Debit

Task 2.3

a) £360

VAT of £63 is 17½ % of net amount

Net amount = (£63/17.5) x 100

= £360.00

b) £423

Net amount	£360.00
VAT	£ 63.00
	£423.00

or:

VAT of £63 is 17½ % of net amount

Gross amount = (£63/17.5) x 117.5

= £423.00

Task 2.4

– Double entry errors
– Transposition errors
– Calculation errors

Task 2.5

Account name	Debit £	Credit £
Bad debts	**240**	
VAT (W1)	**42**	
Sales ledger control account		**282**

W1

£240 x 17.5% = £42

Task 2.6

Any **THREE** from:

- Staff may see confidential information e.g. salaries.
- The accounting records may be stolen.
- The accounting records may be damaged e.g. floods.
- The information in the accounting records may be leaked externally e.g. to a competitor.

Task 2.7

Error	Capital expenditure ✓	Revenue expenditure ✓
Purchase of a delivery van	✓	
Purchase of office stationery		✓
Cost of redecorating the office		✓
Repair to delivery van		✓
Purchase of specialist refrigeration equipment for storing flowers	✓	

Task 2.8

Account names	Dr £	Cr £
a)		
Sales returns	500	
Sales		500
b)		
Office expenses	250	
Bank		250
c)		
Discount allowed	388	
Bank		270
Suspense account		118

Task 2.9

a)

Sales ledger control					
Date 2008	Details	Amount £	Date 2008	Details	Amount £
01 Nov	Balance b/f	48,125	30 Nov	Bank	28,327
30 Nov	Sales	37,008	30 Nov	Discount allowed	240
			30 Nov	Purchases ledger control	2,316
			30 Nov	Balance c/d	54,250
		85,133			85,133
01 Dec	Balance b/d	54,250			

b)

	£
Sales ledger control account balance as at 01 December 2008	54,250
Total of subsidiary (sales) ledger accounts as at 01 December 2008	(54,163)
Difference	87

*Note:

Credit will be given for this task even if the incorrect figure is used for the purchases ledger control account balance provided that it is consistent with the answer given in Task 2.9 a) above.

c)

VAT has been overstated on an invoice.	
VAT has been understated on an invoice.	
A sales invoice has been entered in the subsidiary ledger twice.	
A sales credit note has been entered in the subsidiary ledger twice.	✓
A receipt from a customer has been omitted from the subsidiary ledger.	
A receipt from a customer has been entered in the subsidiary ledger twice.	✓

Task 2.10

Cash book

Date 2008	Details	Bank £	Date 2008	Cheque no.	Details	Bank £
01 Nov	Balance b/f	5,466	03 Nov	110870	Roberts & Co	6,250
24 Nov	Bevan & Co	1,822	03 Nov	110871	J Jones	1,164
24 Nov	Plant Pots Ltd	7,998	06 Nov	110872	Lake Walks Ltd	2,250
21 Nov	**BBT Ltd**	**10,000**	10 Nov	110873	PH Supplies	275
24 Nov	Petals Ltd	2,555	17 Nov	110874	Peters & Co	76
			21 Nov		Insurance Ensured	500
			24 Nov		Rainbow Ltd	88
			28 Nov		Balance c/d	17,238
		27,841				127,84
29 Nov	Balance b/d	17,238				

Bank reconciliation statement as at 28 November 2008	
	£
Balance per bank statement:	7,769
Add:	
Name: Bevan & Co	1,822
Name: Plant Pots Ltd	7,998
Total to add	9,820
Less:	
Name: PH Supplies	275
Name: Peters & Co	76
Total to subtract	351
Balance as per cash book	17,238

PRACTICE EXAM 2 – UNIT 3

FIRST FASHIONS

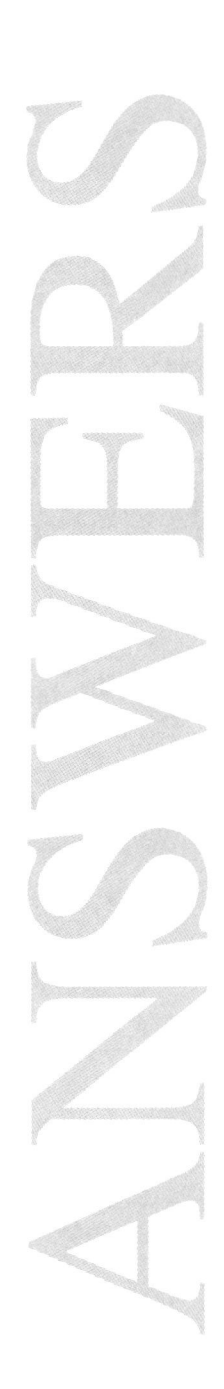

Tasks 1.1– 1.4

SUBSIDIARY (SALES) LEDGER

Sharif Clothing

Date 2008	Details	Amount £	Date 2008	Details	Amount £
30 June	Balance b/f	4,963	30 June	Sales returns	188
30 June	Sales	3,055	30 June	Balance c/d	7,830
		8,018			8,018
1 July	Balance b/d	7,830			

Andrews & Company

Date 2008	Details	Amount £	Date 2008	Details	Amount £
30 June	Balance b/f	3,210	30 June	Balance c/d	3,633
30 June	Sales	423			
		3,633			3,633
1 July	Balance b/d	3,633			

Linens Ltd

Date 2008	Details	Amount £	Date 2008	Details	Amount £
30 June	Balance b/f	21,695	30 June	Bank	6,445
30 June	Sales	9,964	30 June	Discount allowed	250
			30 June	Balance c/d	24,964
		31,659			31,659
1 July	Balance b/d	24,964			

Denton Designs

Date 2008	Details	Amount £	Date 2008	Details	Amount £
30 June	Balance b/f	5,425	30 June	Sales returns	1,739
30 June	Sales	2,115	30 June	Balance c/d	5,801
		7,540			7,540
1 July	Balance b/d	5,801			

MAIN LEDGER

Motor vehicles

Date 2008	Details	Amount £	Date 2008	Details	Amount £
30 June	Balance b/f	10,110	30 June	Balance c/d	38,710
30 June	Bank	28,600			
		38,710			38,710
1 July	Balance b/d	38,710			

Bank savings

Date 2008	Details	Amount £	Date 2008	Details	Amount £
30 June	Balance b/f	15,245	30 June	Balance c/d	17,745
30 June	Bank	2,500			
		17,745			17,745
1 July	Balance b/d	17,745			

Sales

Date 2008	Details	Amount £	Date 2008	Details	Amount £
30 June	Balance c/d	445,388	30 June	Balance b/f	432,148
			30 June	Sales ledger control	13,240
		445,388			445,388
			1 July	Balance b/d	445,388

Sales returns

Date 2008	Details	Amount £	Date 2008	Details	Amount £
30 June	Balance b/f	5,400	30 June	Balance c/d	7,040
30 June	Sales ledger control	1,640			
		7,040			7,040
1 July	Balance b/d	7,040			

Sales ledger control

Date 2008	Details	Amount £	Date 2008	Details	Amount £
30 June	Balance b/f	174,163	30 June	Sales returns	1,927
30 June	Sales	15,557	30 June	Bank	6,445
			30 June	Discount allowed	250
			30 June	Balance c/d	181,098
		189,720			189,720
1 July	Balance b/d	181,098			

Discount allowed

Date 2008	Details	Amount £	Date 2008	Details	Amount £
30 June	Balance b/f	2,650	30 June	Balance c/d	2,900
30 June	Sales ledger control	250			
		2,900			2,900
1 July	Balance b/d	2,900			

Hotel expenses

Date 2008	Details	Amount £	Date 2008	Details	Amount £
30 June	Balance b/f	3,994	30 June	Balance c/d	4,169
30 June	Bank	175			
		4,169			4,169
1 July	Balance b/d	4,169			

VAT

Date 2008	Details	Amount £	Date 2008	Details	Amount £
30 June	Balance b/f	13,762	30 June	Sales	2,317
30 June	Sales returns	287	30 June	Bank	18,653
30 June	Balance c/d	6,921			
		20,970			20,970
			1 July	Balance b/d	6,921

First Fashions
Trial balance as at 30 June 2008

	Dr £	Cr £
Motor vehicles	38,710	
Stock	18,754	
Bank current account	6,249	
Bank savings account	17,745	
Petty cash control	75	
Sales ledger control	181,098	
Purchases ledger control		90,218
VAT		6,921
Capital		68,781
Sales		445,388
Sales returns	7,040	
Purchases	278,100	
Purchases returns		15,350
Discount received		1,907
Discount allowed	2,900	
Wages	45,426	
Motor expenses	3,276	
Office expenses	5,382	
Rent and rates	18,000	
Hotel expenses	4,169	
Subscriptions	450	
Professional fees	1,263	
Miscellaneous expenses	648	
Suspense account		720
Total	**629,285**	**629,285**

SECTION 2

Task 2.1

a)

Petty cash reconciliation	£	p
Balance of petty cash control account	75	00
Cash in hand	66	50
Difference	8	50

b) Any **THREE** from:

- There are errors in the petty cash control account
- The cash has been counted incorrectly
- An incorrect figure has been transferred from the petty cash control amount to the reconciliation
- An incorrect figure has been reimbursed but not recorded
- The difference of £8.50 has been reimbursed but not recorded
- Theft of petty cash
- An incorrect amount of cash has been reimbursed

Task 2.2

a) Any **ONE** from:

- Sales were less than purchases during the period
- There had been an overpayment of VAT in the previous period.

b) £19,250

Workings: £129,250 × $\frac{17.5}{117.5}$

Task 2.3

A banker's draft is a cheque where the funds are taken directly from the financial institution rather than the individual drawer's account. It is also called a bank cheque.

Task 2.4

a) Any **TWO** from:
- Computer
- CPU
- Modem
- Router
- VDU
- Printer
- Mouse
- Keyboard

Credit would be given for other valid reasons

b) Any **TWO** from:
- Accuracy
- Speed
- Efficiency
- Automatic

Credit would be given for other valid reasons

Task 2.5

Suspense account

Date 2008	Details	Amount £	Date 2008	Details	Amount £
01 July	Sales	945	30 June	Balance b/f	720
			01 July	Rent and rates	225
		945			945

Task 2.6

First Fashion would use non trade debtors' control account if it had income from a source or sources other than its usual trade e.g. consultancy or rent.

Task 2.7

Error	The trial balance will balance	The trial balance will NOT balance
The entries in the main ledger to record a sales invoice were duplicated.	✓	
The entries to record payment of an electricity bill have been reversed.	✓	
The motor expenses account has been added up incorrectly.		✓
A purchase invoice was entered correctly in the purchases ledger control account but incorrectly in the purchases account.		✓
A customer did not take the discount offered.	✓	

Task 2.8

Account names	Dr £	Cr £
a)		
Discount allowed	50	
Discount received		50
b)		
Bank savings account	200	
Bank current account		200
c)		
Bad debt	2,800	
VAT	490	
Sales ledger control account		3,290

Task 2.9

a)

Purchases ledger control					
Date 2008	Details	Amount £	Date 2008	Details	Amount £
30 June	Bank	33,106	01 June	Balance b/f	85,299
30 June	Discount received	1,000	30 June	Purchases	39,300
30 June	Purchases returns	275			
30 June	Balance c/d	90,218			
		124,599			124,599
			1 July	Balance b/d	90,218

b)

	£
Purchases ledger control account balance as at 1 July 2008	90,218*
Total of subsidiary (purchases) ledger accounts as at 1 July 2008	90,218*
Difference	6*

*Note:

Credit will be given for this task even if the incorrect figure is used for the purchases ledger control account balance provided that it is consistent with the answer given in Task 2.9 a) above.

c)

One of the accounts in the subsidiary ledger has been understated.	✓
One of the accounts in the subsidiary ledger has been overstated.	
One supplier has offered a discount.	
First Fashions has underpaid a supplier.	
First Fashions has overpaid a supplier.	

Task 2.10

Cash book

Date 2008	Details	Bank £	Date 2008	Cheque no.	Details	Bank £
01 June	Balance b/f	12,050	02 June	136408	Stone & Company	629
20 June	Laura Laing	5,210	02 June	136409	Barker Ltd	500
20 June	DVM Ltd	850	06 June	136410	Belt and Braces	6,425
21 June	Matthew Mann	624	10 June	136411	DRL Ltd	348
20 June	Remnants Ltd	3,400	16 June	136412	Philip Gee	175
20 June	Bank interest	20	17 June	136413	David Kay	216
			20 June		Property Maintenance	725
			20 June		LDM Ltd	100
			20 June		Bank charges	15
			20 June		Balance c/d	13,021
		22,154				22,154
22 June	Balance b/d	13,021				

Bank reconciliation statement as at 21 June 2008	
	£
Balance per bank statement:	7,578
Add:	
Name: Laura Laing	5,210
Name: Matthew Mann	624
Total to add	5,834
Less:	
Name: Philip Gee	175
Name: David Kay	216
Total to subtract	391
Balance as per cash book	13,021

PRACTICE EXAM 3 – UNIT 3

PARKER PAINTS

Tasks 1.1– 1.4

SUBSIDIARY (PURCHASES) LEDGER
High Gloss Ltd

Date 2007	Details	Amount £	Date 2007	Details	Amount £
30 Nov	Balance b/f	12,564	30 Nov	Bank	10,150
30 Nov	Sales	893	30 Nov	Discount allowed	300
			30 Nov	Balance c/d	3,007
		13,457			13,457
1 Dec	Balance b/d	3,007			

The Paint Shop

Date 2007	Details	Amount £	Date 2007	Details	Amount £
30 Nov	Balance b/f	2,398	30 Nov	Sales returns	188
30 Nov	Sales	2,585	30 Nov	Balance c/d	4,795
		4,983			4,983
1 Dec	Balance b/d	4,795			

Decorators World

Date 2007	Details	Amount £	Date 2007	Details	Amount £
30 Nov	Balance b/f	2,309	30 Nov	Sales returns	705
30 Nov	Sales	1,175	30 Nov	Balance c/d	2,779
		3,484			3,484
1 Dec	Balance c/d	2,779			

Homes of Class

Date 2007	Details	Amount £	Date 2007	Details	Amount £
30 Nov	Balance b/f	15,091	30 Nov	Bank	2,520
30 Nov	Sales	14,100	30 Nov	Balance c/d	26,671
		29,191			29,191
1 Dec	Balance b/d	26,671			

MAIN LEDGER

Office equipment

Date 2007	Details	Amount £	Date 2007	Details	Amount £
30 Nov	Balance b/f	20,168			
30 Nov	Journal	1,500	30 Nov	Balance c/d	21,668
		21,668			21,668
1 Dec	Balance b/d	21,668			

Sales

Date 2007	Details	Amount £	Date 2007	Details	Amount £
			30 Nov	Balance b/f	302,975
30 Nov	Balance c/d	318,935	30 Nov	Sales ldgr control	15,960
		318,935			318,935
			1 Dec	Balance b/d	318,935

Sales returns

Date 2007	Details	Amount £	Date 2007	Details	Amount £
30 Nov	Balance b/f	13,657			
30 Nov	Sales ledger control	760	30 Nov	Balance c/d	14,417
		14,417			14,417
1 Dec	Balance b/d	14,417			

Sales ledger control

Date 2007	Details	Amount £	Date 2007	Details	Amount £
30 Nov	Balance b/f	125,775	30 Nov	Sales returns	893
30 Nov	Sales	18,753	30 Nov	Bank	12,670
			30 Nov	Discounts allowed	300
			30 Nov	Balance c/d	130,665
		144,528			144,528
1 Dec	Balance b/d	130,665			

Discount allowed

Date 2007	Details	Amount £	Date 2007	Details	Amount £
30 Nov	Balance b/f	1,350			
30 Nov	Sales ledger control	300	30 Nov	Balance c/d	1,650
		1,650			1,650
1 Dec	Balance b/d	1,650			

Repairs and renewals

Date 2007	Details	Amount £	Date 2007	Details	Amount £
30 Nov	Balance b/f	6,000	30 Nov	Journal	1,450
			30 Nov	Balance c/d	4,550
		6,000			6,000
1 Dec	Balance b/d	4,550			

Stationery

Date 2007	Details	Amount £	Date 2007	Details	Amount £
30 Nov	Balance b/f	134	30 Nov	Journal	50
			30 Nov	Balance c/d	84
		134			134
1 Dec	Balance b/d	84			

VAT

Date 2007	Details	Amount £	Date 2007	Details	Amount £
30 Nov	Sales ledger control	133	30 Nov	Balance b/f	22,535
30 Nov	Balance c/d	25,195	30 Nov	Sales ledger control	2,793
		25,328			25,328
			1 Dec	Balance b/d	25,195

Tasks 1.5 and 1.6

Trial balance as at 30 November 2007

	Debit £	Credit £
Motor vehicles	18,000	
Office equipment	21,668	
Stock	4,950	
Cash at bank	5,762	
Petty cash control	100	
Sales ledger control	130,665	
Purchases ledger control		34,918
VAT		25,195
Capital		72,502
Loan from bank		15,000
Sales		318,935
Sales returns	14,417	
Purchases	198,540	
Purchases returns		564
Discounts received		337
Discounts allowed	1,650	
Repairs and renewals	4,550	
Stationery	84	
Wages	56,320	
Heat and light	2,984	
Motor expenses	3,871	
Hotel expenses	2,577	
Bad debts written off	2,500	
Miscellaneous expenses	1,313	
Totals	467,451	467,451

SECTION 2

Task 2.1

a) 1 December 2007

   Tutorial note: With a BACS transfer there is no clearing therefore the money is available immediately.

b) There is no cheque to pay in at the bank so no need to visit the bank
   Time-saving as no paying in slip required
   Greater security as no paperwork
   No time delay due to the clearing system

   (Note that only one advantage was required for the task)

c) Debtor

Task 2.2

a) Invoices for a particular customer cannot be found easily – for an invoice to be found the invoice number must be known.

b) Filing sales invoices for individual customers together in alphabetical order.

Task 2.3

Petty cash

Date 2007	Details	Amount £	Date 2007	Details	Total £	Stationery £	Postage £	Motor fuel £
1 Nov	Bal b/f	100	7 Nov	Postage stamps	20		20	
			15 Nov	Pens and pencils	18	18		
			22 Nov	Petrol	10			10
			30 Nov	Envelopes	15	15		
			30 Nov	Bal c/d	37	33	20	10
	Total	100		Total	100			
1 Dec	Bal b/d	37						

625

Task 2.4

a) Asset

   Tutorial note: HM Revenue and Customs owe Parker Paints money therefore they are a debtor which is an asset.

b) Credit

c) Debit

   Tutorial note: When the money is received it is debited to the bank account and credited to the VAT account to remove the VAT debtor.

Task 2.5

CAL

Tutorial note: The code appears to be the first two letters of the organisations first name and the first letter of its second name.

Task 2.6

1. Calculations are done automatically therefore eliminating arithmetical mistakes and the need to check figures.

2. Once data is input all relevant accounts will be updated.

3. The system will produce reports such as aged debtor analysis automatically.

Task 2.7

a) A **standing order** would be set up to repay a bank loan in equal monthly instalments.
b) A **direct debit** would be set up to repay a bank loan by variable amounts each month.
c) A **bank overdraft** would be arranged when short term borrowing is needed.

Task 2.8

JOURNAL

Account name	Dr £	Cr £
a) Light and heat	200	
Bank		200
b) Hotel expenses	1,600	
Bank		1,600
c) Suspense	450	
Miscellaneous expenses		450
Suspense	285	
d) Sales ledger control		285

Tutorial notes

a) This expense has been omitted completely and therefore the bank or cash-book must be credited and heat and light debited with the expense.

b) As these entries have been reversed then what must have been done is to credit hotel expenses and debit the bank account (cash book). These need to be not only reversed out but also the correct entries put in so the double entry is for twice the original error, £1,600.

c) The miscellaneous expense account has been debited with £450 too much. Therefore there must be a credit to that account. There have been no other errors so the debit entry must be to the suspense account.

The sales ledger control account needs to be credited with this missing receipt and again the other side of the entry must be to the suspense account.

The journal entry could also show the two separate entries in the suspense account as one entry:

Debit	Suspense account	735
Credit	Miscellaneous expenses	450
Credit	Sales ledger control	285

Task 2.9

a)

Purchase ledger control

Date 2007	Details	Amount £	Date 2007	Details	Amount £
30 Nov	Bank	21,342	1 Nov	Balance b/f	40,550
30 Nov	Discounts received	128	30 Nov	Purchases	18,365
30 Nov	Purchases returns	2,527			
30 Nov	Balance c/d	34,918			
		58,915			58,915
			1 Dec	Balance b/d	34,918

b)

	£
Purchases ledger control account balance as at 1 December	34,918
Total of subsidiary (purchases) ledger accounts as at 1 December (W)	31,962
Difference	2,956

Working – total of individual ledger balances

	£
Paint Partners	20,876
Colour Coordinates	9,321
JBM Ltd	3,243
Barker & Co	(325)
Interior Moods	(1,153)
	31,962

c) The difference is £2,956. Half of this amount is £1,478 which is the total of the two debit balances (£325 + £1,153). Therefore it is likely that this difference has been caused by the balances to Barker & Co and to Interior Moods being listed as debit balances when they are in fact credit balances.

Task 2.10

a), b) and c)

Cash book

Date 2007	Details	Amount £	Date 2007	Cheque number	Details	Amount £
01 Nov	Balance b/f	4,320	01 Nov	01872	Colourways Ltd	450
20 Nov	LBG Ltd	4,000	01 Nov	01873	Barker Boards	321
21 Nov	Reeves & Co	3,674	07 Nov	01874	CHG Ltd	1,098
22 Nov	Cool Designs	2,350	08 Nov	01875	Paint It Ltd	2,963
05 Nov	**Colour King**	**7,930**	15 Nov	01876	G Smith Ltd	998
23 Nov	**Bank interest**	**25**	22 Nov	01877	C Coombs	362
			14 Nov	**DD**	**Wellborough DC**	876
			21 Nov	**DD**	**Lewis and Laine**	290
			23 Nov		Bank charges	27
			23 Nov		Balance c/d	14,914
		22,299				22,299
24 Nov	Balance b/d	14,914				

d) **Bank reconciliation statement as at 23 November 2007**

Balance per bank statement:	£12,215
Add:	
Name: Reeves & Co	£3,674
Name: Cool Designs	£2,350
Total to add	£6,024
Less:	
Name: Paint It Ltd 01875	£2,963
Name: C Coombes 01877	£362
Total to subtract	£3,325
Balance as per cash book	£14,914

PRACTICE EXAM 4 – UNIT 3

THE STUDIO

Tasks 1.1– 1.4

SUBSIDIARY (PURCHASES) LEDGER

Snap It

Date 2007	Details	Amount £	Date 2007	Details	Amount £
30 June	Balance c/d	20,225	30 June	Balance b/f	2,600
			30 June	Purchases	17,625
		20,225			20,225
			1 July	Balance b/d	20,225

DND Ltd

Date 2007	Details	Amount £	Date 2007	Details	Amount £
30 June	Bank	4,875	30 June	Balance b/f	5,594
30 June	Discount received	125	30 June	Purchases	611
30 June	Balance c/d	1,205			
		6,205			6,205
			1 July	Balance b/d	1,205

Camco Ltd

Date 2007	Details	Amount £	Date 2007	Details	Amount £
30 June	Purchases returns	1,363	30 June	Balance b/f	4,325
30 June	Balance c/d	4,513	30 June	Purchases	1,551
		5,876			5,876
			1 July	Balance b/d	4,513

Field Films

Date 2007	Details	Amount £	Date 2007	Details	Amount £
30 June	Purchases returns	987	30 June	Balance b/f	10,326
30 June	Balance c/d	18,739	30 June	Purchases	9,400
		19,726			19,726
			1 July	Balance b/d	18,739

MAIN LEDGER
Fixtures and fittings

Date 2007	Details	Amount £	Date 2007	Details	Amount £
30 June	Balance b/f	9,750	30 June	Balance c/d	21,750
30 June	Bank	12,000			
		21,750			21,750
1 July	Balance b/d	21,750			

Purchases

Date 2007	Details	Amount £	Date 2007	Details	Amount £
30 June	Balance b/f	224,750	30 June	Balance c/d	249,590
30 June	Purchases ldgr ctrl	24,840			
		249,590			249,590
1 July	Balance b/d	249,590			

Purchases returns

Date 2007	Details	Amount £	Date 2007	Details	Amount £
30 June	Balance c/d	3,382	30 June	Balance b/f	1,382
			30 June	Purchases ldgr ctrl	2,000
		3,382			3,382
			1 July	Balance b/d	3,382

Purchases ledger control

Date 2007	Details	Amount £	Date 2007	Details	Amount £
30 June	Purchases returns	2,350	30 June	Balance b/f	31,534
30 June	Bank	4,875	30 June	Purchases	29,187
30 June	Discounts received	125			
30 June	Balance c/d	53,371			
		60,721			60,721
			1 July	Balance b/d	53,371

Loan from bank

Date 2007	Details	Amount £	Date 2007	Details	Amount £
30 June	Balance c/d	15,250	30 June	Balance b/f	250
			30 June	Bank	15,000
		15,250			15,250
			1 July	Balance b/d	15,250

Discount received

Date 2007	Details	Amount £	Date 2007	Details	Amount £
30 June	Balance c/d	2,525	30 June	Balance b/f	2,400
			30 June	Purchase ldgr ctrl	125
		2,525			2,525
			1 July	Balance b/d	2,525

Insurance

Date 2007	Details	Amount £	Date 2007	Details	Amount £
30 June	Balance b/f	1,825	30 June	Balance c/d	4,575
30 June	Bank	2,750			
		4,575			4,575
1 July	Balance b/d	4,575			

VAT

Date 2007	Details	Amount £	Date 2007	Details	Amount £
30 June	Purchases	4,347	30 June	Balance b/f	17,239
30 June	Balance c/d	13,242	30 June	Purchases returns	350
		17,589			17,589
			1 July	Balance b/d	13,242

The Studio
Trial balance as at 30 June 2007

	Debit £	Credit £
Motor vehicles	13,625	
Fixtures and fittings	21,750	
Stock	7,113	
Bank current account		4,812
Bank savings account	1,000	
Petty cash control	100	
Sales ledger control	86,421	
Purchases ledger control		53,371
VAT		13,242
Loan from bank		15,250
Capital		32,174
Sales		305,029
Sales returns	3,444	
Purchases	249,590	
Purchases returns		3,382
Discount received		2,525
Wages	32,650	
Heat and light	1,762	
Motor expenses	1,985	
Insurance	4,575	
Repairs and renewals	328	
Office expenses	2,614	
Advertising	1,800	
Miscellaneous expenses	1,028	
Totals	429,785	429,785

SECTION 2

Task 2.1

Invoice calculation

INVOICE CALCULATION	£	p
Price of goods	1,200	00
Trade discount of 10%	120	00
Net invoice total	1,080	00
VAT	179	55
Invoice total	1,259	55

Workings:

Invoice total after trade discount	1,080.00
Settlement discount 5%	54.00
	1,026.00

VAT = 17.5% x 1,026.00 = 179.55

Tutorial note: The Examiner noted that the calculation of VAT with a settlement discount was not well done. Remember that when calculating VAT you assume that the discount will be taken and calculate the VAT on that basis, but you do not reduce the actual amount of the invoice itself. If the customer does take the invoice then you make the adjusting entry through the discount allowed account.

Examiner's comments: The Examiner also noted that a number of candidates entered the payment as £960 rather than the monthly figure of £80.

Task 2.2

Each cheque has to enter the clearing system. In the clearing system, each cheque is passed to the bank of the drawer (the person who wrote the cheque and paid it to the Studio) and that bank pays the funds to the Studio's bank. This takes several days.

Task 2.3

C   Sales
     VAT   ✓
     Bank

Working

The double entry is

Dr	Bank (£60 x 1.175)	£70.50
Cr	VAT (£60 x 0.175)	£10.50
Cr	Sales	£60.00

Task 2.4

Report or document	To a customer	To a supplier	To a manager
	✓	✓	✓
Statement of account	✓		
Aged debtors analysis			✓
Remittance advice		✓	
VAT report			✓
Delivery note	✓		

Task 2.5

PETTY CASH CONTROL

Date 2007	Details	Amount £	Date 2007	Details	Amount £
1 June	Bal b/f	100	17 June	Taxi fare	12
			20 June	Coffee and tea	17
			29 June	Postage stamps	30
			30 June	Balance c/d	41
	Total	100		Total	100
1 July	Balance b/d	41			
1 July	Bank	59			

Tutorial note: The total petty cash expenditure is £59 pounds and at the end of the month the petty cash tin would contain vouchers to the value of £59 and £41 cash. The vouchers would be removed and filed and a cheque raised for £59 cash which is paid into the petty cash tin.

Task 2.6

Capital expenditure is incurred when purchasing or improving the fixed assets of the business, ie assets that are not bought with a view to resale (such as purchases of goods that the business trades in).

Revenue expenditure is incurred in the day to day running of the business.

Tutorial note: The Examiner noted that many students gave examples of capital and revenue expenditure rather than an explanation of the terms. Make sure that you read the question and do what is asked.

Task 2.7

Account name	£ Debit	£ Credit
Travel expenses	90	
Heat and light	140	
Suspense account £(90 + 140) (see working)		230

Working

	Actual entry*		Correct entry		Adjusting entry	
	Dr	Cr	Dr	Cr	Dr	Cr
Travel expenses	£10		£100		£90	
Cash		£100		£100		
Suspense	£90					£90

* including suspense entry of £230 (90 + 140)

	Actual entry*		Correct entry		Adjusting entry	
	Dr	Cr	Dr	Cr	Dr	Cr
Heat and light			£140		£140	
Cash		£140		£140		
Suspense	£140					£140

Tutorial note: The alternative method of reversing the incorrect transaction and then recording the correct one is also acceptable.

Task 2.8

	Account names	Dr £	Cr £
a)	(see working)		
	Motor expenses	600	
	Bank		600
b)	(see working)		
	Petty cash	75	
	Bank		75
c)	Bad debt	400	
	VAT	70	
	Sales ledger control		470

Working

	Actual entry		Correct entry		Adjusting entry	
	Dr	Cr	Dr	Cr	Dr	Cr
Motor expenses		£300	£300		£600	
Bank	£300			£300		£600
Electricity	£75		£75			
Petty cash		£75			£75	
Bank				£75		£75

Tutorial note: The alternative method of reversing the incorrect transaction and then recording the correct one is also acceptable.

Task 2.9

a) **Sales ledger control**

Date 2007	Details	Amount £	Date 2007	Details	Amount £
1 June	Balance b/f	73,154	30 June	Bank	5,410
30 June	Sales	21,726	30 June	Discount allowed	252
			30 June	Sales returns	2,797
			30 June	Balance c/d	86,421
		94,880			94,880
1 July	Balance b/d	86,421			

b)
	£
Sales ledger control account balance as at 1 July 2007	86,421
Total of subsidiary (sales) ledger accounts as at 1 July 2007 (W)	86,366
Difference	55

c) Any **TWO** from:

Check all subsidiary ledger balances have been correctly included in total.

Check all relevant entries have been correctly included in sales ledger control account.

Check all accounts have been totalled and balanced correctly.

Tutorial note: The Chief Assessor noted that part c) was answered poorly. Many students tried to give reasons why the amounts differed (which was the normal type of question in previous sittings) but on this occasion the questions asked for two actions to trace the difference. The Assessor points out that in future this part of the question will take different forms and students should be aware of this.

Working

	£
LM Trent	24,325
Better Plates	10,943
TML Ltd	8,657
Shutter Box	32,641
Gray & Co	9,800
	86,366

Task 2.10

a) – c)

Cash book

Date 2007	Details	Bank £	Date 2007	Cheque number	Details	Bank £
15 June	PKL Ltd	4,000	1 June		Balance b/f	635
20 June	Beaker plc	3,245	1 June	07315	Abby Photos	483
21 June	Bissell & Co	2,500	6 June	07316	LTL Ltd	2,165
22 June	Gilchrist Ltd	2,416	6 June	07317	Retro Frames	1,233
22 June	Bank int	3	22 June	07318	Tonks & Co	1,020
			22 June	07319	Taylor Agencies	547
			20 June		Hampton CC	135
			20 June		Motor Mania	177
			22 June		Bank charges	44
			22 June		Balance c/d	5,725
		12,164				12,164
23 June	Balance b/d	5,725				

d) **Bank reconciliation statement as at 22 June 2007**

Balance per bank statement:	£1,631
Add:	
Name: Beaker plc	£3,245
Name: Gilchrist Ltd	£2,416
Total to add	£5,661
Less:	
Name: Tonks & Co	£1,020
Name: Taylor Agencies	£547
Total to subtract	£1,567
Balance as per cash book	£5,725

Tutorial notes

a) Note that the opening balance is an overdraft and be careful whether you add or subtract the various amounts.

b) Note also that the opening balance on the cash book does not match the opening balance on the bank statement – the difference being £250. The £250 that appears on the bank statement in the question would therefore have been an item included in the cash book and bank reconciliation for the previous month and should not therefore be included the cash book again this month.